Remapping
Your
MIND

"In this superb contribution to the field of self-transformation through story, Dr. Mehl-Madrona and Barbara Mainguy present important scientific research in approachable language as they demonstrate the intrinsic therapeutic value of story at all levels of our being. The authors have all the qualities of true 'medicine' people—they heal, they bless, they give thanks, they teach, they respect those who approach them for help—and so join the ancient lineage of storytellers who ensure the continuity of life-giving, universal healing wisdom."

JACK ANGELO, AUTHOR OF *SELF-HEALING WITH BREATHWORK: USING THE POWER OF BREATH TO INCREASE ENERGY AND ATTAIN OPTIMAL WELLNESS*

"Our life is a storied life. Where we may have been thrown into an unhappy or even hostile story, we have ways to remap and re-story our lives. I have read each of Dr. Mehl-Madrona's books, shared them with clients and students, and witnessed how his words help transform the inner and outer landscapes of our lives. He shows us how we can experience transformation and transcendence by being able to story our life differently. *Remapping Your Mind* satisfies in every way."

JULIE TALLARD JOHNSON, AUTHOR OF *THE ZERO POINT AGREEMENT: HOW TO BE WHO YOU ALREADY ARE*

Remapping
Your
MIND

The **Neuroscience** of
Self-Transformation through **Story**

Lewis Mehl-Madrona, M.D., Ph.D., with Barbara Mainguy, M.A.

Bear & Company
Rochester, Vermont • Toronto, Canada

Bear & Company
One Park Street
Rochester, Vermont 05767
www.BearandCompanyBooks.com

Bear & Company is a division of Inner Traditions International

*Note to the reader: This book is intended as an informational guide. The remedies,
approaches, and techniques described herein are meant to supplement, and not to be a
substitute for, professional medical care or treatment. They should not be used to treat
a serious ailment without prior consultation with a qualified health care professional.*

Library of Congress Cataloging-in-Publication Data
Mehl-Madrona, Lewis, 1954–
  Remapping your mind : the neuroscience of self-transformation through story /
Lewis Mehl-Madrona with Barbara Mainguy.
      pages cm
  Summary: "A guide to retelling your personal, family, and cultural stories to
transform your life, your relationships, and the world"—Provided by publisher.
  Includes bibliographical references and index.
  ISBN 978-1-59143-209-8 (pbk.) — ISBN 978-1-59143-210-4 (e-book)
  1. Mind and body. 2. Self-actualization (Psychology). 3. Narrative therapy.
I. Mainguy, Barbara. II. Title.
  BF161.M474 2015
  158—dc23
                                                              2014049145

Printed and bound in the United States by McNaughton & Gunn, Inc.

10 9 8 7 6 5 4 3 2 1

Text design and layout by Debbie Glogover
This book was typeset in Garamond Premier Pro with Bauhaus Std, Gill Sans MT
Pro, Helvetica Neue LT Std, ITC Franklin Gothic Std, and ITC Legacy Sans Std

To send correspondence to the author of this book, mail a first-class letter to the
author c/o Inner Traditions • Bear & Company, One Park Street, Rochester, VT
05767, and we will forward the communication, or contact the author directly at
www.mehl-madrona.com.

This book is dedicated to the beautiful ones
who live and have lived the experience.
You know who you are.

And to Stephen Snow, Joanabbey Sack,
Melanie Nesbitt, Mary Moncrieff,
and the women of George Herman House.
To my mother, Susan;
my sister, Sarah;
and my brother, Nicholas—
thank you for everything.
—B.M.

To my son, Takoda Mehl Madrona,
a fabulous artist and a lovely human being.
—L.M.-M.

Contents

Acknowledgments

We want to thank all of our teachers, our elders, the writers, and the researchers who have profoundly advanced our understanding of being human and what it might mean to help people in a good way.

Our bibliography speaks to our fascination with this line of inquiry and to the dedication of the science and academic worlds to the pursuit of discovering the nature of narrative mind. Raymond Mar was a graduate student in cognitive science at the University of Toronto when Barbara was an undergraduate there and first heard his work on the importance of story. We follow his work at the Mar Lab at York University and eagerly read his new writings on the neuroscience of story. Brian Boyd of the University of Auckland, who wrote a landmark account on the origin and importance of fiction, is a source of inspiration, as are Charles Whitehead, Jerome Bruner, Hubert Hermans for philosophy and the dialogical self, Lisa Barrett for understanding emotion, and Roger Schank and Robert Abelson for understanding thought and story. The placebo researchers help us to see the power of our minds in self-healing. The narrative, dance, and movement therapists; Barbara's creative arts therapy work; and my experiences lead us to those whose work takes us to an outer edge of the therapeutic model where acts resist scientific explanation.

Mostly, we are grateful to our clients, those who reach for change, experiment with new ways of being, bring honor to their suffering, and allow us to bear witness.

In all this we find ourselves knowing that the best teaching has come to us around fires, under the sun and stars, in the back of pickup trucks (or under the hood), and stacking chairs and making coffee in community with the elders who drop us a casual line that has us thinking for years. We especially acknowledge John Charles, Sonny Richards, Joe Tione, Marilyn Youngbird, Lloyd and Gracie Elm, and Vern Harper. As one of our friends said, as we burbled excitedly on about brains and minds and plasticity, "Isn't it great that neuroscience is finally catching up to the Lakota."

To all the stories and storytellers, *Hau Mitakuye Oyasin* (we are all related).

Introduction

My books can be seen as logs of my journey as a healer and the discoveries I have made along the way. The first, *Coyote Medicine,* was reluctantly autobiographical. I didn't set out to tell my story. I wanted to hide behind the stories of others, but an editor at Scribner's pulled me out of the background and made me foreground. *Coyote Medicine* became my story of making sense out of being a bicultural person, out of coming to medicine and health care from indigenous origins. It tells the story of how I realized that the indigenous world of my youth, which I had taken for granted, actually had much to offer contemporary, mainstream medicine.

From there I wrote *Coyote Healing,* the book I had initially intended to write, which was about medical miracles I had witnessed and amazing patients I had met. In that book I speculated about the nature of miracles through telling stories about the people who had experienced them. Then, in *Coyote Wisdom,* I started my journey into the world of stories in earnest, for I had realized that story was a common element in all the healings that I witnessed. I wrote about how indigenous healers used story to help people heal.

That led me to *Narrative Medicine,* which told about my discovery that the nonindigenous world was catching up to the Lakota and had also come to recognize the power of story. I wrote about the importance of story in medical practice and how I used story to work with my

1

medical patients. I took this further into psychiatry and mental health in the next book, *Healing the Mind through the Power of Story.*

This book places healing with story in the context of the latest research in neuroscience, which reveals that our brains coevolved with our narrative abilities. Mark Turner, a neuroscientist in the U.K., situates the roots of human mental functioning in story.[1] Story and brain appeared as one in the evolutionary stream. Jerome Bruner, a psychologist and educator of consciousness studies at NYU determined that, "We organize our experience and our memory of human happenings mainly in the form of narrative."[2] We stop events from disappearing by placing them into stories, by consciously incorporating the separate events of our lives into a single unit called a story. The stories we tell repeatedly to an audience become those that are remembered without difficulty. Stories are the way we preserve events in memory that would otherwise be lost, and they are how we connect these events into a unified whole that can be readily remembered.

One of the fascinating discoveries made by modern brain researchers regards the "default mode" of brain functioning—what our brain does when it is on idle. Experiments conducted by neurologist Marcus Raichle at Washington University School of Medicine, and by other groups, demonstrate that the brain is constantly active at a high level even when we are not engaged in focused mental work or focused on the outside world. In fact, the brain's energy consumption is increased by less than 5 percent of its baseline while performing a focused mental task. Raichle coined the term "default mode" in 2001 to describe this resting state brain function.[3]

Research thereafter focused on finding the regions responsible for this constant background activity level.[4] Those regions came to be termed the "default mode network" (DMN). That led to research attempts to identify what the default mode of the brain is—and it is story! The DMN is activated when we daydream, envision the future, retrieve memories, and gauge others' perspectives.[5] It is deactivated when we focus on external sensory signals.

Current neuroscience research is thus affirming what we have already been discovering through our work. We need to understand story, because story is our default mode: it is intrinsic to who we are. Story is what we use to explain our world. Story is what we use to create identity. More than that, increasingly it seems apparent that the stories we tell ourselves literally impact our health.

Most people who come to our family medicine clinic have a variety of wounds and symptoms that are redressed by a multitude of approaches. Often, people present themselves to primary care rather than psychiatry because they would prefer to see their suffering as biological. In the past few years, I have been working with my wife and partner, Barbara Mainguy, a creative arts therapist who shares my understanding of healing.

Barbara's training is in mainstream therapeutic modalities as well as movement, dance, and drama therapy, and she has studied hypnosis and the use of story in hypnosis. She discovered for herself how important it is for people to learn their own sense of agency as author of their life. Sometimes she says that in her work as a therapist, she specializes in holding space for people while they feel uncomfortable at the edge of a new world and a new life. I invited Barbara to work on this book with me to help me lay out in practical terms how we do narrative work for healing purposes. She has contributed to the writing of all the chapters, adding her own understandings and experiences to our discussion.

We believe that any therapy or human service activity can, and probably should, be narrativized, simply through the recognition that story and the structure or template of story underlies all that is human. Each one of us practices story deconstruction and reconstruction every time we reconstruct a memory, but we can become stuck in an automatic narrative that doesn't serve us. When we can change what a story means to us, reconstruct it with new detail and perception, we can break free from old stuck patterns and move forward in constructive ways.

The idea that people can interact together to improve well-being is a story in itself. Cultures tell us how to relieve suffering. In contemporary mainstream North American culture, this means consulting a physician or other health professional. The stories around the consulting room fix the structure of the interaction. Different forms of healing come with their own sets of stories about what can relieve suffering. In the indigenous world, we go see an elder. He or she listens to our stories about our problems and understands our story within a traditional worldview.

It's harder in our postmodern world. When clients come to our office, they have a story to tell. They have a story about what will help and what they want done. We have to find a way to work within that story to see if we can map stories sufficiently closely to interact usefully.[6] Psychologist Michele Crossely tells us that all therapies start with listening.[7] This is medicine's current nightmare—that today's physicians, whether through volition or because of the circumstances of their practice, only listen to any given patient for an average of eighteen seconds.[8]

Our health care system loses time, energy, and money by not appreciating the impact of story on people's responses to suffering. A story is often the answer to the question, "How did you come to think that?" Many approaches to healing become more effective when we not only identify the beliefs that guide behavior and perception, but when we also find the stories that led to those beliefs.

Narrative workers help people to find and gather their stories, to bring them home. We understand that we must listen to you to know what you want, what you think will help. We listen openly, to hear the story you tell about your suffering, but we also listen for a sense of how you construct your stories. Who are the heroes? How much effect can they have on outcome? What is the story of the arrival of the suffering? What might be some clues for the possibilities for change?

In the chapters that follow, you will find illustrations of the following techniques as we present you with accounts of sessions and provide our commentary along the way.

- Listen to the story of the illness. Then listen *beneath* the story. Allow yourself to stay in respectful silence while listening. Refrain from judgment or interpretation, and let the story fall into the space created between you.

- Begin to co-create the treatment narrative. Somewhere in the story you begin to hear clues about the story of healing. Listen for these clues; begin to explore them.
- Be holistic—address mind, body, spirit, community, emotions and relationships, safety, social determinants of health (sustenance). These are the Lakota seven directions or medicine sphere described in *Coyote Healing*. Stories can emerge from any of these dimensions.
- Elicit the stories that explain the behavior or beliefs that the person is living.
- Find out who told these stories and in what context. When did these stories feel true and for whom?
- Explore the beginnings of alternate stories (future life regression, parallel life regression, interviewing other people, etc.).
- Give homework to take the work outside the office into the person's life.
- Construct alternate stories that will produce better outcomes.
- Support the person as he or she tests them out in his or her world.

We express these ideas as part of our way of working with clients, but they offer each of us ways to explore our stories and beliefs and to find and implement alternate stories.

While the focus in this book is what can happen in the sixteen- to twenty-visit time frame, the work is not linear. Different techniques are required at different times, and the correct intervention is the one that opens up the conversation to possibilities and creative outcomes and solutions. In addition, there are no "rules" that we concern ourselves with as far as methods go. We use art, dance, puppets, talk, improvisation, toys, whatever seems to suit the person and the situation. We also use the idea of multidimensions, parallel universes, past and future lives, and the possible presence of ancestors and or other spirits. It isn't necessary to believe in spirits to work in this way; these kinds of interventions can be considered ways of accessing intuition. We find that these ideas help people to imagine change as possible where they otherwise might feel that the world is too finite to be altered.

To do work in a narrative way is to participate in a special conversation. We enter into a creative dialogue to elicit detail, help find openings, look for inconsistencies, and discover forgotten characters, places, and events. More, we help people to begin to imagine future events, create new characters, open up the landscape in which they see their story, and break new ground. We invite fantasy, speculation, and projections into the future. The art of working with story is the art of creating future narratives of success and of reframing past narratives to mine them for new, more versatile and empowering meanings.

Chapter 1 presents both cases and research that illustrate the possibility of discovering our identity narrative and modifying it to a healthier version if needed. It also describes the functioning of the two hemispheres of the brain in relation to language and story. In chapter 2 we explore the fascinating links between memory and story, in our minds and in our lives.

Chapter 3 offers a more in-depth look at the default mode of the brain and how our storying brains are capable of generating multiple "selves." In chapter 4 we look at the intertwined nature of our stories and our beliefs and how they can imprison or release us. Chapter 5 is a more detailed exploration of our capacity for simulation and how it contributes to our carrying the important people in our lives with us wherever we go. In chapter 6 we focus on the powerful role that imagination plays in our capacity to create new stories for ourselves.

We would argue that narrative work is involved in almost all manifestations we see in healing work. We have discovered that our social and individual stories about the power of substance have a tremendous influence on medical treatment and outcome. In chapter 7 we examine the fascinating research on the placebo effect, the nocebo effect, and the art of stimulating self-healing. We also demonstrate how we respectfully work with someone to create alternatives to the story that "real" pain can be seen in X-rays and other imaging studies and that it demands treatment with pain medications, most commonly opiates. Our ever-growing understanding of the mind/body connection affirms our need to learn how to listen and speak to our bodies. Chapter 8 illustrates the dynamic power of movement and healing stories to profoundly modify our physiology and promote health.

Threaded through this book are cogent references to the latest advances in brain mapping and how they support our way of working. For those who wish to explore further, the appendix offers two outlines: one listing the areas of the brain and their story-related functions; the other does the reverse, listing the aspects of the production of story paired with the areas of the brain that accomplish those functions.

It is possible in any practice to create the space to negotiate someone's narrative of suffering and to explore many pathways with them, to find the openings that might lead to a change in direction, possibilities, and choices in life. When we work with someone's story, we discover ways to help them begin to feel and experience what is possible and even begin to shift. We have some core ideas. First, we cannot stress enough the importance of listening. Second, respect for and radical acceptance of the patient's story as a starting point, initially for creating a therapeutic alliance and then for the business of collaborating on story. Meeting clients where they are offers respect and creates space for them to perhaps hear their own story for the first time. Respect and radical acceptance create safety for clients to tell the deeper stories. Good work emerges from this beginning, one of compassion and love.

In this book we share a number of the lessons and methods we have learned and research that supports them. Any practitioner can benefit from incorporating these lessons into his or her healing modality. Every reader of this book can also use these lessons to bring about healthy self-transformation and, through that, to nurture wider and wider circles of social and cultural transformation.

Discovering
the Stories We Live

The sufferer is a poet in search of metaphors adequate to express his predicament.

LAURENCE KIRMAYER

These are all matters we need to know. It's easy to become sick, because there are always things happening to confuse our minds. We need ways of thinking to keep things stable, healthy, beautiful. We try for a long life, but lots of things happen to us. So we keep our thinking in order by these figures and we keep our lives in order with the stories.

DENE ELDER ON
THE PURPOSE OF DENE STRING DESIGNS

We are born into stories, stories about our conception, our history, about who we are supposed to become, about our parents and our families, about our world. We are born into the world as story listeners and story-tellers. We learn language through story, by hearing and telling story. We make meaning of the world by telling ourselves stories about it. The skill of storytelling begins with the first moment we try to navigate our safe passage through turbulent life. At any given moment in time, whether we are aware of it or not, we bring these stories to mind to explain ourselves, to make decisions, to create change. All the time, though we may not be aware of it, we draw upon elements of all these tales to create a master story, a meta-story, a current explanation for our lives.

We all carry a "master identity narrative," our version of the story we tell to explain ourselves. We tell short versions of this story to encourage others to see us as we wish to be seen. This master narrative or identity narrative is a synthesis of many stories we have accepted and repeated about ourselves. Sometimes we are only vaguely aware of the source of some of these stories. We can remember the point and forget where we got the story.

By the time we are young adults, we no longer are aware of the depth and complexity of the woven field of stories we inhabit, and we think our stories are simply "the truth." This sense that they carry some kind of absolute weight leads us to think that they also are a condition for "the way we really feel." This can lead to suffering that we may not understand. Illnesses unfold in us *in the context of these stories.*

An important aspect of narrative practice involves identification of the stories that shaped us and our master narrative. The Lakota speak of these stories as our *nagi.* They believe we are surrounded by a swarm of stories that influenced us and made us who we are today. *Nagi* includes both the stories and the tellers of those stories. It is our legacy. To understand our suffering, we must tap into our *nagi.* Some of the stories we heard taught us to suffer, perhaps needlessly or unnecessarily. Other stories perhaps tell versions of events that may be outdated. As we grow and change, we bring new understanding to our lives and some stories may have become dead weight. To minimize suffering and pain, we need to become aware of the contents of our *nagi.* Through our human capacity to direct our attention, we choose through an act of volition the stories that will guide us most.

The stories that underlie our ideas are mutable. We have created them by pulling together pieces of the different stories that are part of the woven fabric of tales all around us. Once we accept that they are raw material from which we draw, it takes away the constricting parts of our personal relationship to the story, the sense of its "truth," and allows us to consider if we might not need more raw material from which to create our lives, more examples of how things are and can be created.

THE LANGUAGE OF STORY

The way we conceive the world, the ways in which we think, and the ways in which we act in the world, fall into the template of story and its accompanying use of metaphor, the language of story.[1] Metaphor is powerful and activates more of the brain than anything we know. Like the conveyer belts in the baggage area at the Athens Airport, called *metaphorae,* metaphors allow us to more easily carry concepts (luggage) from one place to another. They allow us to understand and experience one thing in terms of something else. Metaphors structure how we perceive the world. They determine what we experience, regulate how we relate to each other, and shape the choices we make.

You can conduct a small experiment—write down the metaphors people use and their illnesses, and you will see how people's illnesses are grounded in their stories that contain the meanings and values that they live. You can do this for yourself as well, or ask a friend or family member you trust to note what metaphors you often use.

Here's an example from our general practice. Terry was a forty-four-year-old woman with a twenty-four-year history of severe, relatively intractable, irritable bowel syndrome (IBS). Upon sitting down in my office, she remarked that she had tried every conventional and unconventional approach to IBS and none had worked. This is a wonderfully daunting way to be approached by a client. She had been to gastroenterologists, the Mayo Clinic, the Cleveland Clinic, other local general practitioners, naturopaths, homeopaths, acupuncturists, herbalists, kinesiologists, psychic healers, shamans, energy healers, Reiki masters, chiropractors, osteopaths, and more. The central character of her story was IBS, perhaps even more central than she in her initial narrative.

I began with the faith that appreciating and then helping her to change her identity story could be associated with improvement in her IBS symptoms. Perhaps the many physicians and healers to whom she had gone had paid less attention to her story and more attention to their stories about what should work. If so, I would be lucky and appear to be more helpful than they.

Our performance of stories is always embodied. We enact our stories in a physical world. The body reacts to the stories we tell ourselves and to the interpersonal performances required by those stories. Our autonomic nervous systems, our hormonal systems, our immune systems respond to the simulations we run in our minds, to the "what ifs . . ." that we ponder. The lives and stories of people suffering from illness are inseparable from the illnesses. They are one and the same. We physically experience our relationships and interactions with others. Illness is dynamic because we are dynamic. Some changes improve illness; others worsen it.

Technique
•—•—•
LISTENING

The French psychoanalyst Jacques Lacan said that the greatest gift we can give someone is to listen fully without judgment or interpretation. When we listen in this way to people, and they observe us listening, together we form an awareness of their story that is greater than they could have had before. The stories occupy space in a heightened way. In this awareness of the stories being told, just by telling them, often clients can see connections previously invisible. Listening provides what is typically a rare opportunity to really speak and experience ourselves being heard, perhaps allowing us to hear what we are saying for the first time. Sometimes, people are surprised by what they say. This is why listening is so powerfully therapeutic. In our language we are nonjudgmental and radically accepting of the story as it is being told.

During the course of our first six meetings, Terry's story emerged. She remembered being a seventh grader in a Catholic School and being very angry with God. She had learned to view God as a white-haired old man on a throne in charge of everything. She was angry with God for not making her life and her family's life better. She thought if she were only more perfect and better behaved, God would smile upon them and make things better. This idea seemed to pervade her life—that God would reward you and take care of all the problems in your life, if you are only good enough. We found a five-year-old Terry suffering under these beliefs as well as a three-year-old Terry, barely aware of the concepts yet comprehending the injunctions.

We went looking for other important characters in her internal mental world—characters telling stories that affected her life. One, whom she labeled the Saboteur, did everything possible to keep her from being happy because: "You don't deserve it. You haven't earned it. You aren't good enough to be happy." She began to reflect on the voices of all her relatives as she grew up, the meaning behind the stories they told her, their notions of life, their misery and pain. These characters resolved into those relatives and their stories that supported the ideas that she had internalized. The message she learned was "Be like us. Be unhappy. Day after day life is the same old thing. Life is drudgery. You live for retirement; then you retire; and then you die." "How depressing," she thought.

Another theme underlying Terry's childhood stories was security. Her parents were children during the Great Depression and therefore insisted that security was the ultimate value and goal. Terry was admonished against taking risks, however small. In telling her story, she realized that she didn't develop IBS until she began working as an IT (computer) consultant, a profession she hadn't wanted and only took because her parents insisted that it was secure. She remembered her mother scaring her into being dependent, living at home, and not venturing into the world. She dreamed of escaping. She recalled everyone in her family throughout her childhood saying, "No, you can't (won't, don't, etc.). You can't do anything unless you're perfect first." These voices included her mother, maternal grandmother, maternal grandfather, father, and seventh- and eighth-grade teachers.

Terry thus grew up with stories about the frightening world and the need for security that influenced her gut years later. We can't escape the stories of our childhood. The best we can do is to identify them and to evaluate whether or not we want to keep them. They have been our best friends for years. Some are not so kind to us, however.

Terry's illness narrative had included the possibility that her life and her stories might be contributing to her illness. Since she had tried every treatment narrative imaginable, she accepted my idea that we could begin by becoming aware of her stories, the stories that lived through her and that she enacted in the world. Becoming aware of those stories, I said, and learning where they originated, would lead us to further ideas about her IBS. This is what we did for six weeks.

We emerged with a new illness narrative: that IBS was somehow related to Terry's doing what she didn't want to do in order to be secure, to take no risks. The plot that emerged was about a woman who didn't feel that she deserved more and settled for what she didn't want because that was safe. We could hypothesize that healing IBS might involve changing this plot. This led to the next phase of our work together, which was co-creating a new story.

Terry wanted a story about her being able to follow her passion, to take risks, and to not need God (or a godlike external expert) to fix her. As she explored and provisionally enacted new stories with this plot over the next ten weeks, the IBS began to change. Her symptoms improved as she began to actively oppose the internalized voices of her family. She reevaluated her job and found a different position in which she had less pressure and responsibility and could be more creative. She reevaluated her relationship and broke with a boyfriend who was barely working and was living off her. She began to explore traveling and reached out to a new set of friends who were more spiritually inclined.

At sixteen weeks her IBS was substantially better and she was actively exploring these new possibilities. We could have stopped there and our work would have been a success. However, we chose to continue four more months, by the end of which her IBS symptoms were gone. This was not magic, just attestation to how our lives, stories, and illnesses are inseparably interwoven. Our guts respond to every thought. That's why we (as did Terry) speak about "gut feelings." We have many metaphors for this, including "gut wrenching," "all twisted up in knots," "sick to my stomach," "that makes me sick," and more.

Terry's changes were qualitatively greater than some. She changed more than just one or two stories; she changed her identity narrative. She took on a new identity, and that new identity did not have IBS.

THE VIEW FROM
COGNITIVE NEUROSCIENCE

A narrative approach values the individual experience and voice and puts a human face on the experience. Personal stories provide a helpful way for us to understand the illness experience and to recognize the uniqueness of each person. A narrative framework provides access to the human experience of time, order, and change, obligating us to listen to the human impulse to tell stories.[2] Recent work being done in the field of cognitive neuroscience supports working in this way.

The ability to mentally represent and experience oneself across time is also known as autonoetic awareness.[3] Projected into the past, this capacity results in a reexperiencing of previous events. However, autonoetic awareness also permits the representation of self-experience in the present and future. The latter is similar to representing one's own experience in a fictional context since the future hasn't yet happened and is imagined.

Personally experiencing oneself in a story is congruent with models being developed in cognitive neuroscience to explain language comprehension, such as the Immersed Experiencer Framework and cognitive psychologist Keith Oatley's theory of simulating narrative experience.[4]

It is also in keeping with research on the development of imagination, which some psychologists, such as Paul Harris, think may provide the basis for the capacity to comprehend narratives.[5] Both the Event-Indexing Model and Immersed Experiencer Framework predict that an even broader network of activations may occur during story comprehension in conjunction with previously mentioned memory and integration areas. When we read or hear a story, we must keep track of the people in the story and connect them to the motivations we have assigned to them. Thus, brain areas associated with inferring the intentions of others should be active during story reading or listening.

Immersed Experiencer Framework

Rolf Zwaan, cognitive and linguistic psychologist and philosopher, writes about the Immersed Experiencer Framework, which helps us comprehend a mind/body theory of story. In his view words automatically activate experiences within the listener or reader of those things to which the words refer. Such activations are not unique to story processing but also occur during sentence and even single-word processing. The continual activation and articulation of specific sensory and motor networks during story comprehension result in their becoming relatively stronger and easier to activate each time they are accessed, which is the neuroplastic basis for learning.[6]

Zwaan tells us that the words we hear activate a wide swath through the brain, including all of the primary sensory areas and any part of the brain that might become active during experience with those things to which the words refer. When we listen to a story, we track multiple possible aspects of that story, remembering our prior experiences to help us gain comprehension when they seem to fit, and suppressing them when they don't.

For Zwaan three concepts appear to underlie story comprehension: (1) words activate broad functional networks that are the same as those activated when we actually experience what it is to which the word refers; (2) currently activated webs interact with previously activated webs and vice versa to reduce the initially broad activations to those that are probably relevant to our current situation and the story we are hearing; and (3) integration into memory occurs via the construction of linkages between these webs.[7] The continual activation and articulation of certain sensory or motor networks during story comprehension may result in the strengthening of areas that are associated with the story as a whole compared to the activations of individual words or phrases. This idea is compatible with Hebbian processes in which learning is associated with the establishment of progressively stronger dendritic connections to nerve axons. The more we use circuitry, the more dense the dendritic connections become, and the more a dirt, country road is turned into a superhighway.

Event-Indexing Model

The Event-Indexing Model of Zwaan and fellow cognitive mental model researcher Gabriel Radvansky proposes that the mental models constructed by listeners or readers are composed of at least five dimensions: (1) temporal, (2) spatial, (3) causal, (4) motivational, and (5) person/object.[8] Any good story tells us who did what, when they did it, why they did it, where they did it, and what motivated them to do it. Television crime dramas are never complete until we can answer these five questions.

INNER SPEECH

The stories that we tell ourselves matter. The inner speech through which these stories are told has been articulated by cognitive researchers Vercueil and Perronne-Bertolotti as "the silent expression of conscious thought to oneself in a coherent linguistic form (i.e., silent production of words in one's mind)."[9] Views vary on the nature of inner speech. The Russian developmental psychologist Lev Vygotsky believed that inner speech comes from children hearing themselves talk and gradually realizing they can talk without moving their lips. In psychosis sometimes one's own inner speech is attributed to someone else. Talking silently requires the ability to create, hold, and manipulate an internal representation of the auditory word form that may be internally generated or triggered by silent reading.[10]

Vygotsky's view was that inner speech and external speech are the same, only that we learn that we can inhibit motor performance. This would be similar to contemporary theories of mirror neurons in which the same areas of the brain light up when we see another person performing a behavior as would be activated if we were performing the same behavior. The only difference is that our motor system is disengaged.

Dreaming is another example of a mental phenomenon in which the motor system is disengaged. The disorders of this uncoupling include frontotemporal dementia,[11] Gilles de la Tourette syndrome,[12] and, in my view, some types of psychosis. In all these conditions, people say things out loud that many of us have thought, but we would never say. The frontal lobes help us to keep ourselves from doing what we would otherwise have the impulse to do. When dementia primarily affects the frontal lobes, this inhibition dissolves. Unlike Alzheimer's dementia, language is preserved until late in the course so this lack of inhibition of inner speech production becomes more noticeable over time. In Gilles de la Tourette syndrome, people find themselves unable to stop cursing. In psychosis people sometimes produce Ulysses-like, Joycean monologues of everything passing through their minds.

However, as is often the case, the neuroimaging studies complicate my and Vygotsky's more simplistic views.[13] Although inner speech and outer speech share a common network of brain regions, they engage some regions in different ways, and they produce separate activations in other regions. People with aphasia (the acquired inability to speak, often due to stroke) can sometimes still talk to themselves but not to others. It is much less likely that they lose inner speech after stroke but can still talk to other people, which has been taken as evidence for the dependence of thought on language.[14]

Vercueil and Perronne-Bertolotti also present the case of a forty-year-old woman with partial seizures who remained alert and aware during the course of her seizures.[15] During these seizures she was unable to recognize words, written or spoken, nor could she write or speak anything but jargon. She had the sense of an ordered inner jargon, which was, however, unintelligible. She wrote: "Incomprehension of inner language (thought is unintelligible), and if I try to repeat inner language out loud, incomprehensible words come out (at any rate I don't understand them!)." Jill Bolte Taylor described a similar experience of wordless, thoughtless awareness during her left-sided stroke.[16] Apparently awareness can exist without worded thought, and a strong relationship exists between inner speech and outer speech.

The Storying Role of the Brain's Hemispheres

The right hemisphere is important for understanding stories. It performs the coarser coding of loose associations that may be more removed in time and space from what is being read or heard, whereas the left hemisphere performs more specific coding of the more immediate and obvious connections. The right hemisphere aids in activating a broad range of inferences, while the left hemisphere narrows down the associations provided by the right hemisphere to what is immediate and obvious to understanding the story.[17] Thus, understanding story requires the collaboration and integration of both hemispheres, consistent with Oatley's idea that experiencing story provides both cognitive and emotional simulation.[18]

The prefrontal cortex processes structured, sequential goal-oriented events in a logical framework. The right prefrontal cortex appears to specialize in the slower processing of loosely associated information such as that found in the themes and morals of stories. The ventromedial prefrontal cortex processes social event sequences, and the medial prefrontal cortex processes predictable event sequences, all of which are important for understanding stories.[19]*

---

*A comprehensive outline of the findings of neuroscientific research regarding the areas of the brain involved in story can be found in the appendix.

Research on understanding story with brain-damaged populations has consistently highlighted the importance of the right hemisphere,[20] although other left-sided brain areas have also been identified as necessary, including the left anterior temporal lobe and the left temporal pole.[21]

Greater right than left frontal activation during narrative comprehension may also indicate a closer parallel with episodic retrieval processes rather than episodic encoding or semantic retrieval.[22] This similarity could reflect actual retrieval processes during reading or that something like the personal experiencing that composes autonoetic awareness occurs during narrative comprehension. Readers retrieve personal memories while reading, and these memories tend to be more actively self-oriented when elicited by stories compared to expository texts.[23] While the retrieval of both autobiographical and imagined memories implicates many similar areas, experienced memories appear to contain more sensory information, while imagined events may evoke more schematic or abstract imagery.[24]

Reading Systems Framework

In the Reading Systems Framework (which seems equally relevant to hearing a story) knowledge of the meanings of words lies in the center of the picture. Knowledge of specific words is integrated into comprehension of a phrase, paragraph, and eventually story. First, we use our knowledge of the component words to make sense out of short stretches of text. Then we build our knowledge of these shorter stretches into a model for the entire story. These processes require linkage between the system that identifies the word and the system that comprehends the phrase in which the word is found, with the person's vocabulary playing the linking role. The way we construe one sentence affects the way we understand the meaning of any given word in a following sentence. Those with more narrative skills (better comprehenders) show immediate use of word meanings in the integration process. Other evidence is consistent with the processes that allow us to understand words being necessary components of the skill sets that allow us to form a more global understanding of an entire story.[25]

The disease process related to the loss of knowledge about words is called semantic dementia. It involves the degeneration of the right (and, as we now know, left) anterior temporal lobes.[26] Although conventionally conceptualized as a disorder of language, people who are diagnosed with this disorder also have problems with behavior and in managing their emotional relationships with other people. They appear to have an impaired capacity to imagine what other people are thinking.

Dementia neurobiologist Mulreann Irish and her colleagues in Australia compared the performance of people who had been diagnosed with semantic dementia on a theory of mind task (determining what other people might be thinking and feeling) with people who were diagnosed with frontotemporal dementia, people diagnosed with Alzheimer's dementia, and with healthy older individuals as control participants. The task was a simple series of cartoons in which people were asked to describe physical scenes and scenes in which characters were interacting with feelings and purposes. In all of the ways they measured, people who were diagnosed with semantic dementia showed marked impairments compared to healthy older adults; however, the most important deficits were those of theory of mind. The greater the deficit, the greater the atrophy in right anterior temporal lobe structures, including the right temporal fusiform cortex, right inferior temporal gyrus, bilateral temporal poles, and the amygdalae.[27] The greater the deficits, the less able the person was to understand the thoughts and feelings of another. All of these functions are linked, and the brain functions as an integrated whole in understanding the story.

HEALING HAMLET?

Healing occurs when the stories we are living change to less painful ones. Take Hamlet, for example. What if he could have found another way to avenge his father's murder in which he didn't die? Is there another alternative that would be equally dramatic but allow Hamlet to live? That would be the type of question we would ask in order to be healing.

If we are suffering, if we are unhappy or have an illness, our distresses are interwoven with the stories we tell ourselves and others over and over, every day. If so, we should identify these stories, discover what we tell ourselves all day long, and become aware of the roles we are enacting. What are the plots, values, characters, and audiences for the dramas we enact? How do we change the stories in which we find ourselves as characters? How do we help our clients find better stories by which to live, stories that involve less suffering and pain?

Wayne is an example of someone whose stories benefited from deconstruction of the narrative, separation into parts, and reconstruction in a more useful way. Wayne was a thirty-five-year-old man with depression (and back pain), who came to me with thoughts of committing suicide. I begin by eliciting the illness narrative. I wondered why Wayne was thinking of killing himself. He responded that he wanted to show some people how badly they had hurt him. Wayne told a story with tragic potential. "People have hurt me and are ignoring me. I'll show them how badly they've hurt me. I'll kill myself. Then they'll really feel bad." I encounter this story frequently, especially among adolescents.

Technique

•—•—•

USE CONCLUSIONS
AS ENTRY POINTS TO STORIES

When presented with a conclusion (as in "the best solution is suicide"), get the story behind it.

I wanted to know how Wayne came to think that suicide worked that way, to show people how much they have hurt the person. "How did you come to think that killing yourself would really get their attention?" I asked.

> **Technique**
> •—•—•
> ### *INTERLOCUTION*
> In keeping with our nonjudgmental, radically accepting stance, our favorite questions are those that open up other possibilities. We don't question the story, rather we enter into its landscape and invite more detail.

"That's what people always say," he replied, "after the person's dead. They go to the funeral and they say, 'I didn't know he felt so bad.' Or they say, 'I would have been nicer to him if I'd known he was suffering so badly.' Or, 'I wish I'd said something to him when he was alive. Then, maybe he wouldn't have killed himself.'"

"Do you imagine them saying that about you?" I asked.

"Of course I do," he responded.

"Could you tell me about the funeral you are remembering?" I asked.

"Sure," he said. "It's as clear as day. It was my cousin, Leslie. He killed himself. Everybody was always picking on him, and nobody knew how much it bothered him. I knew because he told me, but nobody else knew, because they wouldn't believe him. One day he'd just had enough and he blew his brains away. Then they knew what they'd done to him, and they were sorry."

"He was still dead, though, I guess," I said.

"Sure he was dead." Wayne was looking at me strangely.

"It just seems a shame that the only way to get your point across is to end up dead."

"But he sure let them know," Wayne responded, though less strongly and convincingly than before.

"But he was dead in the end," I said.

"But it was worth it," Wayne said. I wasn't sure if he actually believed himself.

"Says who?" I asked.

"Says everyone," Wayne countered, the pitch of his voice rising. He was getting more tentative by the mouthful.

"You mean everyone in the room declared that Leslie was better off dead because now he'd convinced those guys about how much they were bothering him?" I asked, trying to sound a bit incredulous.

"Well, sort of," came the answer, and then we were off and running. Our dialogue became exploring whether or not Leslie had been truly vindicated. Wayne began remembering how some of the reactions weren't so positive. Some people had been angry with Leslie. Was being dead worth the chance to get revenge? After pursuing this for some time, I shifted focus. We identified the stories that could support this conclusion and where they originated. I was ready to change gears.

"Wayne," I said. "What's your daily life like? What's bothering you?"

"Lots of things," he said. "I go to work all day and it sucks and nobody cares about me, and I come home to my family and they're all caught up in their own dramas and they barely notice me. I'm the breadwinner now but nobody seems to care." I pursued that further. Wayne was running the family business that his father couldn't manage anymore, from either diminished capacity or illness or both. Wayne's mother had always worked in the business but her multiple sclerosis was making that very difficult. His sister had just lost her long-term boyfriend to cancer and was staying in the basement and sleeping all day.

Wayne was becoming more isolated. He was taking care of his sister, his parents, the family business, and more. He came home exhausted, walked the dogs, changed the cat litter, and collapsed. I heard him using metaphors like "the weight of the world is on my shoulders." Or at work, he described people as being "perpetually on my back." Wayne's metaphorical back (and his will to live) was breaking. He had no support. He was collapsing under the weight he was carrying. Telling him this directly would not work. I'd have to find a way to help him discover this on his own for it to mean anything. At least I now had a working hypothesis about his distress. I had an illness narrative.

Technique

•—•—•

DON'T GIVE ADVICE—
THE CLIENT BECOMES THE EXPERT

Giving clients advice or making direct interpretations rarely succeeds. Our task is the harder one of finding ways for them make discoveries for themselves. Usually, habitual behaviors have strong and complicated stories behind them. To change those stories requires establishing a new story that is as strong as the old. People tend to build up stories that are layered with values and meaning. The new story has to address those values and create new meaning.

I understood that Wayne had stories from funerals in which it appeared that those who suffered were finally vindicated. I understood those stories, but Wayne had minimized the fact that these vindicated people were now dead. I wanted to explore this idea further but using visualization. Where were the vindicated? Where were they standing? How did they know they were vindicated once they were dead? This touched upon Wayne's stories and the beliefs they supported about what happens after death.

We often offer stories in the middle of a session to seed the creative work that will follow and to inspire and distract. With Wayne I told a Coyote story to inject some humor into his thinking about suicide.

Technique

•—•—•

TELLING A STORY TO MAKE A POINT IS
MORE EFFECTIVE THAN SIMPLY MAKING THE POINT

Stories are simple, powerful devices for whole brain activation. I'm going to tell a story that will make it easier for Wayne and me to talk about suicide seeming silly. The story will create a shared metaphor to which we can return over and over. Stories teach us in ways that direct exposition can never do.

Coyote was hungry and angry. No one was giving him any food. That made him feel bitter, for he protected so many other animals and had outdone himself to make the world a safer place for people when they did come, and, therefore, he deserved some appreciation. He needed a way to show the other animals how little they valued him and how much he was hurting. He crossed over a tall ridge and came upon a wolf hovering over a shape.

"What have you got there, big fellow?" Coyote asked. The wolf just grunted. Coyote gingerly crept over to see what Wolf had under his paw. Whatever it was, it had many little spikes sticking out. It looked like painful eating. Wolf was rolling it over with his paw and every time he touched it, he winced. Finally, Wolf looked up in disgust.

"You eat it, Coyote," he said. "It's too difficult to be worthwhile for me." Coyote had watched Wolf's pain whenever it touched the spiky, thorny thing. Coyote imagined that thing in his mouth.

"No, thanks," Coyote said.

"Well, don't say I never offered you any food," said Wolf. "Some food!" thought Coyote. Wolf trotted further down the valley toward the river where Moose was taking a drink. Coyote wandered back onto the trail. He turned around to look at the ridge in case Wolf had dropped some food, and suddenly the spiky thing stood up!

"Heh," said Coyote. "You're not dead."

"Of course not," said Porcupine. "I was just playing dead."

"Heh, that's pretty cool," said Coyote. "Fooled me. Can you teach me to play dead?"

"Sure," said Porcupine. "Let's go visit my friend Badger. He's always got something good to eat, and we can talk there." They meandered down the trail toward the river. Badger lived alone in a camp downstream and

near the lake. He had lived there for a really long time and knew where to find many good things to eat. Coyote was angry with him for not sharing enough, but to put it in perspective, Coyote was angry at everyone for not sharing enough.

"Hello, Badger," said Porcupine. "I've brought my friend Coyote with me. You must have something good to eat. I'm going to teach Coyote how to play dead."

"I've just roasted some duck," said Badger. "I'll get you some." Coyote was even more miffed when it looked like Badger gave Porcupine a bigger piece of duck than he gave Coyote. "Tell Coyote how you learned to catch duck so good," said Porcupine. That got Badger really excited.

"Porcupine taught me how to play dead," said Badger. "Once I knew how to do that, I got me a big stick and sharpened both edges. Then I climbed down on the rocks by the lake where the ducks like to swim because they think the shore is too rugged for anyone to sneak up on them. I found me a flat place down there near where they swim, and I lay down with my stick close to me. Then I pretended to be dead. After a while those ducks got curious. They wondered who was lying on their rocks. Pretty soon some of them got out of the lake and came up to check me out. Pretty soon they started talking about me. I heard them say, 'He has a very short tail. His legs are very short, too. What is he?'

"I didn't move a muscle. I kept my stick down by my side. Pretty soon the ducks who were checking me out called out to the other ducks, 'Come up and see what this is. He has very short ears. It's hard to see his eyes. They are very small. He has a white spot on his nose.'

"When enough ducks had surrounded me, poking and prodding me with their bills and their feet, I jumped up and knocked them down with my stick. I killed a lot of them. Only a few escaped to waddle back down the rocks into the lake. I didn't follow them, because I had enough. I still have plenty. I carried them back up to my camp and plucked their feathers out. As you can tell, they are very fat and good to eat. Now let Porcupine teach you how to play dead."

Coyote had never realized what an art it was to play dead. You had to lie just right with your legs up in the air at the perfect angle. When Porcupine was satisfied that Coyote could play dead, he announced that he was done. "You are as good a student, Coyote, as Opossum was. And he was my star pupil."

"Okay," said Coyote. "I'm ready. Now what kind of stick do I use?"

"Any kind of stick will do," Badger said. "It doesn't matter."

"I'm going to try it myself," Coyote said. "I'm going to lie down there, too, and get me some duck." Coyote made his own stick and then asked Badger, "How long do you have to lie there?"

Badger told him, "As long as it takes, that is all." Coyote found a stick and sharpened it to look just like Badger's. Then he went down to the rocks. He looked around for a place to lie. He saw where the ducks were swimming and saw what he thought was a good place near them. He was mad at ducks, too. He had killed big scary monsters that had lived in their lake and had made the water safe for them. They should have been more grateful to him. He'd make them feel bad that he was dead, and then he'd jump up and kill them and eat them.

Coyote lay on his back. He played dead for what seemed like a really long time. He thought the ducks should have noticed him by then. He opened an eye and turned his head slightly to look at the water. He played dead some more and then looked again. No ducks had come out. He thought, "Maybe I am being too impatient about looking down there."

Some little ducks had come out of the water. They looked up to where Coyote lay. They said to the others, "Come out and look at this. It is a long one." Some of them came up to see better. They said, "This is a long one. What is it? It has a long tail." They called to the others to come and look. More of the ducks came up. Coyote had not stopped playing dead. They said, "He has a very sharp nose." "His ears are pretty long." More ducks came out to look.

Coyote thought, "Don't they know that it's me, Coyote?"

The Ducks said, "We will touch him to see how that fur feels." They gathered around Coyote and put their feet on him to feel the fur. This *tickled Coyote, and he began to laugh. The ducks jumped away. Coyote jumped up, grabbed his stick and tried to hit them, but he missed every one. They were too quick. He didn't get one.*

"We knew it was you, Coyote, and we knew you were trying Badger's trick. Badger already taught us that trick."

"But didn't you feel bad that I was dead," Coyote said.

"No," the ducks said. "We knew you weren't dead. You were breathing."

He got up and went to Badger's place. Badger saw that he had no meat. Coyote told Badger that the ducks were too smart and had all gotten away.

"Maybe if I were really dead, I could have caught them and they would have felt bad," Coyote said.

"If you were really dead," Badger said, "you couldn't jump up and catch them and you wouldn't need to eat them anyway. If you were really dead, you'd eat spirit food and who knows how that tastes. It's better to be alive and not catch any ducks. You can come over here and eat duck with me and Porcupine if you get too hungry trying to catch those ducks. We'll help you out. And, besides, who cares what those ducks think. They're not worth fretting about anyway. Ignore 'em. Eat 'em if you can."

Coyote thought about that and figured it was good advice. He ate more duck and walked home, figuring he didn't need to be dead when he could practice playing dead, and sooner or later he'd get the ducks.[28]

"That's what you need, Wayne," I said, "a way to play dead without being dead. Stick with me like Coyote stuck with Badger and Porcupine until we find your way. We'll find a way for you to get back at everyone without having to get dead in the process."

I'm now beginning to negotiate a treatment narrative with Wayne, showing the tremendous overlap of these steps, for I still haven't fully gained the illness narrative. Nevertheless, I am suggesting to Wayne that part of the treatment is to find a way to get back at people without having to die. I'm looking for an alternate Hamlet story for Wayne. Suggesting that he didn't need to get back at people would have been too big a leap for him to make. The leap he could make was to imagine getting back at people without killing himself. That was enough to begin with.

Technique
•—•—•

USING THE LANGUAGE OF HYPNOSIS AND
GUIDED IMAGERY TO HELP CLIENTS MAKE CHANGE

Learning happens more quickly in altered states of consciousness. Hypnosis represents a body of work available for healing and centered on the use of language to facilitate change in people's points of view. It is inherent in the art of persuasion and is used all the time by everyone. The more aware we can become of our use of persuasion and the more consciously we direct it with intent, the more helpful we can be to the client.

For me hypnosis, visualization, and guided imagery are synonymous. These are just different words for using the power and tools inherent in language to produce novel experiences that permit the person to make spontaneous change.

Wayne agreed to do visualization in our next session. I began with breathing, as I usually do, giving suggestions for him to relax, to create an openness and a space for change, to give permission to those parts of him who were wiser and more knowledgeable than he to go ahead and create a shift so that all his parts worked better together, some of those parts being those that caused the heart to beat, the food to digest, the lungs to breath. And wasn't it wonderful that he didn't have to regulate those parts and make them function properly because his conscious mind probably couldn't do what these deeper parts, of which he was largely unaware, knew how to do?

Technique

•—•—•

EXPLORE PARALLEL UNIVERSES
WITH IMAGINATION!

I call this parallel life regression, which consists of visiting the road not taken and the life not lived as if another version of us had taken that road and was living that life.

I asked Wayne to remember a time when he had considered suicide. I suggested that we could open a portal to a parallel universe in which he had committed suicide and attend his funeral to see what really happened. Wayne agreed to do that, and we moved forward in time to his funeral. To his surprise people were angry with him for being so stupid. Killing himself didn't have the impact he thought it would have. We tried several scenarios in which he ended up dead, and none of them turned out the way he superficially had thought they would. This is often the case when people seriously go through their own funeral. Suicide is more romantic when not carefully considered. It seems like a better solution than it is.

Now Wayne and I shared a metaphor. I could now ask him whether he was caring too much about what ducks think and if he had mastered the art of playing dead yet. This injected some humor into his thinking about suicide, which paradoxically made it more difficult to conclude.

In subsequent sessions Wayne and I continued to work together to manage his response to "ducks" and his feeling that no one cared. Over time we could laugh about his being willing to die for effect. He realized that he had absorbed a story as a child that suicide was a good way to show people how much they had hurt you. He knew people who had committed suicide for that very reason. He thought it made sense. Through our identification of that story and our evaluation of other possible interpretations of the same events, we made it less likely that he would act out this story. I was able to challenge the successfulness of this strategy both in terms of people actually feeling what you want them to feel and also the satisfaction being completely coupled to being dead and possibly oblivious to the satisfaction.

Wayne began to wonder why he cared so much what people thought of him. He wondered why he felt so burdened by needing other people to like him. He started to want them to just get off his back. As he imagined shucking them off, his back pain began to ease. He got people off his back. This is a common metaphor in states of back pain. Getting rid of the people (metaphorically or literally) is often associated with a reduction in pain.

Next we looked for the stories behind why it mattered so much what people thought of Wayne. I learned that he had grown up in the shadow of a highly successful, highly competitive older brother in a family with highly successful, high-status parents, and Wayne never felt he measured up. His wife had just left him for a more successful, more competitive, wealthier, more handsome (etc.) other man. We had the opportunity then to explore the cultural and familial stories about how we measure ourselves. We got to look at the stories that define success in our culture. We got to look at parallel selves who had made different choices and how their lives were going. Wayne became consciously able to pick a different story and move toward it. He stopped feeling suicidal, and his back pain went away.

Wayne is a typical general practice patient. In sixteen sessions his back pain was 80 percent reduced and he no longer felt suicidal. We continued to work together for four more months, but had we stopped at sixteen weeks, our work together would have been a success. Over the sixteen weeks, Wayne did much of the homework I recommended, identifying the stories and the tellers. He started walking regularly at my suggestion, which also helped. He began to improve his diet. He started taking micronutrients and fish oil. These things also matter and are part of an overall behavioral activation. More radically, some theorists are proposing that back pain and depression (as well as a host of other conditions) can be seen as part of an inflammatory syndrome that should be approached holistically and not as separate diagnoses. Back pain and depression are part and parcel of the same syndrome.

Narrative helped Wayne and me make sense of his symptoms. Through hearing his stories, I came to understand his suffering. Metaphors and stories make sense in a way we can't always explain. They make "common sense," even though we can't always articulate how.

The stories with which we grow up are powerful. Wayne's childhood included particular stories about suicide that formed the foundation for his thinking years later. Terry grew up with stories about the frightening world and the need for security that influenced her gut years later. We can't escape the stories of our childhood. But we can identify them and evaluate whether or not we want to keep them. We can ask if these stories still work in the time and place and age in which we are currently living.

2

Your Mind on Story

Fiction is not defective empirical description, but a species of simulation; just as computer simulation has augmented theories of language, perception, problem-solving, and connectionist learning, so fiction as simulation illuminates the problematics of human action and emotions.

KEITH OATLEY,
WHY FICTION MAY BE TWICE AS TRUE AS FACT

Human experience is embedded in stories, which we understand and produce through our brains.[1] We are insatiable consumers of stories. We find the personal stories of others absolutely compelling, whether as anecdotes or gossip, and spend considerable time engaged with novels, plays, films, and television shows. We become very attached to the storybooks and movies of our childhood. We may form lifelong relationships with characters such as Peter Rabbit, Cinderella, and Squirrel Nutkin. These fictional stories are not frivolous; stories have the power to change our beliefs about the world, whether or not they "really" happened. They do "really happen" in the telling. We can't help but change our ideas to become more congruent with the ideas expressed in stories we hear or read. Stories change us, whether we know it or not.[2]

Understanding a story means being able to respond to the person telling the story. It means linking the story we are hearing to the most relevant stories we have already heard. Empathy and mirror neurons and our understanding of the rules of social encounters clearly play a role in our knowing how to respond to the person telling the story. Fiction, as well as traditional cultural stories, gives us practice in reading the minds of others as we explore multiple layers of intention and their interpersonal complications.[3] Stories provide, "an environment in which versions of what it was like to experience situations and events can be juxtaposed, comparatively evaluated, and then factored into further accounts of the world (or a world)."[4]

HOW DO WE UNDERSTAND STORIES?

When we hear or read a story, our minds actively start recognizing words, parsing sentences, accessing our memory for all possible meanings of each word (semantic memory), understanding the meaning of the word (semantic comprehension), generating all possible associations we might have to what we are hearing/reading, making inferences regarding character intentions, interpreting the intentions of the teller, deciding on the overall meaning, eliminating extraneous information, and more.

The brain processes required for understanding story have been separated into three broad categories: (1) memory encoding and retrieval; (2) integration; and (3) elaboration or simulation. Memory is required to achieve an overall sense of coherence for a story, at least in part by allowing us to track the relations between near and distant clauses within that story. The same neurons associated with hearing a story continue to be active for a time after the story ends, supporting the idea that we hold the story in working memory. The frontal lobe is the brain region that best performs this function.[5]

A great number of brain regions contribute to understanding story.[6] Any brain network that supports language, memory, and even perception is likely to play some role. Neurons in the dorsolateral prefrontal cortex—Brodmann's areas (BA) 6, 8, 9, and 46—have been associated with the processing across time and sensory modalities that is necessary for language processing.[7] These same brain areas are very important for depression (underactive on the left side) and anxiety (overactive on the right side).

The processes of strategic memory retrieval most relevant to story comprehension include: (1) the monitoring and manipulation of the contents of working memory (located in mid-dorsolateral frontal cortex, or BA 9 and 46); (2) the specification or maintenance of cues for long-term memory retrieval and encoding (ventrolateral frontal cortex, or BA 47); and (3) the processes of rejecting or accepting the products of memory retrieval (respectively, ventromedial frontal cortex, or BA 11, 13, and 25, and anterior prefrontal cortex, or BA 10).

Although we can talk about separate brain regions, what really matters is the communication between them. This communication allows them to operate as a functionally integrated system. Frontal and temporal regions play a particularly important role in language comprehension and production. Researchers who study dynamic, on-line (functional/effective) connectivity during language perception tasks using functional magnetic resonance imaging (fMRI) and magnetoencephalography (MEG) have come to the conclusion that distinct linguistic abilities do not rely on separate neural pathways, but rather multiple pathways interact dynamically to support multiple linguistic abilities.[8]

WHAT IS MEMORY ANYWAY?

Memory is essential for understanding and producing stories. Memory is not stored like parts in a warehouse or books in a library, even though much of the general public and many in the scientific community assume it is. Discrete packets of memory for particular events are not placed on shelves with identifying data that allows them to be retrieved easily when needed like books in a massive library. Rather, memory is stored in accordance with emotional salience* and experiential relevance.

Roger Schank and Robert Abelson, cognitive scientists and leaders in the field of artificial intelligence, focused their research on understanding the integrated functioning of our brains. They write that our memories for events, our eidetic memories, are actually indexed by our characterization and evaluation of the given experience.[9] We can understand this by picking a category of experience and seeing what stories come to mind. For example, when Lewis thinks about moving to Maine, he remembers, "the night we spent at the Drayhorse Pub and Inn in Bethel, Maine, and what a lovely dinner we had." He remembers how much this pub resembled an English country inn in Cumbria or Northumberland, where he had spent substantial time. He remembers chatting with the owner about his inspiration to open the inn and with one of the waitresses about her daughter's being stuck in Ontario on her drive back from Michigan due to losing her passport. What also comes to mind is a dinner at the Senator Inn in Augusta in which every course was lobster. Lewis's memory for moving to Maine is full of stories like this, disconnected in time and not organized in any linear or logical arrangement. He can generate a logical, linear story about moving to Maine if requested, but he recognizes that the order of the stories he includes is arbitrary and not necessarily accurate. These memories are stored so differently in his brain than are his tax receipts in various orderly drawers in the file cabinet.

Memory Is Reconstruction

We do not consciously or deliberately construct an index for memory storage. We do not function like computers. We don't systematically record our life experiences and store them on the hard drive. Memory

---

*Salience refers both to how something stands out relative to its neighbors and the degree to which we care about it. Detecting things that are important to us is a key aspect of attention. This "salience detection" helps us to survive by enabling us to focus our limited perceptual and cognitive resources on what seems most important to us.

is reconstruction.[10] This process of reconstruction encompasses selectivity, embellishment, and distortion. In a famous experiment, psychologist Elizabeth Loftus tested witnesses' recollection of details regarding a car accident.[11] Participants were shown a series of slides depicting an accident involving a pedestrian and were instructed to be eyewitnesses. Half of the subjects saw a red Datsun at a stop sign, and the other half saw the same Datsun at a yield sign. After seeing all pictures, participants were asked twenty questions. Among these was a question with a presupposition that either matched or did not match the picture they were shown, that is, "Did a car pass the red Datsun while it stopped at the stop sign?" or "Did a car pass the red Datsun while it stopped at the yield sign?"

Participants were later shown pairs of pictures and were asked to select the one they had seen. Among these was the red Datsun, either at a stop sign or a yield sign. Accuracy was 71 percent when the supposition in the preceding question matched the picture that was actually viewed but dropped to 41 percent when the presupposition was misleading. The results demonstrated that memory is susceptible to suggestion. Memory is not a fixed recording of an event. Memory is reconstructed in the moment by piecing together fragments seemingly related to the event but with large gaps that we fill with whatever seems relevant or likely to construct a coherent story, fitting the demands of our current situation in which we are trying to remember something.

Memory Is Selective

Human memory must be selective to function well. One aspect of this selectivity in memory is the recognition that some events need to be added to our more general memory about classes of events (restaurants, classrooms, forests) while others need to be told as new stories, causing them to be saved in our story-based memory. Memory is looking for knowledge that tells it something about the nature of the world in general. Facts or isolated events must achieve significance to be stored, which means that they must become part of a story.

Telling the Story Creates the Memory

We stop events from disappearing by consciously incorporating them into a single unit called a story. For stories to be told without a great deal of effort, they must be accessible as a unit. Without connectedness of the events into a unified entity, stories would have to be reconstructed each time they are told. This would become more and more difficult as the connections between events fade from memory over time. Without a telling, without a rendition, memory is not formed or stored. These stories contain more than events; they express our points of view, our philosophy of life, our values and valuations of others, our assessment of others' goals and beliefs, and so much more. Story-based memory, then, expresses our points of view and philosophy of life.

We construct memory by telling stories to others (or at least rehearsing the telling). It resembles remembering dreams. If we tell our dream upon awakening, we remember it. We feel compelled to tell stories to others about the experiences that matter to us. I remember what I say to others. The more I tell a story, the more it gets etched into long-term memory. The stories we tell repeatedly to an audience become those that are remembered without difficulty.

NEGATIVE STORIES

Stories are the way we preserve events in memory that would otherwise be lost, connecting these events into a unified whole that can be readily remembered. But sometimes the stories and the events they preserve are causing us to suffer, particularly when the stories are negative.

In fact, as memory and emotion researchers Kensinger and LeDoux tell us, our brains have a bias toward remembering the negative.[12] This bias toward remembering the negative helps us survive since it's more important to remember what's dangerous and potentially lethal than to remember positive experiences. This tendency to give more salience to negative experiences appears to work at both the cellular level (one-celled animals demonstrate these tendencies) and at the level of complex organisms with brains (mammals).[13] At the cellular level, axons in neural networks associated with negative affect grow faster and bigger and have more dendrites. These bigger, faster, and more connected networks are like interstate highways compared to country roads. The faster, larger connections have a more intense effect on behavior.

These "negative affect" or danger-remembering neural networks are typically connected to the amygdalae, the area of the brain that manages fear and panic. These "superhighways" to and from the amygdalae allow us to react quickly to possibly dangerous situations without the frontal, thinking cortex having to get involved. The connections from the medial prefrontal cortex to the amygdalae are smaller. Information travels slower, like on a country road. If the brain suddenly perceives a risk of being bitten by a snake on the path while hiking, these superhighway connections allow us to jump faster than the speed of thought.[14]

Beaudoin and Zimmerman, family psychologists in the Bay Area, remind us that we are biased toward negative affect at the outset, because we are literally wired to pay more attention to the negative. We have a disproportionate number of neural networks that favor negative affect.[15] They point out that clients struggling with depression, anxiety, or anger may emphasize and enhance this bias. They may consciously rehearse negative interpretations, pay them more attention, and may have fewer experiences of a happier state.[16] This lopsided development creates what they have described as negative superhighways.[17]

As Beaudoin and Zimmerman comment, once negative affect is generated, the prefrontal cortex creates an explanation to account for the experience. This explanation of our negative emotion and experience can become an identity narrative, or who we think we are. We tend to notice what fits our identity narrative and miss what Michael White called counter-narratives, or examples of times when we behaved differently from the story we tell about ourselves. Under stress or duress, these bigger, more developed neural pathways and the stories that are

associated with them are more likely to be activated rapidly, with predictably negative results.[18]

This dynamic is very clear in Claire's case, from her first visit to my
office, when I ask her "What brings us together today?"

Technique

•—•—•

INITIATE THE CONVERSATION
IN AN EMPOWERING WAY

We choose not to ask how we can help, but to ask, "What brings
us together today?" It begins the discussion with an emphasis on a
collaborative relationship and presumes that people have some say
in the journey to come. It guides them to tell us how they view their
own ability to act in their own healing.

In the modern shortcut that people use these days, Claire first presents with her diagnostic labels. Claire tells me she has attention deficit
disorder (ADD), is highly sensitive, and has post-traumatic stress disorder
(PTSD).

Claire assumes that I know what she means by the labels, but in
fact, I don't. This is not because I haven't trained in their meaning, but
because I am aware of their vagaries and because I want to remain open
to the possibilities she is presenting. Too often when we hear a label, it
sends us immediately into a particular pattern of responses. This is very
useful in emergency medicine, not as useful in psychiatry. That is why
it is important to go beyond labels.

Technique

•—•—•

LOOK FOR THE EXPLANATORY STORY

We need explanatory stories. They serve as a kind of narrative top-
down driven way of processing information we otherwise find hard
to accommodate into our world.

Claire tells me about burying the memory of blunt force trauma at age thirteen. Her mother pushed her face first onto the floor and then beat her on the head with a wooden clog. She remembers being defenseless on the ground while her mother "knocked her lights out." She describes running away to keep her mother from killing her. Other families took her in. "Nobody said anything about anything in those days. There were no human service agencies, because we were middle-class America."

Claire doesn't understand why she's unhappy. She needs an explanation. She finds herself talking to her brother about his terrible experience with their mother. She remembers her own terrible experience. She's having a headache. Suddenly it seems very logical that the event that she is now remembering is the cause of her troubles. Claire has concluded that her problems all stem from this beating her mother gave her, which caused traumatic brain injury and PTSD. She tells me she suffers from excruciating headaches. (I should note here that Claire had been tested extensively for damage that may have resulted in her symptoms but nothing had ever been found. There is of course no baseline measure to assess brain damage. The trauma effects are obvious.)

In our practice we begin with radical acceptance. We never argue with people. We don't dispute their explanatory story. We may offer other possibilities of interpretation, drawing on our own training and knowledge, and hold up a mirror to reflect the story back, but we never tell someone we think he or she is wrong. By working in this way, we encourage people to let us into the world of stories they have created for themselves.

In my own worldview, I doubt that one event conditions a lifetime, but I do believe that one event can stand for many and that we remember one event to represent the many. I could believe that Claire's poor relationship with her mother affected her life—not just due to one event that she painfully remembers, but because of many events that she may not even readily recall. We all often remember one event that becomes representative. We think of it as the signal story that becomes powerful as a stand-in for multiple events, all now coalesced emotionally into one vignette/memory. It's a kind of synecdoche, letting one story stand in for the whole narrative.

Claire elaborated that she thought her mother had "knocked some screws loose." She related that she had already been having a hard time at school. She was bullied for her large hair. When she came home with a bad report card, her mother called her stupid. Relatives called her the black sheep of the family. She accepted that definition and self-labeled as a loser. She recalled that from the time of the beating forward, she had stayed in other people's houses and come home only when necessary. She said that her father didn't know any of this. Nor did her siblings. During this time her headaches were debilitating, though she never mentioned her family difficulties to any of the many doctors consulted about her headaches.

Claire dramatically asserted that she had never woken up happy after that beating. It had given her a fatalistic view of the world that "it's going to end and we're all going to die." This had become her life ever since, she said, leading her to make choices that led to a series of totally exhaustive depressions and "crappy jobs."

Claire's beating had happened forty-six years earlier when she was thirteen years old. Clearly the episode was extremely wounding, and now her fearful narrative about her head injury was tied into her tightly woven story of the futility and hopelessness of effort. It seemed to seal her fate; she had become convinced that it added organic damage to psychological damage and meant that she would never emerge from the gloom of her sense of failure.

Technique
•—•—•
ROOT OUT ONE EXAMPLE OF SUCCESS

When people can only focus on failure, I sometimes gently ask them if they can tell me about any one moment in their lives when they felt as though they had a handle on things, that they had created a success, felt better. We then investigate what was going on at that time.

I asked Claire if there had been any time in her life, any time at all, when she had felt better. Claire offered a story about change. She talked about a major shift in her evaluation of her childhood, when—after years of feeling terrible—she had suddenly realized that she had been smart to run away. She felt relieved to have this revelation that she was not a complete failure and had actually done something right. She proudly announced that she was lucky to be alive.

She also reported that lately she had started to feel better, not as guilty. She said she had a joyful epiphany and freedom from her past, but still had this sense of pain, and that she was not going to live to enjoy her life because of her head injury. Meanwhile, the head injury explained why she couldn't meditate and feel calm and peaceful. It explained her continual experience of being violated. It explained her feeling like "a nervous wreck" in public, always having to carry tissues in her pocket. It explained her not wanting teachers to call on her because she didn't know anything, and it explained her ADD.

Technique

•—•—•

CLARIFY GOALS

We need to clarify and agree upon goals as early as possible. Having clients set the goal empowers them and involves them in the process. We need to establish how we will know that we have accomplished what we set out to do. We like to think of it as pondering what story might be better than the one the person is living.

Claire told me that she wanted to release her heavy burden. She wanted to become "dignified." I asked her to think about what the achievement of this goal would look like. How would we know when this goal was accomplished? What could we do together to accomplish her goals? I asked her to report back to me in the next session.

When Claire returned she had thought more about what we should do together. Before elaborating, however, she began repeating, almost verbatim, the story she had told me previously. Perhaps she feared I had failed to remember it, though I had asked her permission to write it down in our session. Perhaps she had been to other practitioners who had indeed forgotten what she had told them. More likely, she was in the habit of repetitively telling this story, as people often are when they arrive at what Dan McAdams of Northwestern University calls a "defining moment."

When this happens it is a clear signal to us that the story is representative of something and that it is a well-rehearsed and likely effective story for clients to get what they want. Part of our work is finding out what makes a version of a story become rote. We often find that the story is a marker, an anchor for a causal relationship between the story and what it *causes*. Often we find that these stories are in a way protected, as the things they cause are in their way protected. Without the story something might change. With the story the situation cannot be fixed. Because the wounding event was real, and cannot be changed, and the outcome stems from that, there can never be reparation. We work gently with these stories to see if we can change the story of cause.

Claire again told me about staying away from home but having to come back into the home, complaining again about the lack of family protective services when she was a child, and describing again her mother's verbal abuse. She described being called a dummy and hearing repeatedly that she never did anything right. Again she described having trouble at school after her mother beat her on the head, but not knowing why. She remembered putting her head on the desk at school and drooling. She recalled being bullied in school for having curly hair and poor grades. She'd have headaches and visit the doctor only to be told to take two aspirins. She recalled feeling noble in her silence about her mother, not wanting anyone to know what a creep her mother was. She repeated how this beating had affected her emotionally her whole life. She said she still has headaches and foggy brain.

Finally, Claire drew breath. She made a pitch for needing amphetamines.

People like quick-acting drugs that change their state. These include benzodiazepines, which are like alcohol, stimulants like amphetamines, and opiates. Claire told me her favorite activity was to be in her bed, asleep, adding chronic depression to her list of sufferings. She wondered if she needed some type of brain chemical therapy to excite her dopamine?

Technique
•—•—•
NEGOTIATION

Once we get the story that explains the illness and understand the client's treatment narrative, we enter a phase of negotiation in which we endeavor to shift the narrative toward treatments that we believe could be more effective.

Claire asserted again that she had permanent brain damage. She said she could read three chapters of a textbook and not retain anything. Shaped by modern culture, Claire seeks a story for her life. Clearly she has experienced trauma, but more, she has been shaped to see her unhappiness and dissatisfaction in medical terms. She feels she is ill. If she were not ill, she would be happy and satisfied. Hence, she is searching for the illness or illnesses that match her symptoms. She wants confirmation of that and a drug to make her better. When I asked what "better" meant to her, she answered, "less tired; happy and perky." When we appreciate how she is embedded in the dominant cultural narratives, we see that she has made a marvelous effort toward self-explanation.

I was open to prescribing a drug for Claire if it seemed like it might help more than harm, but I didn't really think a particular drug existed to make her perkier, less tired, and happier. She thought amphetamines would do this. I didn't want to prescribe amphetamines, because I didn't think her symptoms really matched any condition for which we're authorized to prescribe amphetamines. Also, I'm not fond of the "better living through chemicals" approach. If a drug were demanded, I would pick bupropion, because it can be stimulating, mood-elevating, and attention-improving.

However, I really wanted to move the dialogue toward lifestyle changes that Claire could make. I explained to her that amphetamines were not really indicated for what she was describing according to current state guidelines. I mentioned bupropion but also said that some other approaches could be very helpful. Claire said that once she was studying for final exams in college and someone gave her a "Black Beauty," which made her feel "great"—energetic and smart. She thought, "Wow, I need a prescription for that." I remembered that Black Beauties were amphetamines and did my best to explain that feeling great wasn't necessarily therapeutic and that many drugs of abuse make one feel great, which is why they're so readily abused.

I gave my well-rehearsed speech about the value of exercise, changing diet, doing yoga, meditation, t'ai chi, chi gong, visiting friends, writing, praying, painting, and more, for feeling happier, perkier, and less tired. Claire responded that maybe she needed hormones. I answered that we could explore that at a future meeting. Claire was still trying to get medication. She responded that she knew friends who were taking amphetamines that helped them feel better. I suggested perhaps some doctors were overmedicating their clients. She said she didn't know any doctors who don't overmedicate.

She thought she deserved amphetamines, because of her highly sensitive system. I shared more of the state guidelines and told her that we'd have to do neuropsychological testing to confirm a diagnosis of ADD or ADHD, and even then, we should try at least two noncontrolled-substance approaches to attention problems and that she would have to come to our attention-training group twice monthly. She decided that maybe she would start with the bupropion. I wrote her a prescription for 100 mg of the sustained release form.

Next we talked about diet. I talked about how helpful anti-inflammatory diets are for the symptoms she presented, which could be the consequence of excess inflammatory load. That got her attention. "I do feel like I've got too much inflammation," she said. I gave her the address of a website describing an anti-inflammatory diet and talked about some of the recommended herbs and spices, especially curcumin (turmeric), bromelain, coenzyme Q10, burdock root, and more. That led to a discussion of the inflammatory theory of depression.[19] I was hoping to hook her with this story.

I told Claire how, when we are stressed, our immune cells produce molecules called pro-inflammatory cytokines. They're great for fighting off infection, but if it's just the stress of chronic unhappiness, that's not so great. These molecules act upon our brains, making us feel sick and tired and unhappy. I named some of the colorful characters in this parade of molecules that make us feel sick, including interleukin-1 alpha and beta, tumor necrosis factor-alpha, and interleukin-6 (IL-6). I explained how their effect on the brain, which makes us feel sick, may paradoxically help us to recover (at least from acute illnesses), by putting us into a state of rest and repair. However, exposure to these pro-inflammatory cytokines on a long-term basis leads to the symptoms of depression.

Claire was impressed with this story and shared that her diet was primarily meat, potatoes, and bread. We ventured into ideas of eating more vegetables, fewer grains, and eating other proteins like fish, chicken, and even vegetarian sources. I had her interest now and thought she would actually visit the websites for which I gave her addresses. Now we are on the road toward building a therapeutic alliance. My offering Claire an alternative explanatory story of healing allows some useful information to come her way. Next, we can begin to address management of her traumatic past and the scars it has left behind. If Claire makes some changes in her diet and begins to feel better, psychotherapy and group participation can begin to address some of her other wishes.

In these first two visits, Claire didn't get everything she wanted. She didn't get confirmation that her mother's beating of her had caused all her problems, and she didn't get amphetamines. However, she did get to be heard, she did start a relationship in which she could have a dialogue about her ideas, and she did glimpse some ways in which her treatment narrative could change. That's what the general practice of medicine is all about—the negotiation of stories for the benefit of the patient.

THE URGE TO STORY

We are social creatures. The success and popularity of Facebook confirms this. Whatever happens to us, we want to tell others about it. We have multiple reasons for telling. We may want to improve our social standing. We may wish to influence someone to do something for us—give us a loan, give us a job, go on a date, marry us, or let us into the country. We design our stories to accomplish the social purposes we have in mind. We notice the stories that work and the stories that don't. We keep telling the stories that work, and we modify or delete the stories that don't work. We build a repertoire of stories to use in social occasions for specific purposes.

The more successful people are at getting what they want, the larger their repertoire of stories from which to choose, and the more astute they are at matching story to audience. We call this narrative competence. The greater our narrative competence, the more popular, successful, or sought after we are. We notice those who lack narrative competence, such as people who get diagnosed with schizophrenia or people diagnosed with autism. These people are not so able to tell a good story or recognize when a story is not working (the error-detection system is faulty in schizophrenia and autism), so they are not so able to modify or change the story they are telling.

When we tell a story, we search memory for relevant episodes or vignettes to weave together. Inevitably, we find more associations than we need and must discard episodes that fit less well into the effect we wish to have. Narrative competency, or being able to construct and tell a good story, requires both a widespread search and an evaluative process that selects the most salient items from that search, discarding the rest.

The orbitofrontal cortex is crucial for this discard function. In order to compose a story, someone must want to hear it. Even in the real-time telling of the story, audience reaction changes it. We want the story that elicits the desired response from the audience. When this isn't forthcoming, we change the story.

THE PARADOX OF
UNDERSTANDING STORIES

We tell stories for many reasons. We show we have understood a story we have received by telling that story back. The storyteller can assess how well he or she has been understood by comparing the two stories. Thus, we tell stories to show that we have understood stories.

In life we are often looking for stories to tell back to show that we have understood. When we find them, processing stops, and we wait to tell our story. We only incorporate what we have heard into memory when we feel that our own stories are inadequate in some way, for example, if our story is missing a piece. Such pieces can be supplied by other people's stories. We may find a story inadequate when we use it to exemplify a belief that we are not quite sure we hold. We are willing to consider new stories as evidence for or against those beliefs and, therefore, to record and to remember better the stories of others.

The odd paradox to all this is that we are less likely to learn directly from someone else's story than we are to modify our own memories to incorporate some aspects of those stories we are hearing. When we hear a story, we are reminded of our own similar stories. The story we heard is recalled in terms of the story of which we were reminded. Thus, we rarely recall the stories of others easily. Generally, other people's stories don't have the richness of detail and emotional impact that allows them to be stored in multiple ways in our memories. They do, however, provide enough details and emotions to allow them to be more easily stored than if the teller had simply told us his or her belief.

We learn from others' stories, but more and better if what we hear relates well to what we already know, prompting us to remember and review our own stories. This is equally true in the reading of fiction. We hear best from others that which we personally have already heard or experienced. Retrieving personal memories that occur as associations to a story is what provides the richness and emotional depth we expect from literature or the theater. Our memories tend to be more actively self-oriented when elicited by what we consider to be fictional as compared to what we consider to be news.[20]

DYNAMIC MEMORY

Roger Schank proposed the concept of dynamic memory, which changes in response to what it understands over time. When we have a new experience that appears related to what we already know, perhaps updating it, perhaps overriding it, we add that experience to our memories. For example, information from a new play we have just seen updates what we know about plays in general. Or traveling to make home visits to patients tucked away in hidden recesses of the county updates stories about the roads of the county and causes our memory to add new information about those roads to existing knowledge about the county.[21]

Pieces of memory structures, once altered, update those same pieces occurring in other structures. Thus, for example, if you learn something about tipping in a restaurant in France, that new information updates how to tip in a taxi and at a hotel. The way this happens is through sharing of standardized smaller knowledge structures, of which "France" would be one, and "tipping" would be another even smaller structure. Through such structures, and through the sharing of smaller structures by larger structures, we build up event memory. Whenever we use a particular body of knowledge in our interactions with the world, that new experience alters our preexisting knowledge.

I took advantage of dynamic memory in the way I worked with Tina, who suffered from drug and alcohol abuse. I saw her when she was just getting out of jail and uncertain what direction to take.

"What's wrong?" I asked her.

"I'm an addict," she said.

"What does that mean?" I asked. That irritated her. I was supposed to know what it meant. I tried a different tack. "When did you start drinking?" I asked her.

"When I was twelve," she said. "I got into my dad's vermouth and all the pain disappeared. I loved it. I'd drink and I'd run outside and fly about the yard like an eagle. The pain went away. I was numb and I loved it." There's a story here about her pain, but that will come later. I decide to continue tracking this story of drinking.

"Then what happened?" I asked.

"I found drinking buddies. We started with two by fours and moved on. Initially it was one for all of us, then one for each of us, then eight or ten of them, and more. Who knew how much we could drink? It came to pass that I only knew people who drank. Why would I be interested in people who didn't drink?"

"Then what happened?" I asked.

"Then came the drugs," she said. "Cocaine was my magic. It was the best feeling in the universe. Nothing was better than that. Pretty soon the only people I knew were the people who could give me cocaine or who could get cocaine from me."

"Then what happened?" I asked.

"I was the Empress of the Universe. I knew no fear. I was in control of everything that moved, of all that I could see, of everything in my world."

"Then what happened?" I asked.

"I ended up in jail," she said. "That was such a crash. My world ended. They said that I had no healthy relationships. All my relationships were about giving or getting drugs. That was my world. Nobody cared about anything except the next high. And, in jail, the high was over."

"Then what happened?" I asked.

"I came to see you," she said. She was being quite literal. She had walked from jail to my office.

Technique

•—•—•

NEGOTIATE SHAME

Shame is the enemy of change. When the client feels shame, we need to transform that to heroism. Turn the journey to the office into one of heroic, even epic proportions. Dragons can help, as can witches, trolls, werewolves, and gargoyles.

Part of narrative practice is to show people other ways to view their story, other ways to spin the same factual events.

"Let me tell you your story back to you as I understand it," I said.

"Okay," she said.

"Once upon a time, there was an orphan princess whose real parents had died. She had been stolen by an evil sorcerer and farmed out to peasants who cared not for her. She suffered greatly. She lived in a shack at the edge of the village and had to do the bidding of the peasants who owned her. Her feet were covered with sores, her hands with blisters. Whenever the villagers saw her, they beat her with sticks. She had to toil from sunrise to sunset on whatever task the evil peasants gave her. Sometimes they made her do things that didn't matter just for the sheer pleasure of seeing her work and suffer.

"One day she discovered a magical potion in the home of the peasants that made all the pain go away. Even though she still had the sores and the blisters and the bruises, suddenly all the pain was gone. She was numb. She was so grateful for that potion. She tried to get more and more of it and share it with her friends, with the other servants she knew who were also in pain. Suddenly life had become bearable. This was wonderful. She was helping all her friends who were in terrible pain just like her to be numb and free from suffering. That was great even though they still lived at the edge of the village and weren't really accepted by the majority of people in the town.

"Then, one day, something miraculous happened. A great and powerful wizard appeared at their doorstep, announcing that he had a magic white powder that was so much better than their liquid potions. 'Just breathe this powder,' he said, 'and you will not only be free from pain, you will be all-powerful. You will be invincible.' At first, she was skeptical, but when she tried it, she discovered that all he said was true. She wanted more and more of this magic powder. At first she shared it with her friends, but as time went on, she wanted more and more of it for herself.

"She now lived in a wonderful world, free from pain, free from disability, happy. All was fine, until one day the unthinkable happened. The magical world had disappeared around her, just like the story of the knight who found the Grail Castle only to awaken in the morning in a field of grass covered with the morning dew. She, however, awoke in a jail cell. Apparently she had been betrayed. The wizard was actually an evil warlock, and the power had been an illusion. When they let her out, she came straight to my office."

Tina loved this story. It painted a different picture of her life using the same details. Tina's story held social stigma and rejection. My story captured the goal of her drinking and using drugs—to relieve unbearable suffering. We legitimately use legal drugs to do this. Tina had used illegal drugs and alcohol. The distinction is in some ways arbitrary, imposed by governments and authorities. Had Tina been in a different social class, perhaps she would have been taken to a psychiatrist and been given psychotropic medications. Or perhaps she would have ended up on the same regimen. Regardless, we can ennoble her story.

My story transformed a story of shame into one of heroism. The alcohol and drugs had deceived her, for sure, but in her noble search for freedom from suffering and pain. Certainly I had her attention, which is the first step in any healing process. Healing (making whole again) requires attention and rapport. My story had provided both. As a novel perspective, it got her attention and even showed compassion toward her, so we built rapport.

Tina started to share the rest of her story with me. She had grown up poor with four brothers and a younger sister. Her mother had died when her youngest sister was one year old, leaving her, as the oldest, and a girl, to care for the family, despite her youth. Her father was a rough man, loving, but largely absent in his grief and his work. He modeled the story of the magic potion by drinking away his sadness and loneliness. He didn't notice when his brother molested Tina, who had no one to protect her. Sadly, this is a common story. The result was a wounded young woman, whose life was one of relatively continual pain with no models for soothing except her father's example of drinking, which worked.

Now we had to find alternate strategies for pain management. The magic potion had worked to a point but at too high a cost. She had no friends except for those who could score drugs from her or sell her drugs. She had gone to jail. She had no place to live and no possessions. She had no income. Life objectively looked bleak. She was moving from jail to a shelter. She was thinking of applying for Social Security disability income. She needed community.

Technique

•—•—•

INTRODUCTION OF COMMUNITY

Large group meetings are wonderful for promoting change. The more people there, the easier change will be. The more we can bring the world of the client into the wider world, the more we can change the expectations of the audience and the more the person will change. The group becomes a kind of "care team" and can be very helpful.

We need comrades to support new behaviors. We change because the people around us expect us to be different. If we remain isolated, we stay the same. The audience is required for a new play to go forward. In my view being with others would bring about Tina's recovery much faster than being alone, which might never work.

I knew about a healing circle Tina could join. Led by a colleague at the local Unitarian Church, no appointment was needed and no fee was charged. All Tina had to do was go. If she went long enough, she would connect with people and begin to build friendships. I knew of other resources for her. The Mental Health Association offered free peer counseling and support groups. Another agency offered a no-fee group once a week. Groups were also available at the shelter.

However, Tina's story about other people was saturated with shame, leading her to avoid others and to isolate herself except when drinking or using drugs. At first Tina did not want to be with a group of people. She didn't like people, and people didn't like her except "under the influence." My task was to introduce the idea that we need other people and that other people need us. The importance and value of community for Tina's healing was a hard concept for her to accept.

To understand her feelings, I needed to hear what Tina had heard as a child about other people. I learned that her father didn't trust others and was a suspicious man, perhaps overly so. He didn't want anyone, not even his brother, to know his business. I already knew he was not an emotional man. He didn't share his thoughts or his feelings with his children. He didn't want anyone to see him "weak." For him (or as he was interpreted through Tina's eyes), other people were a threat, a source of discomfort, a stressor. His audience was always critical, never warm and accepting. If we only ever perform for cold, critical, distant audiences, we can lose our enjoyment of the theater. Tina and her father only played for rejecting audiences. Alcohol and drugs mitigated that. I needed stories to inspire her to connect with other people. I needed stories that would demonstrate people's interdependence on each other, the interconnectedness of all of us, and the idea that we can be in whatever state we are and still be acceptable to others. I needed stories that would emphasize taking help from others.

Technique

•—•—•

INDIRECT TELLING

Direct confrontation rarely works. Telling stories with suggestion through metaphor is more effective.

When faced with stubborn refusal, I just keep telling stories without telling the person the meaning of the story or what I intended. Here's an example of a story I told Tina around the time of the turning point. The idea was to build a new identity based on being helpful to others to resist substances and crime in opposition to the old identity of substance abuse and crime to support her habits. I continued to find stories in which she could identify with heroes who did right to oppose evildoing. Imagine that you are Tina listening to the Penobscot (Maine) story of Rabbit calling a truce! This is a very traditional story.[22]

Once upon a time, when Glooscap still walked among the Wabanaki in physical form, there lived two lively animals. Keoonik the Otter, and Ableegumooch the Rabbit, who were forever playing tricks on each other.

One day, when Otter was swimming, Rabbit ran off with a string of eels he had left on the shore. Otter had thought he had hidden those eels really well, but he had forgotten that Rabbit had a fine nose and could sniff them out no matter where he put them. When Otter saw Rabbit running off with his eels, he rushed out of the water and followed in angry pursuit. Rabbit was fast, but so was Otter, and Rabbit was weighed down by all those eels that were bumping against his back. Otter simply followed the marks made by the eels touching the ground between Rabbit's hops. Suddenly the trail broke open into a clearing in the woods, a lovely meadow. What astonished Otter, however, was the sight of a withered old woman sitting beside a small fire and no trace of Rabbit.

"Kwah-ee, Noogumee," said Otter, using the formal address suitable for an elderly female. He lowered his eyes to show respect and spoke softly. "Did you see a rabbit hopping this way, dragging a string of eels?" The woman was so old Otter feared a puff of wind might blow her to dust.

"Rabbit? Rabbit?" muttered the old woman. The sun reflected off her almost translucent skin. "What kind of animal is that?" Otter could see the blood highways in her hands and arms. He explained that a rabbit was a small brown jumping creature with long ears and a short tail. He tried to draw a picture of Rabbit with his paws. "I saw no such animal,"

the old woman grumbled, "but I'm glad you came along, for I'm cold and sick. If I had seen that thing that you called Rabbit, I would have asked him, but since I did not, you will have to do. Now please gather a little wood for my fire."

Obligingly, Otter went off to do so. He toiled hard and long at cutting firewood for the old woman until he was exhausted. Returning with the wood, he stared around in surprise. The meadow was empty. The old woman was gone. Only the plant people stood guard around the meadow. On the spot where the old woman had sat, he saw the mark of a rabbit's haunches, and familiar paw prints leading away in to the woods. Again at the spot of each hop the eels had made their mark. It was then that Otter remembered that Rabbit was very clever at changing his appearance and fooling people.

"Oh, that miserable rabbit!" cried Keoonik and set off again on the trail. Despite his exhaustion from cutting all that wood, he ran along the path lined with old maple. This time the tracks led straight to a village of the people, where Otter could see Rabbit in conversation with a thin, sad man wearing the feather of a chief in his hair string. The village itself was run down with a sad air and the people were thin and gaunt. Wily Otter cut himself a stout stick and hid behind a tree. He was prepared to jump out and give Rabbit a thwacking until Rabbit gave him back his eels. In due time Rabbit came strolling down the path, his face creased in an absent-minded frown.

Otter was ready for him. He jumped from behind the tree onto the path with a howl that would have made any ninja proud. He brought that stick down on the Rabbit's head with a thud, and Rabbit collapsed on the grass.

"That should teach him," thought Otter, with satisfaction, and he sat down to wait for Rabbit to recover. He had to wait longer than he had expected and was beginning to worry that maybe he had hit Rabbit too hard and had killed him or permanently damaged him, when Rabbit starting coming to his senses and then slowly staggered to his feet with a dazed expression. Rabbit had a plaintive look of complete bewilderment on his face. "What did you do with my eels?" demanded Otter. He made his voice as self-righteous as he could and tried to look foreboding.

"I gave them to the people," muttered Rabbit, exploring the bump on his head with a groan. Rabbit plopped back down on the soft forest floor to nurse his bump. "Why did you hit me like that, you silly creature?" Rabbit stretched and collected his dignity. "Those people are starving," he said. Rabbit showed a look of genuine and total compassion, rare for this furry trickster. "For many moons someone has been stealing their food."

"Just the same," grumbled Otter, "those were my eels." Rabbit hopped upright and thumped his hind legs on the ground with an air of great determination.

"Otter, we must find the robbers and punish them!"

"We?" asked Otter in astonishment.

"Yes, you and I," said his companion firmly. "Let there be a truce between us until we discover the thieves." Otter thought that Rabbit was a fine one to complain of people stealing other people's food! However, he too felt sorry for the Penobscots.

"All right," he agreed. "We'll have a truce," and they shook hands solemnly. Then they started back to the village to ask the Chief what they might do to help, but when they were still some way off, they saw the Weasel and the Mouse talking to him. These two animals were so troublesome that even their own families would have nothing to do with them.

"Let's listen," whispered Rabbit, drawing Otter behind a tree.

"We will find those robbers for you, Chief," they heard Weasel say. "Don't you worry about a thing."

"You can depend on us," chimed in Mouse.

Rabbit nudged Otter, "Did you hear that?"

"I heard," said Otter. "So the people don't need our help after all."

"I wonder," said Rabbit thoughtfully.

"What do you wonder? And why are we whispering?"

"Shhh! Let's think about it a little, Otter. Have you any idea how those two get their living? They sleep all day and go hunting only after dark."

"Some of us like to hunt after dark," Otter said fairly.

"Well, but listen," said Rabbit. "All the fur robes in the camp have

been chewed and scratched and spoiled. What animals chew and scratch wherever they go?"

"Weasels and mice," answered Otter promptly. "Very well. Let's follow them and see what happens." So Otter and Rabbit, keeping out of sight, followed Weasel and Mouse a very long way, to a large burrow in the side of a hill where a number of other weasels and mice of bad reputation were gathered. All greeted Weasel and Mouse and listened to what they had to say, while Rabbit and Otter, hidden behind a blueberry bush, listened too.

"We were very sympathetic," smirked Weasel, "and said we would help them."

"So now they won't suspect us," said Mouse, and all the mice and weasels chortled gleefully.

"It is time now," said Weasel, "to call all the animals together and plan the conquest of the Penobscots. For we are smarter than the people and deserve to have all the food for ourselves."

"Very true!" all shouted.

"How will we get the rest to join us?" asked Mouse.

"The smaller ones will be afraid to say no to us," declared Weasel. "We will use trickery on the others. We will tell them the Penobscots plan to destroy all the animals in the land, and we must unite in order to defend ourselves."

"Then, with Wolf and Bear and Moose to help us," cried Mouse, "we'll soon have all the people at our mercy!" Otter and Rabbit could hardly believe their ears. Someone must warn the people.

"Come on," whispered Otter, but Rabbit only crouched where he was, tense and unmoving. The fact is, he wanted to sneeze! Rabbit wanted to sneeze more than he ever wanted to sneeze in his whole life before, but he mustn't sneeze—the sound would give them away. So he tried and he tried to hold that sneeze back. He pressed his upper lip, he grew red in the face, and his eyes watered—but nothing was any good.

"Ahhhhhh-ahhhhhh-choo!" Instantly, the weasels and mice pounced on Otter and Rabbit and dragged them out of hiding.

"Spies!" growled Weasel.

"Kill them, kill them!" screamed Mouse.

"I have a better plan," said Weasel. "These two will be our first recruits." Then he told the prisoners they must become members of his band or be killed.

Poor Rabbit. Poor Otter. They did not wish to die, yet they could never do as the thieves wished, for the Penobscots were their friends. Rabbit opened his mouth, meaning to defy the villains no matter what the consequences, and then his mouth snapped shut. He had heard a strange sound, the sound of a flute piping far away, and he knew what it was. It was the magic flute of Glooscap, and the Great Chief was sending him a message.

Into Rabbit's head came the memory of something Glooscap had said to him long ago, half in fun, half in earnest. "Rabbit," he heard again, "the best way to catch a snake is to think like a snake!" At once Rabbit understood. He had to think like the mice and the weasels, feeling the greed and selfishness that was in them. That gave him a plan.

"Very well," Rabbit said, "we will join you. Those people are certainly very cruel and dishonest. They deserve the worst that can happen to them. Why, only yesterday"—and here he gave Otter a secret nudge—"my friend and I saw them hide away a great store of food in a secret place. Didn't we, Otter?"

"Oh, yes, certainly," stammered Otter, wondering what trick Rabbit was up to now. The weasels and mice jumped about in mad excitement. "Where? Where? Where is this place?" "Take us there at once!" cried Weasel, licking his lips.

"Certainly," said Rabbit, starting out toward the woods. "Just follow us." Mouse was right at their heels, but Weasel shouldered him aside. Then each animal fought to be in front, and in this way all rushed through the forest, across the meadows, down into the valleys and over the hills, until at last, pushing and panting and grunting, they all reached the bottom of a grassy hill. Rabbit pointed to a pile of rocks at the top. "You will find the wealth you seek up there," he cried. "Hurry, hurry! The best

will go to those who get there first." Away they all went, each struggling to be first. Then Rabbit and Otter stood aside and watched as the wild mob scrambled up the hill, up and up until suddenly, too late to stop, they found themselves teetering on the edge of a cliff, with nothing in front of them but space and the sea far below. Those who were first tried to stop but were pushed over by those crowding behind. So, screaming with terror, down they all went, headlong into the sea.

"Well," said Otter, peering over the edge of the cliff with a shiver, "their nations are well rid of them."

"So are the Penobscots," said Rabbit. "And now that together we have saved our friends from the mice and the weasels, Otter, let us go home together in peace as good neighbors should."

"I'm willing," said Otter, but he had no sooner taken a step than he sprawled on the ground. Rabbit had tripped him.

"That's for the knock on the head!" Rabbit laughed, and made for the woods. Picking himself up furiously, Otter was after him, shouting, "Just wait till I catch you. I'll teach you to play tricks!" Their truce was over. And Glooscap, looking down from the tallest mountain, laughed at their antics, for he knew that with all their mischief, there was no greed or spite in the hearts of Otter and Rabbit, against the people or against each other.[23]

At first it seems too simple. I'm just telling Tina stories. I'm actually doing more than that, because each story is told in a persuasive manner with suggestions toward the desired goal of constructing a new post-substance identity of someone who can cooperate with others for a common goal.

Healing is always and primarily social. It happens in communion and communication with others and not alone. Healing is primarily social because humans are primarily social. Electromyograph studies show that our faces automatically make invisibly small muscle contractions in response to pictures of human facial expressions, even when we are unaware of what we have seen. "Apart from immediate danger, nothing captures our attention like the actions of others around us."[24]

Eventually, Tina went to the healing circle. To her amazement she enjoyed being there. The talking circle appealed to her as a non-threatening way to communicate. She began to form real relationships with people who didn't need drugs or alcohol to cope with each other. Participation in community is crucial to continued recovery and progress past depression. We need an audience. We need to see an audience seeing us to understand fully what we are doing. We develop the capacity to step back one more step (which is self-awareness) to see ourselves seeing others seeing us. The presence of the audience helps us to see social information from the perspective of other individuals or other times, places, and conditions. We must receive the feedback from the facial expressions and other gestures of those who hear us that we have changed and are changing and will continue to change.

We must immerse ourselves over and over in the performance and rehearsal of healing so that it will happen. Once is not enough. We must practice and perform over time for healing to occur. We and our audience must come to believe in the transformative story. The recent neuroscience of this can be found in the work of Keith Oatley, Raymond Mar, and Maja Dijik, three researchers who have been working to understand the way stories inspire social learning.

Just as our seemingly individual illnesses emerge from social processes and events, our healing requires other people's involvement as well. That is why we endorse the saying, "to change a habit, change the habitat." Through the talking circle/healing circle, we were changing Tina's social habitat. The way for Tina to recover was not a logical consequence of her diagnosis, but was a path coconstructed by all of us interacting within her environment.

3

The Collective Self

The stories people tell have a way of taking care of them. If stories come to you, care for them. And learn to give them away where they are needed. Sometimes a person needs a story more than food to stay alive. That is why we put these stories in each other's memory. This is how people care for themselves.

BARRY LOPEZ, *CROW AND WEASEL*

Our minds and selves are formed by stories. "We" are the product of all that has been told around us and about us, as well as the stories we tell ourselves, either by repeating ones we have heard or creating our own new ones. We make sense of things we don't understand by placing them into a familiar story structure.[1] "We organize our experience and our memory of human happenings mainly in the form of narrative."[2]

To understand who tells the stories within our minds, we need to shift our perception of how we are constructed. Psychologist Paul Roberts suggests that rather than thinking of ourselves as unique, discrete individuals, we need to shift to understand ourselves as a complexity of our relationships, memories, culture, inventions, and experiences, moving through time. We need to think of ourselves in a way that is less literal.[3] This is an indigenous way of thinking that locates us embedded in a swarm of stories, moving along through time. A moving target for attempts at understanding. Contemporary psychology speaks of the disorders of the self. In the work we are presenting, we suggest instead that one of the selves is mismatched for the relationship he, she, or it is supposed to be managing and needs to be swapped out for a more appropriate self for that task. The perspective we are presenting is highly indigenous and does not conform to the rational, Cartesian framework. It has its contemporary nonindigenous proponents, including in the work of the Russian philosopher Mikhail Bakhtin and, more recently, in the dialogical self theory proposed by Hubert Hermans, emeritus professor of psychology at the University of Nijmegen and a primary developer of the dialogical self movement.

We think of the self as a map created by the brain to separate the "me," which I can locate in the physical body that I can always touch, from the "others," whose physical bodies can always be touched in our minds, but who cannot always be located to physically touch. I need to keep track of my swarm of stories (*nagi*) and remain aware that there are other bodies in my world who have their own swarm of stories and therefore motivations and desires. Like all brain maps, as argued so convincingly by neuroscientist V. S. Ramachandran (with his coauthor, science writer Sandra Blakeslee), our "me" map is somewhat arbitrary and is created by the experiences we have.[4] From a neuroscience perspective, no intrinsic "self" exists that can be found or discovered. No Platonic essence can be found. Rather, the brain is designed to manage the sensory impressions we receive, wherever they originate.

According to neuroscience our identity or sense of who we are is a story constructed primarily in the medial prefrontal cortex (mPFC), which links together separated fragments of experience into a coherent narrative with continuity.[5] Indeed, this brain area is part of a default circuitry that represents the brain's resting condition—that of daydreaming and storymaking, playing with "as if" scenarios, revisiting past scenes and constructing alternate scenarios or simulations of what could have happened had we acted differently or what might happen the next time we encounter this person or situation if we act differently.[6]

DEFAULT MODE OF THE BRAIN

The default mode of the brain is important to our understanding of story. The default mode brain circuit is active at wakeful rest and is deactivated during goal-oriented activity when another network, the central-executive network, takes over. "The default mode network (DMN) manages introspection that is independent of the outside world, as well as thought about ourselves, while the central-executive network produces action."[7] The default mode is also implicated in many other kinds of experiences, "including memory, self evaluation, prospection, theory of mind, moral reasoning, and spontaneous thought."[8]

The default mode network is composed of a number of subsystems, each of which has its own role to play, as indicated in the table below.

SUBSYSTEMS OF THE DMN	
Brain Area	**Function**
Part of the medial temporal lobe	Memory
Part of the medial prefrontal cortex	Theory of mind*
Posterior cingulate cortex	Integration of sensory modalities[9]
Adjacent ventral precuneus	Gathers sensory information, and possibly information that is within us[10]
Medial, lateral, and inferior parietal cortex	Visual processing, motor planning, activates recall of autobiographical memory and when we think about other people's thoughts (without reference to physical characteristics)[11]
Ventromedial prefrontal cortex (VMPFC)	Mentalizing or creating a theory of mind; perceiving other people; [12] representation of knowledge about the self[13]

*"Theory of mind" refers to the ability to attribute mental states—beliefs, intents, desires, knowledge, and so on—to ourselves and others and to understand that others have beliefs, desires, and intentions grossly similar to our own but potentially different in the specifics.

The posterior cingulate gyrus is the part of the brain that discerns information that is emotionally relevant to the self. It interacts with the anterior cingulate gyrus, which integrates emotional information with thought, and with the medial prefrontal cortex, which allows for self-reflection and the regulation of emotion and arousal. The posterior cingulate cortex, with its strong connections to medial temporal lobe systems, has also been linked with episodic and autobiographical memory retrieval,[14] visuospatial mental imagery, prospection, and self-projection.[15]

The default mode network is thought to generate spontaneous thoughts when our minds are wandering and gets involved in creativity.[16] Regions belonging to this network are engaged when we are relating to other people.[17] This overlap between the DMN and the "social brain" has led to the proposal that the DMN is strongly associated with thinking about social relationships.[18]

When we are at rest, then, this network is active; that means our minds are "wandering," or focused on internal cognitions such as remembering stories of our past, creating stories about ourselves in the future, and entertaining stories that show us how other people are thinking and feeling. The default network allows us to use the stories of our past to imagine possibilities that might emerge from our social interactions.[19]

However, for most of us, activity in the default network is reduced when we are performing a task.[20] Currently, research is continuing in many places to try to understand when the default network is activated and when it is deactivated and what the implications might be. Researchers have examined activation in those with schizophrenia, who appear to have brains that do not deactivate the default network easily.[21] Other researchers have found that in autism, the network activation is very low, which could explain deficits in social processing.[22] Alzheimer's disease researchers have found that the default network is preferentially attacked by the buildup of beta-amyloid that characterizes the disease.[23] Dr. Ruth Lanius, who researches the complex systems involved in posttraumatic stress disorder at the University of Western Ontario, has reported that her team found that many aspects of network activity, including social processing and self-referential processing, were diminished or offline in long-term trauma sufferers and in people diagnosed with PTSD.[24] Meditation practice is associated with increased activity across the default mode network.[25] Impaired control of entering and leaving the default network state is correlated with old age.[26] Infants lack the default network, which appears around ages nine to twelve years.[27] Children who have experienced trauma often lack an inner world of imagination and show little symbolic play. This may be due to interruptions in the transmission of information across the default network.[28]

Another network that is involved in processing is the salience network (SN). This network impacts the way we select the things that have personal significance for us, out of all the possible signals we receive from sensory information. The salience network is most activated when we need to overcome challenges. It is linked to a sense of intention and purpose, both of which impact our ability to solve problems and achieve goals. This network integrates highly processed sensory information with somatovisceral information from the body to guide attention and decision making.[29] The salience network is thought to be activated when daydreaming must stop and we need to focus on a task that needs to be done or an outside stimulus that needs our attention. Damage to the salience network can interfere with motivation and planning.[30]

DEVELOPMENT OF THE SELF

We form our stories about ourselves by watching other people watching us and becoming aware that they are forming a story about us (theory of mind). In this dialogical way we come to self-awareness and the realization that we need an identity narrative, a story about ourselves. Stories train us to use our theories of mind. Brian Boyd, a narrative theorist from the University of Auckland and author of the foundational text

On the Origin of Stories, guides us in our understanding of the way we as children develop a meta mind:

> Children between one and two start to entertain multiple models of reality, to recall the past and recognize it as *no-longer,* to anticipate the future and recognize it as *not-yet,* and to enjoy pretense as *not-really.* But although they can reason within these frames, they cannot yet clearly understand the relationships between one model and another. Only during their fourth year do they begin to develop fully human metarepresentational minds, which allow them to understand readily past, present, and future; real, pretend, supposed, or counterfactual; and the perspectives of others and even their own in the past. . . .[31]
>
> A metarepresentational mind allows us, among much else, to understand what others might know or infer from what they see or hear, and how that knowledge may affect what they do. We can use this understanding for the purposes of cooperation—for example, in explicitly teaching others—or of competition.[32]

Lisa Zunshine from the University of Kentucky, who has studied the way our mind's cognitive abilities are at work when we form ideas about other people in literature, suggests that stories challenge and enhance our abilities to infer the intentions and desires of others, because stories multiply our experience of levels of intentionality and the complexities of human relationships.[33]

THE THEORY OF THE DIALOGICAL SELF

This is the theory that our minds are full of multiple avatars, representing real people and playing key roles in our simulations of real relationships in the outer world. One could say that we have invented computer video games in our own image. We create maps of our social landscape, populated by these avatars for use in our simulations. In dialogical theory the self is accepted as "culture inclusive" and culture as "self-inclusive."[34]

Hermans, respected dialogical-self theorist, argues that increasing complexity in society leads to problems for the self. Migration, mobility, and contact with other ways of understanding the self stimulate greater uncertainty and expansion of self-structures through a dialogue between local and global positions, and the confrontation between these proliferate several voices and counter-voices. Identifying educational encounters, tourism, Internet communication, media, migration, and political interconnections between people as accelerating, the authors argue that the forces (both social and natural) bring fresh challenges in their wake.[35]

Professor of psychology and director of Georgetown University's Conflict Resolution Program Fathali Moghaddam declares that in the study of human dynamics, inter-subjectivity (the relationships between self and other) is only one dimension of reality. An integral portion of human activity is transacted at the collective level. He terms this process "inter-objectivity" to imply those dimensions of culture or society that characterize people's understanding of others and claims that in fact, inter-objectivity would also configure inter-subjectivity among people. For instance, prevalent beliefs about individuality, autonomy, and self-control in everyday life would form the basis for evaluating a person as difficult, self-indulgent, or mentally ill. Depending upon the degree of dissonance tolerated by society, the manifestations of fluidity and flexibility of individuals will be assessed.[36]

THE STORIED NATURE OF THE SELF

Dalhousie University psychology scholar John Barresi, who studies identity, believes that stories form only in the revisiting of a personal encounter. In real time we are caught in the experience. Only upon reflection on the experience do we create a story about what happened.[37]

Philosopher and psychologist William James, whose interests ranged from economic theory to medicine, also worked on identity. James conceptualized the "self" as a source of permanence beneath the constantly shifting set of experiences that constitute conscious life. He argued that our sense of self or personhood is a conglomerate of everything that is considered to be our own. He posited an explanatory "me," which makes sense of the "I" acting in the present moment.[38] "Me" is a story my brain invents to make sense of my experience.

The "me" of William James is formed through the linkage of episodic memories and experiences across time with a kind of glossing or erasure of the gaps between memories so that it seems as if we are continuous and coherent. In addition to appearing to support this self-creation by making the necessary linkages to support an identity across time,[39] the medial prefrontal cortex also appears to support other self-forming capacities, including memory for self-traits,[40] memory of the traits of others who are similar to us,[41] reflected self-knowledge,[42] and aspirations for the future.[43]

"Me" is clearly culture bound as are all my maps. My social learning trains me how to perceive and what to believe. Observation teaches us that people can be quite different according to the context in which they are behaving and that context is an extremely powerful influence over what we do. This is confirmed by the Stanford prison experiment in which students pretending to be guards became so excessively cruel to students pretending to be prisoners that the study had to be terminated lest harm occur. Similarly, Zimbardo's electric shock experiments demonstrated that people would deliver a potentially lethal shock to another human being (played by an actor who received no actual shock) just because a person in authority (a white coat, at Yale University) told them to do so. Boyd wrote, "Purposes arise not in advance, but as possibilities materialize."[44] As we told a client who was bemoaning the unpredictability of her life, "our lives unfold in accordance with whom we meet and what happens in our encounter, neither of which can be predicted in advance."

Like Hermans, we are challenging both the idea of a core, essential self and the idea of a core, essential culture.[45] Self and culture represent a multiplicity of positions among which dialogical relationships can be established. When we work with clients, we dialogue with all the characters included in their *nagi* or self. Their presentation to the world, and the story that they will enact, is determined by collaborations and coalition formations with all the internal characters or voices of their minds. Our social relationships are asymmetrical and hierarchical. Some voices have more power than others, particularly those granted legitimacy by the dominant voices of the epoch. Our work in healing is often political in that we support minority voices to be heard despite the potential objections of the dominant cultural voices.

In the clinical stories we present, and in comparison with other contemporary works with clinical stories, we shift attention from a core self to zones of contact in which self-coalitions enact stories that produce certain feedback from the world of others outside the individual. Implicit in the idea of the *nagi* is the complexity that arises from every story ever told in a person's life being important. This leads to uncertainty, for we can never hear all the stories—that would require the same amount of time as the person's life up to this moment. We must pick and choose representative stories, and our choosing can be biased and lead us to miss that which really matters.

We have internal (meaning silent) conversations with the characters or avatars that fill our minds. These imagined characters are mapped from real life people with whom we interact, have interacted, or wish to interact. They can be quite vivid visually, auditorally, and kinesthetically. We can have such powerful internal experiences that our hearts race and our faces turn red. More importantly, when the medial frontal lobe (that part of the brain that appears necessary to maintain a coherent, consistent, historical self) is damaged, we become a multitude of seemingly separate voices and characters, each struggling to be heard and to achieve primacy over the others.[46]

Hermans proposes that these characters with their voices engage in quasi-independent dialogue, producing a view of the self as a heterogeneous society created through narrative activity.[47] In my experience, most people can experience this when they reflect on how their minds actually operate, but in ordinary life, we are trained to minimize this dialogue and to view ourselves as autonomous, single selves. Hermans suggests that imitation is the first evidence of the recognition of others. Indeed, animals imitate and the study of imitation led to the amazing discovery of mirror neurons, which may represent the neurobiological substrate of empathy.

PLAYING WITH AVATARS

Here is a story about a woman, Donna, with low back pain. Back pain is the most common presenting complaint to physicians, so it often shows up in the plot. We do the usual physical exams and make sure there are no problems that would benefit from surgical intervention. We refer to physical therapy, massage, orthopedic practitioners, osteopaths, and so on. But there are times when, no matter what treatment is given, there seems to be something in the way of success. How do we extricate the stories that are connected with that?

I began by asking about the pain, when it began, what it feels like, and how it progressed. Donna told a typical biomedical story in which the pain came from excessive twisting at work as she turned to talk to her clients who sat beside her and then back to her computer. These types of purely mechanical stories are common in the beginning. The initial illness narrative and treatment narrative are straightforward and biomechanical. She turned wrong and her back hurt. She needs some form of manipulative or manual therapy to put her back into order. I can prescribe that, but it's my habit to look for more.

Technique

•—•—•

EMOTIONAL INVESTIGATION

Explore the emotions around the time the symptom began. What were the important relationships? What was happening in them? We use an idea espoused by Jaak Panksepp, a neuroscientist who researches emotion, who coined the term "affective neuroscience." While we prefer the idea of emotions as networks, as suggested by emotion psychologist Lisa Barrett (of whom we will say more later in the chapter), we respond to Panksepp's idea of emotions as signals that alert us to the progress of our goals. When we have negative emotions, our goal-seeking may not be going well. Positive emotions tell us things are working in a way consistent with our happiness.[48]

When Donna finished the story, I asked her what she felt in her life at the moment she first felt the pain. This is a risky question. Not everyone is sufficiently cognizant of his or her emotional states to be able to answer this question. My intuition was correct. She remembered feeling "torn." I asked her how she was torn. She said she felt torn between doing what she should and doing what she wanted. She was caught in a dichotomy.

"How are you torn?" I asked. She said she had essentially no relationship with her husband and, at the time her back pain had begun, had met another man who paid attention to her and with whom she thought she could be happy. However, she said she shouldn't be attracted to someone outside the marriage. I detected a bucket load of "shoulds." I asked her to tell me her "shoulds."

"I should make the best with what I have," she said. "I should stay with my husband. The 'shoulds' always win." She continued to say that her husband paid her no attention even when she told him she had something important to say. She told a story about telling him that flowers in a garden won't grow without sunshine, water, fertilizer, and weeding. He had no clue about this metaphor. He said that he was happy and didn't understand what she was saying.

Next I wondered who in her family would endorse "making the best of things"?

She answered that most everyone in her family would endorse that position and having the approval and acceptance of her family was very important to her. She reminded me that she was an independent person (in seeming contradiction to what she had just said) and that she didn't go to others for help. She said that when she got distressed, miserable, or unhappy, she worked ferociously in her garden or found a hobby to occupy her time and attention.

"What does your husband do when he is distressed?" I asked.

"He drinks," she responded. In answer to my question about what they did together, she said, "Sometimes we watch television or visit our grandchildren." Then she said, "I feel bad even thinking about divorcing him. He provides well."

"So thinking about divorcing him makes you a bad person?" I asked.

"Yes," she agreed. "Divorce is shameful." She proceeded to recount the stories of her relatives and their long marriages. Her parents had been married for sixty years. Her sister had been married for forty. "People in my family stay married for a long time," she said.

"Everyone?" I asked. I was playing at being incredulous.

"Most of my cousins are divorced," she answered. In this way we were getting to her overgeneralizations, which are usually present when we use words like "everyone" or "all" or "no one."

Technique

•—•—•

OBSERVATION OF LANGUAGE

It's useful to pay attention to the subtleties in the language people use and to work toward specificity. The more detail we can bring into descriptions of feelings, the more we can find the stories that are behind them.

I explored what it meant to feel "bad," since "bad" isn't actually a feeling. "Feeling bad," she said, meant "feeling unacceptable, such that no one would want to be around you."

Of course, unacceptable is not a feeling either—it's a judgment. We explored her feeling some more and came up with "feeling isolated and lonely." That is a clearer idea for us to explore. There are many more interesting ways to explore feelings of isolation than there are ways of exploring feelings of unacceptability.

> ### Technique
> • — • —•
> ### WHO'S TALKING?
> When there's internal conflict about an issue, dialogical self theory works well. We begin by looking in a dialogical way at internal conflict, by asking about the group of storytellers that can be identified in the individual's inner landscape.

Donna identified a part of her she came to call "Mother Superior," who came from her Catholic grade school past and represented whatever the Church thought. Next she identified a part of her that she called "me," who believed that superior people stay married, no matter what. Then she identified a weaker voice, who she called "me, too," who believed that it was okay to get divorced if the relationship was miserable. She found a part she called "Joy," who believed that divorce was much better than staying miserably married. This led her to a part she called "Spoiled," who believed that divorce was undesirable because it would erode her lifestyle. Her husband made good money, and she had much stuff she would have to relinquish if she divorced. She had a desirable level of security that would disappear. Finally, she found "Faith," who believed that she would be rewarded in heaven for suffering through this marriage on Earth.

> ### Technique
> • — • —•
> ### INVITE THE CHARACTERS TO DIALOGUE
> Once we have the avatars that are fighting, we can create dialogue with them—through gestalt therapy, drama therapy (with masks, puppets, or plays), guided imagery, dialogue, journaling, and more.

We began a dialogue among these parts and searched for additional supporters. Mother Superior began by saying long marriages are serene. "You do everything together, enjoy each other's company, and talk lots. If it's not so, you pretend that it is."

Joy reminded her of all her relatives who had divorced and were much happier as a result and suggested that these relatives would support her and would not reject her as unacceptable.

Spoiled got support from her husband. It worked well for him for her to think this way, and he encouraged it through gifts and trips. Her family members in her same faith who were long married also supported that position. Plus, her husband thought they had a perfect marriage.

Through continued work we identified that this internal arguing inside her mind by the characters who represented the important people in her life made her tense. In fact, the more she listened to it, the more her back began to ache. The remainder of our work together consisted of dialogue with her many parts about what to do.

Each "part" or avatar represented a point of view, a collection of beliefs, which is supported by a set of stories. The stories, like the avatars, are in conflict. Negotiation is needed to resolve or at least highlight that conflict. No wonder Donna had pain. Within her consciousness was constant argument about what to do. Leave her husband or stay with him. Live her own life in the marriage and ignore him or try to engage him and pull him into what mattered for her. Put herself first and her potential greater happiness versus put appearances and the marriage first and her potential greater stability. Take risks or keep quiet and have security. There's no resolving these dilemmas easily. We would have to do more dialogue.

My approach is to create a round table in imagery or in an actual room with each of the avatars represented in a physical form. This can also be done with virtual reality software, on paper, with puppets, or even with a group of people. Each avatar presents its position and tells some of the stories about life experiences that support that position. When all have spoken, we ask if any other characters in the mind have opinions. We can add other avatars to the table if any speak up. We keep going around the table and hearing the stories that support the various positions. I call this a "talking circle" within the mind.

I guide the person to choose a master of ceremonies or a chair of the board to represent the identity narrative (the character we have invented to explain who we think we are). That avatar can negotiate with the others, forming coalitions when necessary to support the highest good, which is sometimes elusive in its determination. It can participate in further guided imagery to explore the path of greatest peace.

With Donna we had avatar gridlock. No decision was possible. I tried another tack. I wanted to help Donna generate a counter-narrative that would strengthen her sense of agency. I sometimes use guided imagery to engage the client's imagination. I asked her internal characters if I could do some guided imagery with Donna and they agreed.

Technique
•—•—•
PLAYING WITH STORY

Playing with story or imagining ourselves as a different character in our life dramas dislodges our usual, habitual way of being just enough to alter our state of mind. Once this shift has occurred, an assignment to practice the change accomplishes the purpose of behavioral activation, a necessary element to change.

I began with a relaxation induction, using hypnotic technique to get to the flow state and to avoid as much as possible the routine areas of consciousness, in which we plan trips to the grocery store, strategize how to win a game, or otherwise face challenges. Then I began to guide Donna on a meditation about the greatest peacefulness in her life. Where and when had she found that? I reflected on the concept of peacefulness, and we explored which avatars had the most peaceful stories. With whom would she align if she were to aim for peacefulness and to reduce suffering?

Donna and I met twelve times. Through those sessions she clarified for herself that she was not going to leave the marriage, no matter what, and that affairs were not an option for her. She was going to live her life independently of her husband whenever possible. She was angry, but not enough to cause trouble or to risk her security. As she became clearer about her intentions, she also began to take better care of herself. We focused on radical acceptance of her situation and on consciously getting the conflicted voices "off her back." Over the course of the twelve weeks, her back stopped hurting. Our goals had been met—her back was no longer caught in the tangle of her emotions.

UNDERSTANDING
EMOTIONAL EXPERIENCE

As our work with Donna illustrates, a single word (e.g., fear, happiness, sadness) is often used to refer to the many different instances of an emotion category, which may explain why it is routinely assumed that within-category variability either does not exist or that it is unimportant. However, in order to understand human emotional experiences, it is essential to study the tremendous variability that exists within common emotion categories. This was the essence of William James's charge to psychology over a century ago.[49]

For example, feelings of fear can emerge when excitedly engaging in a sword fight, when beginning to feel a sore throat, when frantically running away from a moose, or when asking for a date. Psychologist Lisa Feldman Barrett, in her lab at Boston College, has been proposing a much more complex idea of emotions. Rather than assuming that emotions are nouns, singular and identifiable categorically, she proposes that they are rather what she calls "conceptual acts."[50] Rather than looking for the biological signatures of commonly understood emotion categories,[51] she looks at systems and structures involved in emotional experiences, and proposes that emotions arise in a network of physiological and conscious activity. In her words, "A psychological construction approach predicts that tremendous variety in emotional life exists because our nervous systems produce countless possible emotional experiences."[52]

In research projects in cooperation with fellow emotion researchers Christine Wilson-Mendenhall and Lawrence Barsalou, she describes emotions as grounded in "core affect"—a person's fluctuating level of pleasant or unpleasant arousal. Participants' subjective ratings of pleasure versus displeasure and of arousal evoked by various experiences of emotion correlated with neural activity in the orbitofrontal cortex and the amygdalae, respectively. These correlations were observed across diverse instances within each emotion, as well as across instances from all three emotions. "Consistent with a psychological construction approach to emotion, the results suggest that neural circuitry realizes more basic processes across discrete emotions. The implicated brain regions regulate the body to deal with the world, producing the affective changes at the core of emotions and many other psychological phenomena."[53]

Emotion and the DMN

The default mode network plays a central role in emotional experiences.[54] DMN serves a broad role in the context-based conceptual processing that occurs during complex categories of mental experience (e.g., emotions, beliefs, attitudes), which are dynamically constructed using prior experience to direct physiological, perceptual, and motor response.[55]

The brain regions that comprise the DMN integrate information across modalities and across time to produce inferences tailored to the socio-emotional situation.[56] The anterior cingulate and fronto-insular cortex hubs of the salience network participate in a variety of emotional experiences (both positive and negative), as well as other experiences involving subjective feelings of affect and agency.[57]

Studying Typical versus Atypical Emotional Responses

A group of researchers have embarked on an intriguing line of questioning, wondering what happens when emotional experience becomes confounded by an interpretation that may be incongruent with the way we typically experience that emotion. Typicality refers to how good an example a particular instance is of its category. For example, in North America, robin is a more typical example of the category bird than penguin, which is an atypical example.[58] Some theories imply a one-to-one relationship between emotion categories and their evaluation: fear and sadness are unpleasant, and happiness is pleasant.[59] However, we often experience our feelings with more ambiguity. "Less typical fear experiences, for example, are sometimes pleasant: the scary thrill of zipping downward on a rollercoaster or the jittery exhilaration of performing before a crowd. Less typical happiness experiences are sometimes unpleasant: the exhausting relief of finishing a time-consuming project or the freeing reprieve of a friend's comforting words when distressed (i.e., when the relative shift toward feeling pleasant tends to make the feeling tone simply less unpleasant)."[60]

Wilson-Mendenhall and colleagues at Northwestern University invited participants to immerse themselves in scenarios designed to induce either atypical or typical experiences of fear, sadness, or happiness, and then focus on and rate the pleasant or unpleasant feeling that emerged.[61] To examine the variability within these three common emotion categories, Wilson-Mendenhall et al. manipulated one aspect of emotional experience for each test. They compared unpleasant fear, unpleasant sadness, and pleasant happiness with what they called atypical emotional experiences such as pleasant fear, pleasant sadness, and unpleasant happiness.[62] Because the same parts of the brain work together to create diverse emotional experiences,[63] the researchers hypothesized that the same parts of the brain would be engaged across the three categories of emotional experience. They believed that the atypical emotions would put greater demands on the default mode network, "driving" it harder and decreasing processing efficiency.

What the researchers found was that as long as the emotional scenario was paired with the predictable (typical) value, the network behaved normally. For fear and sadness, as scenarios became more unpleasant, the network behaved within the range it typically would. As happiness scenarios became more pleasant, typical processing occurred.

When the participants were exposed to scenarios inducing atypical fear, sadness, and happiness experiences, the DMN worked much harder. There were no cases where brain regions worked harder during the typical scenarios. This greater activity observed for atypical versus typical emotional experiences in the default mode network (including the medial prefrontal cortex and the posterior cingulate cortex) suggests that atypical instances indeed require greater conceptual processing.

This effect was also observed in the salience network (including the anterior insular cortex and anterior cingulate cortex). This suggests that atypical instances place greater demands on integrating shifting body signals with the sensory and social context.

What is useful for us in this idea is to understand that when someone is asked to interpret emotions in a way that is atypical, it has an impact on the speed and efficiency of his or her story (meaning-making and social organizing) circuitry. This results in coping strategies that can be slower, hard to learn, and hard to access.[64] The researchers suggest that behavioral change would be supported by proper characterization of these atypical instances of emotions. They proposed the importance of this in their own words: "Learning to categorize atypical 'fuzzy' instances of emotions and to differentiate between instances within an emotion category is important for mental health because it supports identifying and changing dysfunctional patterns of behavior."[65] We can entertain many ideas for therapy when we consider this research. Not least is the notion that the feeling of relief that comes from the work in therapy to locate and understand emotions might in part be truly the result of lessening the workload and stress involved in the processing work needed to sustain atypical emotional experiences.

In our practice this was revealed in Barbara's work with Jill. Jill was the child of a couple who were drug dealers. She grew up in at atmosphere of deception and was routinely forced to reinterpret the experiences of her life in ways that did not feel congruent. This happened, too, when she was sexually assaulted by her uncle and, when she reported it, disbelieved by some of her family and encouraged by others to be "understanding" so as not to disrupt. This had led to many years of emotional dysregulation and difficulties with all kinds of human relationships as she struggled to find a home for her feelings. If we consider the research, her salience network and her default network were likely both struggling to make meaning, as her abilities to self-reflect, to be motivated, to learn successful coping skills, and to sort out what feelings were "real" were compromised.

Added to Jill's suffering was pain that seemed to move around her body, never staying in the same place.

In the story work they did together, Jill and Barbara worked with an idea that the pains that moved were stories looking for a home, a place to live in her body, but finding nowhere to settle in. Jill was a young adult, and had one child who had been taken away by social services. More than anything she wanted a home, so that she could at least have visitation with her son. Creating a home had proven to be more difficult than she had imagined. She understood that "home" to her was a place of fear and insecurity, so together she and Barbara looked for a place to put things that she might put into a home. They spent most of the first year playing with "small world" trays, sandboxes with little figurines that can be set in scenarios. Jill would come to the office and create "homes."

Before and after the sessions, Barbara would encourage her to dance in a dialogue with her pain, to see where it might go, and to see if Jill could begin to direct the pain to go where she wanted it to. Gradually, Jill began to speak and write about her emotional experiences; as she did she found that information she had forgotten came back to her.

"I guess I was pretty confused," she said one day.

"That makes sense. Confused sounds like a reasonable thing to be in these circumstances," Barbara told her.

Jill began working with a dialogue between confused Jill and clear Jill. Together she and Barbara collected elements of both Jills. The more they gave them form, the more Jill could differentiate between feeling confused and clear. She found a hat that she thought clear Jill would wear and began more and more to dress like "clear" Jill.

It wasn't easy for her. More than anything she wanted her father to acknowledge what had happened to her, what his brother had done, and to believe her. She tried over and over again to reach out to him, but he resisted all of her offerings. This continued maintenance of the family lie could disrupt Jill easily and quickly if she wasn't on guard. If she gave in to it, the need to be believed could consume her and derail her healthy coping behaviors. She grew to have more and more understanding and clarity, and her mother, now separated from her father, finally said that she believed her, but there was still a vulnerability to contend with as far as her relationship with her father was concerned.

As Jill got healthier and healthier, she became more able to maintain a relationship with her father on her own terms. She decided that she wanted a connection with him even if he didn't believe her. At first he resisted contact, using Jill's previous involvement with drugs and "chaotic life" as his reason. Jill was furious at this unfair accusation, given her father's past. As her chaos diminished and clarity rose, he finally agreed to meet with her, and they had a father and daughter lunch together, avoiding all difficult subjects and agreeing that they wished each other well. After that visit Jill came to terms with her father's inability to hold space for her emotions. She stopped trying to seek his company. When he died a short while later, she felt a sense of closure.

Life is not always fair, but if we can find a way to disentangle our confused feelings and come to a sense of congruence, we can hold our peace even in the face of others' inability to do so.

4
Stories, Beliefs, and Anomalies

There are no truths, only stories.

THOMAS KING,
GREEN GRASS, RUNNING WATER

God turns you from one feeling to another and teaches by means of opposites so that you will have two wings to fly, not one.

RUMI, *THE ESSENTIAL RUMI*

We have been told that our approach is highly compatible with other schools of therapy or healing, including cognitive-behavior therapy (CBT). We believe it enriches and deepens CBT by identifying the stories that support the beliefs that may be problematic. We approach beliefs as conclusion statements drawn from a story. A belief is the point of the story, the conclusion you want me to draw when you tell the story to me. If suffering comes from perception, as the Buddhists say, then we must look to find the filters (stories) that hold our expectations about the world, for we see what we expect to see. Our expectations tell us where to direct our attention. Those elements of the world to which we do not attend are not perceived. Our expectations arise from the stories we repeat to ourselves, the stories that formed our beliefs.

Identify a belief, and we should be able to find stories that exemplify that belief. These beliefs in turn activate the stories that led to the formation of those beliefs. When we hear a story, we look for the many possible beliefs inherent in that story. We find these beliefs by sorting through the beliefs we already have. We are not as concerned with what we are hearing as we are with finding what we already know that is relevant. Understanding a story means being able to follow what is going on by relating what we are hearing to what we already know. We compare what we are hearing to other experiences we have had.

Picture it this way. We have a list of beliefs, indexed by type of experience and meaning. When a new story appears, we attempt to find a belief that relates to it. When we do, we find a story attached to that belief and compare the story in memory to the one being processed. Our understanding of the new story is a function of the old story. Once we find a belief and connected story, we need do no further processing; the search for other beliefs is co-opted. We rarely look to understand a story in more than one way. The mind does not easily pursue multiple paths.

Our large brains function well to infer the implicit beliefs that lie within the stories we hear. We determine what will happen next and what beliefs are being conveyed. Our understanding of the neuroscience of how this happens is still evolving. Hearing a word activates memories of all our experiences linked to that word.[1] These words activate the same functional brain networks that were activated when we had the experiences associated with that word. Karl Pribram enjoys both neurosurgery and research psychology, and his ventures into understanding consciousness help us here. He invokes a holographic memory theory, in which the memory pattern (patterns of neuronal excitation and inhibition) of a word activates other similar patterns, which is association.[2]

Then our brain searches for inconsistencies between the memories recalled and the immediate context of the story we are hearing. Successful inhibitory selection, a function of the orbitofrontal cortex, may be an important part of understanding story. It could be that increasing comprehension is associated with greater elimination of extra details that come to be irrelevant to an ever-improving sense of the story and what it means. A second, more strategic integration process inhibits recalled information that seems irrelevant, leaving only that which may aid comprehension remaining in working memory.[3]

WORKING MEMORY
AND MENTAL MODELS

Working memory is required for text or story comprehension.[4] The multicomponent model of working memory[5] includes a temporary storage area, known as the episodic buffer, which integrates, manipulates, and maintains complex information involving multiple sensory modalities. This buffer also permits the modeling of hypothetical situations and theoretically forms a foundation for telling and understanding story.[6] The functions performed by this component of working memory appear to require the right frontal lobe.[7] The mid-dorsolateral frontal cortex also plays a role in ordering events sequentially in time, processing sequential information, and integrating information across time.[8] The orbitofrontal cortex plays an important role in removing extraneous information; similarly, the anterior cingulate is involved due to its association with motivation.[9]

When we hear or read a story, we develop mental models for what the words or text represents or describes.[10] We begin with an initial, more or less automatic and indiscriminate broad activation of information potentially relevant to the word or clause that we have just read or heard, relatively unrelated to context.[11] Potentially, our entire range of life experience can be called into play. We hold cues in working memory that we use to retrieve and elaborate our real-world knowledge from long-term storage. However, the act of forming a mental model is considered to be different from the extensive elaborating or "filling in" we do for gaps or points of indeterminacy in a story which we will look at more closely in the next chapter.

Stories provide cues for constructing mental models of referred-to processes and content.[12] For the most part, studies involving conversational language (storytelling) use other lower-level language tasks as a comparison or control. In this way brain areas engaged during narrative but also active during sentence-level presentations, such as semantic processing or the encoding of stimuli into long-term memory, are somewhat taken into account. Probably multiple brain regions contribute to narrative comprehension and production. Any network that supports language, memory, and even perception is likely to play some role.

Structure Building Framework

The Structure Building Framework proposes that listeners or readers: (1) lay a foundation within which new information received will be represented, (2) map new information onto related previous information, and (3) shift and create new foundations when incoming information is less coherent with previous structures. The goal of the listener or reader is to build a coherent mental representation or model of what is being communicated.[13] The building blocks for these structures are neuronal networks associated with memory. Networks are enhanced when the information they have is needed for further structure building. Networks are suppressed when the information they have becomes unnecessary or irrelevant. These networks may be holographic, as in Karl Pribram's theory of memory, mentioned earlier.

REMOVING STRUCTURES THAT BLOCK

While our working memory and the processes that build it up enable our functioning as individuals and in society, some of the belief structures that are created become blocks to our health. Kevin's story is a good example of doing the kind of forensic story work that uncovers beliefs that are preventing change. Kevin told of a meeting with his Department Chair at the University of Nebraska. The Chair was a study in business casual and good grooming. Kevin saw it as a pitched battle. The Chair had stacked the deck throughout his career to be the winner.

In spite of the fact that Kevin's arguments had inspired high praise from his committee, the Chair had taken exception to Kevin's work and withdrew his financial and academic support. Kevin stood up for himself because he knew he was onto something that would impact the world of economics. The Chair had the potential to crush Kevin because he had final say. As Kevin put it, "he could turn me into someone unimportant." In keeping with a fledgling belief, Kevin tried to "radiate loving kindness," but found it impossible. "Not easy," Kevin said. "I feel like a guy who didn't get anything. Good guys don't finish first. Usually the bad guys percolate upstairs because they're willing to do the things that would bother most folks." Kevin left his academic training.

This had happened sixteen years previously, but it was as real in his mind as if it were happening right now.

Kevin had come to see us for a multitude of medically unexplained symptoms. He was tired. His muscles ached. He felt weak. He had no stamina. His digestion was poor with reflux, pain, and constipation alternating with diarrhea. Over the past few years, he had gained a lot of weight, in part from lack of exercise.

When he quit business school, he found Roy, a Marine recruiter, who was happy to engage Kevin's creative services. He told us that he trained as a sniper and traveled to places he'd never imagined to kill people he'd never known. His tours of duty took him to Afghanistan, Kuwait, Iraq, Somalia, and other places he couldn't tell me about. He had also qualified as an underwater demolitions expert. For twelve years he worked his way up the ranks. During this time Kevin began to climb mountains, finding that to be a source of continual enjoyment. He told us that he also embarked on a hedonistic journey of "women, fun, and power lifting." In his twelfth year with the Marine Corps, Kevin collapsed. His metaphor was that his pilot light had gone out and he couldn't start his stove.

He had been to multiple major medical centers: Harvard University, Cleveland Clinic, and the Mayo Clinic, to name a few. Kevin had also received a host of diagnoses, none of which satisfied him. At Mayo the doctor told him he needed to eat better but didn't produce anyone to tell him how to eat better, nor did they go into any of his stories of eating. Mayo just called him chronically malnourished. He was diagnosed as having chronic fatigue syndrome, which is a polite way that medicine has developed for saying, "you have no energy and we don't know why, but we'll agree that it's because of something." He had also been offered diagnoses of fibromyalgia, multiple chemical sensitivities, and more. Kevin had come to me because he had given up on conventional medicine.

Barbara and I met with Kevin together. During our first meeting, Kevin told his story of rebelling against the adversities of graduate school by becoming the kind of man who could turn his antagonists into cowering fools. He had taken pride in doing things no one in his graduate program could imagine (and if they could, he felt they would admire him). He continued to reflect on his involvement with authority figures who had tortured him. "I set myself up for a pretty tough existence this time," he said. "I probably need to forgive all the people involved in this drama," Kevin remarked, "but I'm not going to do that." He had rebelled in his own creative way until his body failed him.

With a sense of hopelessness about his diagnosis, Kevin gave up on life and began to enjoy overindulging in awful food. He could no longer fit into the interesting cars he used to enjoy driving. He couldn't think of anything that could be fun. Mountain climbing was no more. The quest for status didn't impress him. He had enjoyed shooting, but now that he wasn't able to blow up things underwater or shoot people, life held no interest for him.

The first session often belongs to the client. People come with a story to tell. They have rehearsed it and honed it to be just what they want to say and it involves recounting a package of familiar events and details that are the "usual suspects" in their repertoire. It has a mixture of purposes. People generally want us to like them. They want us to empathize with the depths of their suffering.

People sometimes want to convey to us their preferred treatment narrative, what they know will help them. Kevin's first visit was more in the way of an anti-treatment narrative—nothing and no one had helped him or could help him. In the same way that he had rebelled against business school and joined the Marine Corps to be as opposite as possible from where he had been, we felt that he was telling us he was rebelling against conventional medicine and coming to us, whom he saw as ensconced in indigenous healing and alternative medicine, as a complete opposite.

We were faced with a mysterious illness narrative, in which fate or destiny seemed to be the villain who had dealt him a bad hand at the peak of his military career. He carried some sense of Greek tragedy, of Achilles, of warriors who were felled at their prime for no reason of their own—perhaps the trifles of the gods and being unlucky to be around them when they were in a bad mood. The treatment narrative was nihilistic—"I dare you to try to help me because nothing will."

Our first step could be to renegotiate the treatment narrative and to find something that we could agree might work. In the second session, we explored what we could do that appealed to Kevin. He rambled and digressed and told entertaining tale after tale, so that it wasn't until the third session that he announced he wanted to attend a purification ceremony. That made sense, for it had a manly sort of appeal, a potential for extremes, though that rarely happens, but a sense of being challenged, which is what Kevin had chosen for himself for most of his life. My working illness narrative for Kevin lay in that direction, "one challenge too many."

The Role of Ceremony

Kevin was in luck, because we were going to a purification ceremony led by a Dakota elder that very next Saturday night and could take him with us. Kevin enthusiastically agreed.*

We met him at the office parking lot on Saturday afternoon. He left his car, and we were off. Ceremony begins with the making of prayer ties. People sit around a table laden with colored cloth and tobacco. Sage burns while tobacco is wrapped in small squares of cloth and tied onto a string. The general rule of thumb is to tie 28, 51, 105, or 176 pieces of cloth onto a string of the color corresponding to the direction from which one needs most help.†

Kevin sat at a table of men on the rear deck of the house, making prayer ties. Some of us were practicing a new song we were learning. Women's voices floated toward us from the kitchen, as the door between us opened and closed. Men and women changed into their lodge clothes, shorts and t-shirts for the men, loose cotton sweat dresses for the women. Though it was an overall warm September afternoon, a slight chill served as a reminder that winter was coming. At around 6:30 p.m., word suddenly came from the firekeepers that the stones were ready and the elder, Charles, made his way slowly to the lodge with his "sacreds." The rest of us hurriedly made last minute bathroom visits, and made our way to the lodge site. We lined up around the lodge, first women, then men, and prepared to enter. One of the firekeepers kept smudge (sage burning in a number 10 tin can) nearby to "wash off"

---

*Kevin was paying privately outside of health insurance. As such, he didn't need a diagnosis and we didn't need to generate CPT (current procedural terminology) codes for what we were doing. We simply called it "individualized instruction in self-healing" and billed a previously arranged fee by the hour. Thus, we were free to bring Kevin with us to the purification ceremony (for which, of course, we did not collect any fee, though we encouraged Kevin to make a donation to the family for the cost of wood burned). When clients use insurance, we would have to make a diagnosis, generate a CPT code, and the limitations on what we could propose would be much greater.
†This has been described in more detail in *Coyote Healing* (Mehl-Madrona, *Coyote Healing,* 61).

the people with smoke before entering. When all were inside, Charles started the singing while stones were brought in.

Charles is Dakota from Wisconsin. In his tradition all the stones are brought into the lodge all at once in the beginning. The lodge heated up and the ceremony began with music. Charles's lodge has fantastic singers, and singing inside the circle-shaped lodge sounds like music being sung in a cathedral.

Charles opened the door four times to denote different periods of the ceremony. To his credit Kevin stayed inside the entire time. The group sang a welcome song for him and made sure he knew that he was part of the spiritual family now and could come anytime he wished. He no longer needed me to bring him. Charles sometimes channels in the fourth "round," or time of door being closed, and he had messages for Kevin that didn't make particular sense to me but seemed to be deeply meaningful to Kevin. Kevin had brought a sleeping bag to use on the floor of the living room for after the feast. Kevin had a good time at the feast and was still chatting with people when we turned in.

The next morning I nudged Kevin awake amidst other snoring forms and we slipped out of the house to our truck. I asked Kevin what he thought. Kevin replied, "That sweat lodge was kind of fun."* "What really felt good was to be around people of good intention." I invited Kevin to say more about that as we rolled through the darkly green Connecticut countryside, alongside beautiful brooks and the occasional lake.

A Closer Look at Beliefs

What had deeply impressed Kevin was the camaraderie of men. He said he had never experienced men together as we were, outside of

---

*Elders, especially Vern Harper in Toronto, Canada, have counseled us to stop calling this ceremony "sweat lodge." Vern says that's what the English called it, and we never had a term that could be translated in that way. In Lakota the word is *inipi,* which means, "breath of life ceremony." It's for purification and prayer. The sweating is a means of eliminating toxins and not the goal.

the military or athletics. In those settings it was always competitive, where men looked at each other with the attitude of "I can take you" or comparing themselves in terms of who's bigger, stronger, better, quicker, brighter. To be with men in a challenging way (coping with the heat of the *inipi*) without the competitiveness was an entirely new experience for him.

We were still in the phase of negotiating a sharable treatment narrative, and it seemed that one part of that story might be finding new ways to relate to others in community. I proposed that Kevin make a list of all of his beliefs about how men relate to each other as he went through the days until our next meeting so that we could explore his stories about masculinity.

Technique
•—•—•
WHO DO YOU IMAGINE YOURSELF TO BE?
A shorthand way to get people's stories and to find their ideal heroes is to ask them about what movie you can watch to understand them and who were the characters with whom they identified.

When I asked Kevin these questions, he responded with a list of action films like *Rambo*. Characters with whom he really identified consisted of anyone played by Jean-Claude Van Damme, Charles Bronson, and the *Die Hard* version of Bruce Willis.

When Kevin returned for his next session, we realized that part of the treatment narrative might be the establishment of a beneficial, noncompetitive relationship with another man. Maybe this is what he was seeking? We didn't know how aware he was of this possibility. We decided to run with this idea and see where it took us. Barbara recused herself from our conversation.

I began by asking Kevin about his research into his beliefs about men, and he produced a notebook in which he had jotted ideas as they came. He summarized by saying that all of his previous ideas involved competing or defeating each other. In previous conversations we had discovered that this story of male bonding had been present in his family, where his father kept that kind of relationship with him, in constant competition. On his own he had experienced teamwork, but as what he envisioned a pack of wolves to be like—any member of the team could turn on any other member in an instant if they didn't do their job (this isn't actually what happens in a pack of wolves; they're more compassionate to each other). The *inipi* and our conversations were challenging him to rethink how men could relate to each other.

Technique
•—•—•
GIVE HOMEWORK

If possible every session should end with a homework assignment. People need to bring the work out of the consulting room and into their worlds and lives. They need to keep the learning active. This is called "behavioral activation" and has been shown to be quite effective.

I offered him the possibility of researching men and their relationships during the next week by being alert to men who were relating cooperatively and even interviewing them if possible to learn more about their motivations and desires. He agreed to do that. Kevin did his homework. He took it seriously. Not all our clients do that. Kevin returned with another notebook full of observations and interview data. He was becoming aware that some men valued other men for their unique qualities and what they brought to a relationship and not because of fear or intimidation. I wondered where he could practice relating differently to men. He said he was returning to the *inipi* ceremony. He thought he could form a decent relationship with Charles and learn something from him. I supported his doing that, saying it was a marvelous idea.

We had negotiated an implicit treatment narrative of my assisting him to change his stories about men and their relationships, through homework, through our relationship, and through his developing relationship with men and Charles in Charles's *hocokah*.*

Then Kevin asked me if I did channeling like Charles did. I answered that I was learning and that I did it somewhat differently. I explained that I did a more Cherokee version that I had seen my grandfather and his friends do in which men sit around in a circle. After an opening song and a prayer, the spirits are invited in and the men all smoke cigars to make a tobacco offering (tobacco is sacred). When a man received a message from spirit, he stood up and delivered that message and then sat back down again. The group continued to smoke in silence until another message was received and delivered. Kevin asked if we could do that, and I agreed.

At the next meeting, we went outside to the gazebo in the park, and sat down on the wood floor. I blessed/cleansed us with sage and we sang a four directions song. I invited the spirits to come and enjoy our tobacco and help us if they could. I sang another song, and then we lit our cigars with a short prayer. We sat together in silence, smoking, until each of us had a message we felt the need to communicate. Kevin received several messages. He heard that maybe subtle things could be more satisfying than high speed. He heard that cigars are fun (as long as you don't inhale). He heard that he should explore chi gong and other similar martial arts that could be sustained into advanced age. He heard that he needed a "slow burning martial art that changes over time as you change, some kind of real basic procedure." I barely heard anything. When we finished our cigars, I thanked the spirits for coming and sang a thank you song. Kevin felt connected to me, he said, in a way that he never had before to another man, like we were friends, working together on a project, but not competitively.

---

*A *hocokah* is a circle or an altar and refers to a group of people who work with the same elder and often come together to do ceremony with each other and to support each other's healing and capacity to live life in "a good way."

> **Technique**
> •—•—•
> ### EMBODIED NARRATIVE
>
> It is always interesting to explore the way we embody our stories. We literally perform these stories, and like good actors, we take on the physical character of them. By looking at the narratives that shape our movements and the way we hold ourselves, we can often begin to create change. When a person can physically experience a different embodied story, it can create change from the outside in.

Barbara will often teach people how to negotiate their internal stories using dancing, movement, or improvisation. She invites them to begin exploring in whatever scale they are comfortable with. Our next step was to invite Kevin to work in a physical improvisation, exploring metaphors that arose from his body, in the hope that he might connect to his body in a different way and discover some of the internal characters who were activated in his physical self. Kevin was doubtful at first, but willing, and she promised that they would work in a way that felt okay for him. Kevin began awkwardly, walking around the room. She walked around with him.

As they moved about the room, she asked, "What images, colors, dynamics come to mind?"

After some ambivalence Kevin eventually said he saw red, and he identified it with his anger. Kevin related that his father supported his vision of himself as a superman and, since he had left that life, was having real difficulty treating him with respect. As he said this, he spoke of himself with derision: "I don't really care, it doesn't matter what I think." Barbara is always interested when she finds someone telling themselves that they don't matter. Sometimes, she invites people to imagine their younger, foolish selves and to offer them kindness, and she is always amazed at how difficult people find it to do.

Barbara asked Kevin to let that statement determine the way he stood. He stood with his shoulders down, shuffling his feet. She asked him to repeat the phrase, while she experimented with different dynamics of movement, sometimes standing on furniture, sometimes crouching. She worked at different distances away from Kevin, asking him to let her know when the dynamic felt like his relationship to anger. Finally they found a place that made him feel like he did when his sense of anger was aroused. She encouraged him to explore this dynamic, and they moved together in a kind of dance.

They worked with the image of Red. Barbara asked Kevin to give Red a body. Kevin decided that Red was a fast talking, type-A character who drove around in a bright red convertible. Paunch-bellied, Red liked to pick fights with everyone. He was loud and obnoxious and felt extremely justified in hurting those around him because he felt that his treatment in the world had been unjust. Barbara worked with him using movement to explore that sense of injustice. She used a group of exercises she calls the Hero Series, which uses different poses and ways of walking to explore power dynamics. Kevin began to get into it and improvised with Red, but then he began to feel how exhausting it was to live as Red and embody his approach to the world.

They began to develop another character, no less a hero, who could take his place managing "unjust" relationships. In this work Kevin imagined a monk, a little like the character played by David Carradine. He liked that image better. He agreed to begin to involve the monk more in decisions around anger. Embodying the monk felt calmer, and he could think straighter. Barbara often invites people to invent a small gesture, something to do when they want to remember that they want to change the energy they are embodying. The small reminder gesture acts as a physical reminder, creates a physical shift that reminds the body to make the change. Kevin created a gesture with his thumb that he could do when he felt Red elbowing his way to the front. Kevin also got a metal replica of a red Corvette, which he kept in sight in his home as a reminder to keep the dialogue going with his anger.

In addition to our narrative work, we always encourage people to make lifestyle changes to support their new reality. Kevin was beginning to feel inspired enough to bring some of these practices into his life. A little later Kevin started taking a t'ai chi class and was quite satisfied with his capacity to engage in this form even given his limited energy. He also began to eat a healthier diet.

Technique

•—•—•

EXPLORING FUTURE SCENARIOS

"Future life regression" can be quite useful as a means to explore stories of possibility and to mitigate a pessimistic future prediction. It is based on the idea that we have multiple, parallel lives in other parallel universes, and through visualization, we can visit one or more of these lives, to find out what happened when other choices were made than those that we made for ourselves in this life. People's regrets are often quite powerful. The roads not taken sometimes hold more sway over people than the roads taken. It's not hard for us to imagine parallel lives of who we might have been had we taken a different path. Whether we are actually visiting those lives is not, of course, important. Even if we visit them in our imagination, it is a worthwhile journey. This imagination can be deeply therapeutic—to tell the story of who we could have been. In this process we use guided imagery, visualization, and sometimes, if the person is willing, some hypnosis.

I asked Kevin if he would like to try a future life regression. He thought it sounded fun, so we agreed to proceed. Our goal was to check out some future versions of Kevin and to find out how their paths would be different from his. I wanted to explore other possible outcomes than his current path.

After an appropriate relaxation period and an induction of imagery, Kevin found a parallel self who worked with horses. As he explored that man's life, he found that he hadn't previously realized how interesting big working horses could be. He saw that version of him happily surrounded by horses, doing some blacksmithing. This man lived a comfortable, rural life, surrounded by the physical challenges of managing animals who had wills of their own and weighed more than he did.

Next Kevin visited a version of him who lived in the Caribbean and spoke Spanish. This Kevin was excited by all the cool places that version of him had found to hang out. Not all these places were safe. Business had brought him to the islands in the first place. This version of Kevin had a business transporting fresh food to hotels. Kevin said that this was the version of him who had graduated from business school. He liked this version of him, but wasn't as attracted to him as he had been to the horseman.

Next Kevin found a third version of him who had gone to medical school in Europe. That was appealing because of his interest in chemistry. This version of him had spent much time working in chemistry, physics, and math. Kevin said how much fun it was to work in that way. Science was kind of neat. He followed the life of this version of him into being a physician. He liked him but wasn't excited in the end by this man's life either.

When we were done, I asked him what he'd learned. He said he realized that his regrets about not having finished business school or gone to medical school could be released, since he wouldn't have enjoyed the lives that these pursuits would have given him. He preferred the more solitary horseman, though this version of him lacked for companionship. "I'd like the horseman's life," he said, "if I had a wife."

"There must be some stories there," I said, "about why you're not with anyone?" Kevin nodded vigorously.

"Oh, the stories I could tell," he said.

I asked him to write them down for our next session. "Write me some stories of loves that didn't turn out," I said. "Let's explore the men-women thing next time." Kevin agreed and was off. We had just turned the corner into a new chapter of his life—relationships with women.

Kevin returned with stories about love gone awry. He had the usual assortment of betrayals and unrequited loves: the one who got away, the one who didn't wait for him to come back, the one who went off with his best friend. His stories about women were as rich as his stories about men had been. They reinforced a view of women as untrustworthy and dangerous, especially the more desirable they were. We were in the midst of the stories that supported his beliefs about women, which were keeping him from actually having a good relationship. After hearing these stories, I challenged him to find someone who had a good relationship, one that he could admire, and to interview this character to learn how that had happened. Kevin agreed, though he smiled and said he didn't know if he could find anyone with a good relationship. He sheepishly admitted he had adopted a view of women: "use them and leave them."

It took an extra week for Kevin to find someone whose relationship he respected. He interviewed this man over a pint at the local pub and got his story. When he presented it to us, he said it was fairy tale. He had trouble believing it was true, though the man told it as if it were. My feedback to him was that I found it entirely plausible, to which he responded, "You must have lived in a very different world than me." I agreed that this was most definitely true.

Next came an exploration of more stories about how men and women relate. He accepted assignments of watching a variety of movies, including dreaded chick flicks (romantic comedies). We began to sort out a variety of possible ways of being with women. It was then that Kevin announced he was ready to date again.

"How are you going to do that?" I asked.

"I don't know," he answered. "I don't know how to meet women outside of base bars."

We proceeded to brainstorm about interests he had that might bring him into contact with women. I told him the story of a client who discovered that women liked men who went to cooking class. We talked about the importance of doing something you like where women might be instead of looking for women primarily. Kevin's assignment was to figure out what that might be.

In these meetings Kevin changed his preferred stories about men, women, men's relationships with each other, men's relationships with women, and how he wanted to fit into these stories. He explored what his preferred ending would be. By this time we were twenty visits into the work together, steadily changing the story Kevin told about himself and his relationships. His medical symptoms progressively had diminished during this time, even though we didn't really talk about them.

On a rating scale called the MYMOP-2 (My Medical Outcomes Profile, Version 2), his main symptom (fatigue) had dropped from 5 on a scale of 0 to 6 to 2.5. His second most bothersome symptom (muscle pain) had fallen from 5 to 2. The degree to which his symptoms interfered with his activities of daily life had fallen from 5 to 2. His overall quality of life went from 3 to 5 on a 0 to 6 scale, where 6 is best and 0 is worst. This happens more often than not with medically unexplainable symptoms when we address the underlying source of the misery in people's lives.

While the focus in this book is what can happen in the sixteen- to twenty-visit time frame, over the next while, Kevin would periodically work with us for a few weeks at a time. He did go to cooking class and discovered what I told him—women like men who know how to cook vegetables. Consistent with his overall approach to life, he found a special energy machine that finished curing his fatigue and pain. When we last heard from him, he was almost entirely free from pain, energetic, and enjoying his life of dating and continuing to explore what he wanted to do.

DEALING WITH ANOMALIES

Brian Boyd, our story theorist from New Zealand, has argued that our storytelling capacity coevolved with our need to manage social nuances, which are more important for our thriving and surviving than for any other species by far. We expect people to be able to tell a story that explains their beliefs and desires. We want to know what motivates them. If they don't tell us a story, we create one for them. This is how badly we need a story to explain others' behavior.[14]

When people don't behave as we expect them to do, we start running simulations in which we can pose various interpretations of their behavior and decide which one(s) feels most accurate to us. The results of these simulations depend upon how well we have constructed a story about the other person. The simulations we run require memory calls, requests to get information from memory that will be of use in making our simulation plausible. The call to memory is for episodes or vignettes that bear some superficial similarity to our memory (the story we have constructed) about the social situation or interaction we are trying to explain.

The details we recall in our stories are often quite different from the story we told or wrote immediately after an event. Places, people, time, and context can change quite significantly. What is similar is the "point" or "points" we make with the story, which typically relate to goals, plans, themes, or lessons learned. Salience matters, because we don't make points that fail to relate to the beliefs we already hold. Instead, we seek stories that verify our beliefs. When a new story matches what we already believe, it can easily be absorbed into our memories giving us the sense that we have understood the story.

Thus, when my client, Hope, ran a simulation of a telephone call in which her husband told her he wasn't coming home when scheduled, she asked herself, "Are there any similar events in my memory?" When we do this, we are asking ourselves whether we can find a story like the one we are simulating, at the broadest level of interpretation. We can match new stories to old ones on the basis of identical goals. Therefore, one question we can expect people to ask themselves is: "Do I have a story in memory where the main goal is the same as that being pursued in the story I am hearing?"

Our Brain's Anomaly Detector

Anomalies get our attention. They activate the "anomaly detector" in our brains, which tells us when something isn't like it's supposed to be.

When our anomaly detector alerts us to the unexpected, it causes us to focus our attention on that phenomenon. We are driven to explain why we were wrong in our expectations, if only to silence the anomaly alarm. This is probably wise and has survival success.

A failure to have things turn out as expected indicates a failure in understanding. People desire very much to remedy such failures. We ask ourselves questions about what was going on. After our attention is focused and in explanatory mode, we may even have to construct a new story from elements of several old understood stories. These old stories are the memory base and they represent our beliefs. A belief under this view is a point of view we can illustrate with a number of good stories. (They tend to be of the form: "You know X never works out. Remember that old example of X we both knew? And there was another type of X I saw once, too.")

We scan our associational networks for indices that indicate similarity to what we have previously encountered. With the help of Brodmann's areas 11 and 25 of the brain, we eliminate those stories that are the least relevant. We settle upon a collection of stories that are at least close and potentially plausible. My favorite humorous example of this is the movie *The Gods Must Be Crazy*. In this movie a Coca-Cola bottle falls from the sky into a remote village in Africa. The locals have never seen such a thing, and the movie is about their efforts to generate a story to explain what has happened. We are always performing variations of this comedy to quiet the anomaly detector in our brain.

Consider our client, Hope, we were discussing earlier. She has many stories about being defective and unacceptable in some way. Then, an anomaly happens. Her husband goes to a sporting event with the college team he coaches. The event is the last of the season, and he decides to remain afterward. He is in Wyoming and she in Vermont. This has never happened before. It is anomalous. She needs an explanation. She generates possibilities: (1) he is having an affair, (2) he is leaving her, (3) he doesn't care about her.

Considering these possibilities reminds her of other stories in which people left her. Her father died when she was in high school of a heart attack. Her mother implied that she had broken his heart with her bad behavior (dating, marijuana, drinking—all relatively mild compared to some students of her time). That reminded her of stories about her having failed to perform up to her level of competency. In entertaining these stories, she came to the conclusion that she had been a bad wife and that he was punishing her by staying away, looking for an affair or actually having one, showing her how unimportant she was.

Scripts

We all understand differently—this much is obvious. The reason we understand differently is that our memories are different. In order to understand anything, we must find the closest item in memory to which it relates. Brain pattern research pioneers Schank and Abelson claimed that understanding new events requires us to find the correct knowledge structure and to use that structure to create expectations for what events were likely to take place.[15] In Hope's case she brought out her script about what husbands normally do when they go out of town on business, and staying much later for what seemed like a vacation did not go with that script. Therefore, it qualified as an anomaly.

Our knowledge structures are somewhat idiosyncratic. For example, each of us has his or her own conception of "husband" based upon our own experience of having or being one, based upon our parents' experiences, our friends' experiences, what we have seen in movies and read in books, and so on. Much drama occurs when we assume that each of us means exactly the same by the word "husband." If two people with widely different stories about being a husband marry, they are doomed to frequent alarms in their anomaly detectors.

To explore this further, I reversed the possible accusation. I asked Hope if her fears could relate to her desires. Given the way our "theory of mind" brain works, we infer other people's beliefs and intentions based upon what we would feel were we performing the same behavior. "Is there a part of you who wants to leave Mike? Maybe that part of you—secretly from the other parts of you—is also thinking about having an affair? Maybe that part of you has a very tiny voice and can barely be heard? Maybe she's so tiny that when she speaks, her words are almost imperceptible, but they do register and you interpret them as Mike's intentions and preparations instead of yours? We all have parts of us that are contrary to most of our other parts, and sometimes it's important to showcase them, to let them speak.

Hope thought for some time. Had she not had some experience in working in this manner, she would have immediately denied feeling this possibility, because most of her avatars want to stay with her husband, but she had learned to accept the parts of herself that seemed unacceptable (to society, to her family, to the parts of her who represent society, church, family, etc.) and to invite them to speak. Feeling conflicted often involves suppressing an unacceptable voice. If we tie up and gag one of our inner characters, he or she will still struggle against the ropes and make sounds to be rescued. We still hear him or her. Hope had learned enough radical acceptance of her internal voices to entertain this possibility. "Maybe . . ." she responded with a rising tone, as the word lengthened and progressed. This was my invitation to offer some hypnosis and guided imagery techniques to find that part of her.

As Hope stilled her louder voices to listen for the quieter ones, she came upon a part of her who was an adventurous teen, the part of her just finishing high school, and looking at the world as a great adventure, and preparing for a great love of epic proportions. "Maybe she's my inner romantic," she said.

"Is that what you'd like to call her?" I said.

"No, let's call her Jean" (an adventurous friend from high school who is still living large).

"Okay, so what's Jean's perspective on all this?"

"Jean is like saying, 'What the f**k! What happened to this great romance you promised us? I'm not giving up that dream. Trade in Mike for a new model!'"

"That sounds unacceptable to someone else within you," I said. "Who rises up to counter Jean?"

"My mother!" (I think everyone on this planet has internalized the voice of their mother as a character within our menagerie! This is probably why moms got so much play in the early days of psychoanalysis.)

"What's your mother got to say?"

"She's saying, 'Don't even begin to think that way. You were married in a church. You're living a respectable life. Don't even think of anything so scandalous.' She named me Hope, after all."

"So your mother would say, 'No matter how distant and unhappy you and Mike are, you have to stay in the marriage, because that's the respectable thing to do.'"

"Right."

"Are there other parts of you, who are unhappy in this relationship? Maybe they're friends with Jean?"

Hope chuckled, "There's 'Our Lady of Infinite Patience.' She likes to stand on a pedestal and look holy. She would do well in front of a Catholic school or a church. She keeps giving Mike 'another chance.' No matter how many times his coaching or his sports interfere with the rest of our life together, she gives him another chance. No matter how many times he walks out on couple's therapy, she gives him another chance."

"So who is this part of you who keeps concluding that the problem is because you're a bad wife?" A bit more reflection allowed a character to emerge, whom she called "All the Women in My Family."

"'All the Women in My Family' say with one loud, unified voice, 'If you're not a good enough wife, your man will leave you and run off with someone else and you'll be left destitute with hungry children and no way to feed them.' That's a story I heard a lot growing up. That happened to women in our family, in the past. That was one of the great fears of my grandmother's generation and probably also my mother's."

"Checklist," I said. "No hungry children for you. No possibility of being destitute. Able to support yourself on your own merits. Probably not likely to become one of the Les Miserables, the homeless waifs roaming the city, without Mike."

"Probably not," she said.

Further discussion during that session led to her strengthening the voices who would describe her as being a patient, loving person with limits. We reviewed some of the examples that led to the "you better be a good wife" story, and Hope began to relax about her fears that Mike would run off or have an affair. She ended the session joking that maybe that would be for the best, since it would solve her difficulties with "Our Lady of Infinite Patience," who took spiritual satisfaction in forever giving Mike another chance. More work remained, but progress had occurred and Hope left with some homework for writing dialogues among these characters about possible futures and how all of them would react. She looked forward to this assignment as creative time that also nurtured her. The journey continued.

5

Meeting the Storytellers

Art is fire plus algebra.
JORGE LUIS BORGES, *FICCIONES*

Once we have identified the stories we are living, we need to discover the voices inside our minds. Richard Schwartz, the author of *Internal Family Systems Therapy,* writes that our minds contain internal representations of the members of our families. Memory is narrative. Our memories of the important people in our lives are laid down as stories. As young children we internalize and practice and repeat these stories. A way of understanding this that comes closer to contemporary neuroscience is to say that we create simulations or representations of the important people in our world.

We rehearse and "reperform" these stories in our minds or in the public arena so frequently that they become automatic. We forget who first told them or that we invented the story to hold on to some memories of happenings, and we assume that these stories are actually truths. Behind every statement of fact we make about ourselves lies a story and a character from our past who was the source of that story. Schwartz noted that therapy did not fully help people until they also changed their internalized characters. Here is an example:

Juliette came to me for help with ulcerative colitis. She was a forty-year-old woman living near Newcastle, England, and came to Vermont to spend ten days with me. We began by identifying what she told herself over and over about herself. I asked her to tell me some stories that captured how she saw herself. She told about how she always wanted to dance. She would go to dance class in her neighborhood and hide behind the curtains to watch. Eventually the teacher noticed that she kept coming to every class and allowed her to join the class even though the entrance requirement was being six years old and Juliette was only four. The teacher even let Juliette participate in the recital for all the parents even though Juliette was too young to fully memorize the routine. Predictably, Juliette forgot parts of the routine on stage and was terribly embarrassed. She remembered how she tried to cover up her mistakes by forging ahead with great enthusiasm and poise despite not doing what everyone else was doing.

We found this theme repeated often in her life. She applied to art school and made large canvases with great panache even though she lacked the training and technical expertise of her classmates. When she asked how she came to be admitted, she was told that her charm made up for her relative lack of talent. She often heard this theme as in weekend dance classes that she took with students who were able to study every day. Teachers liked her enthusiasm and capacity to throw herself into the dance even if she didn't do it technically as well as the others. We began to formulate this coping style into a character who managed to cover up deficits with charm and enthusiasm. She thought of this character as the four-year-old who got through the recital, now grown up, but still covering up a lack of skill with charm and enthusiasm and "living large."

"This is not necessarily a bad story," I said. "Sometimes we aren't perfect for any number of reasons, and the show must still go on. Forging ahead is a virtue." In a narrative approach, we offer alternative interpretations for the story—different ways of seeing the same events.

Juliette had more stories. She told the story of being her mother's confidante. She listened patiently to the stories told by her mother and her aunties. She was the adult child. Rather than play with friends, she stayed indoors with the older women and heard them out. "They came first," she said. Juliette described the impact of this as making her feel "old before her time." She felt compelled to make her mother and aunts feel better, regardless of her wishes.

Juliette told stories of her grandmother telling her she could never do anything right. Her quilts were never good enough. Her grades were never good enough. She never helped her mother quite enough. Juliette's grandparents were relatively wealthy, while her father never succeeded at anything, though he tried often enough. He had failed at being a musician, at being a carpenter, at being a Marxist, at being a welder, at selling art, at writing newspaper columns, and countless other pursuits. Juliette's story of her father was that he was tormented by the success of his father, who mingled with the rich and famous of his day as their private banker. In fact, Juliette's grandfather was more than a banker—he fixed things for the wealthy, made things go away when that was needed. He was connected, both above ground and below. Juliette was intimidated by him. She felt he occasionally paid attention to her, but mostly she didn't exist for him. Her grandmother formed a constant patter of undermining and invalidating comments. Her defining memory of her grandparents consisted of the time when they were both ridiculing her and she dumped a pot of spaghetti on her grandfather's head. She said his respect for her rose enormously after that.

Technique
•—•—•
IDENTIFY THE MAIN CHARACTERS

The focus of this part of the healing is to help people become aware of their internal characters and the often repeated stories involving those characters.

I started this process by asking Juliette to tell me about her. When she tried to tell a story about her self-identity, she couldn't help but invoke the characters who influenced that story. Juliette's grandfather remained in her consciousness as a character. Within her everyday experience, he continued to speak to her, to criticize her, to ignore her, even though he was actually dead. She had created an internal representation of him—his voice, his words, his appearance. In essence, she had a map of her grandfather, a sort of hologram who continued to appear in appropriate circumstances. She also had a map of her critical grandmother.

We all do this. We internalize the powerful characters of our lives. Surely our brains are designed to do this for survival reasons. We must have a very good "theory of mind" for the people who have power over us. We must anticipate their reactions. Our social survival is dependent upon having accurate stories about how important people in our social environment will react to various scenarios that we create.

The summary line for Juliette's internalized map of herself is that she is someone who lacks talent, but makes up for it by enthusiasm and panache. However, she is never quite good enough and must continually try harder to perform, please, mitigate, placate, and so on. This character is a composite of all the stories she has heard about Juliette and the stories she repeats in her mind about events that happened to her. These stories require a host of characters and voices. There are more voices than just those of her family. The moment we step outside the house, we are ready to acquire new characters and voices. I asked her, "Who else lives in your mind?"

She responded:

Hamid, her lover during graduate school, who was studying journalism and aspiring to work for the *Times of London*

Jamal, a friend who worked for the BBC in London and had been her confidante during graduate school

Sara, a freelance artist

Sheila, a mother figure

Kim, who keeps losing things—relatives, jobs, roommates

Robert, who is *very* fit

Francis, her brother, who was diagnosed with attention deficit hyperactivity disorder and had both extreme reactions and difficulty slowing down

Harriett, her twenty-three-year-old daughter with challenging emotional issues

Her uncle Sheldon, who had open heart surgery this summer and writes plays

Alan, her current boyfriend, a pharmacist doing corporate drug research

Her best friend Susan, with whom Juliette often shared memories of their fathers; she is able to tell Susan stories of things that have shamed her and has a sense that it is healing to tell Susan these stories

And many more!

In her ordinary life, Juliette was telling stories about these people all the time, about what they might do. We call that, "running simulations, or sims." We sim about what would happen if we . . . Fill in the dots with anything. What would happen if Juliette invited Jamal for dinner? What would happen if she tried to seduce Hamid? What would happen if Susan tried to seduce her? She had a number of scenarios, inspired in part by *Cosmo,* about how to make Alan more passionate. She had stories about how she could become half as fit as Robert.

I asked her to tell me about these people. To do so required her to tell stories about them because that's how we communicate.

Technique
•—•—•
POSSIBLE NEXT STEPS

I could now go in many directions. Having identified some characters, I could ask her to search for photographs of them and we could make a collage of these photographs with attached stories. We could also do this using technology. We could use guided imagery in which we invite each of these characters (or some of them because there are always time constraints) to speak for themselves and talk about Juliette and how they got to become "ghosts in her mind." I could tell Juliette a story to seed her to produce other stories.

Technique
•—•—•
A COGNITIVE APPROACH

I decided to take a more cognitive approach of examining the plausibility of the conclusions made based upon the stories that support these conclusions.

My next step with Juliette was to look at the usefulness of her identity stories. How useful is it to believe that she is relatively untalented, for example? I told her about Malcolm Gladwell's book, *Outliers,* in which he asserts that no one is really all that talented. To become proficient we have to apply ourselves for about 10,000 hours to a task. Without those 10,000 hours, no "talent." With them one still has to have luck, for many people have put in their time and not all have been successful, discovered, rich, or won the Nobel Prize. Given the flimsy evidence for Juliette's lack of talent (a four-year-old dancing with six- or seven-year-olds), could she modify that conclusion? "What have you actually spent 10,000 or more hours doing?" I asked.

"I haven't actually done anything," she said. "Like my father, I've started many things, but never taken any of them over the top."

"There's that no-goodnik story again," I responded. "That story goes: 'I'm just like my father who also completes nothing and ne'er does well.'"

"But I haven't done anything," Juliette insisted. "I've studied dance. I've been in a dance company. I've choreographed. I've opened a studio. I've run a business. But have I really succeeded in dance? No. My performances are poorly attended, my classes are small, the studio is barely in the black, and I'm not thrilling audiences worldwide.

"I've studied art and my paintings hang on the walls of my studio, but no one is buying them except for that occasional sale that barely covers the cost of the materials. And now, at the ripe old age of forty, I'm going to medical school, but my ulcerative colitis is acting up, and I don't even know if I'll be well enough to finish. I'd like to be a general practitioner, out on the fells, or some such nonsense. Perhaps treating the people who care for Beatrix Potter's cottage or the farmers of Cumbria. But perhaps I'll never get there for lack of health. So I'm not good enough."

People have a hard time letting go of stories that don't work. They are comfortable. They are certain. Performing them over and over will produce the same results in the future that performing them over and over in the past produced. Therefore, they are predictable. We will almost always pick certainty over the possibility of healing unless we have support to do otherwise. Juliette was no exception.

"That's your story," I said, "but I'm not buying it. Look at my Uncle Rod. When asked what it took for him to become the incredible healer he is, he inevitably says, 'thirty-five years of being a wino.'" I love Rod for owning his past as being part of what generates his present. What if ulcerative colitis is just your gut-wrenching experience of never meeting your expectations? What if letting go of others' expectations for your failure could relax your gut? It might, you know? And you'll only know if you try."

How can I know that the stories I am hearing are linked to her ulcerative colitis? I can't with certainty. However, I have a commitment to the idea of the interconnectedness of everything. Since she came to resolve her ulcerative colitis, whatever happens during our efforts to do so is probably connected to ulcerative colitis. Life out of balance and harmony is simultaneously physically, mentally, and socially relevant. I will feel more certain if the gut finds a way to join our developing metaphors such as "gut-wrenching" or "all twisted up inside." She resonates with having "gut-wrenching" experiences, so maybe we are on the right track. I poke around until the person makes the connections that matter to him or her.

PLEASE SEND US THIS CARD TO RECEIVE OUR LATEST CATALOG FREE OF CHARGE.

Book in which this card was found _____

❑ Check here to receive our catalog via e-mail.

	Company _____
Name _____	❑ Send me wholesale information
Address _____	Phone _____
City _____	State_____ Zip_____ Country_____
E-mail address _____	

Please check area(s) of interest to receive related announcements via e-mail:

❑ Health   ❑ Self-help   ❑ Science/Nature   ❑ Shamanism
❑ Ancient Mysteries ❑ New Age/Spirituality ❑ Visionary Plants   ❑ Martial Arts
❑ Spanish Language ❑ Sexuality/Tantra   ❑ Family and Youth   ❑ Religion/Philosophy

Please send a catalog to my friend:

Name _____ Company _____

Address _____ Phone _____

City _____ State_____ Zip_____ Country_____

Order at 1-800-246-8648 • Fax (802) 767-3726

E-mail: customerservice@InnerTraditions.com • Web site: www.InnerTraditions.com

INNER TRADITIONS

BEAR & COMPANY

Inner Traditions • Bear & Company
P.O. Box 388
Rochester, VT 05767-0388
U.S.A.

What we are doing here can be framed within a larger context that has been called constructive psychotherapy,[1] though we are trying to avoid the term psychotherapy to emphasize that we are addressing the total social person and not just whatever "psycho" is. This field emphasizes complex cycles in natural ordering and reorganizing processes that characterize all development in living systems. We are all active participants in our lives. Within rich contexts of human relationship and symbol systems, people make new meanings as they develop. We use whatever techniques we can find that will assist people to find and refine their sense of balance.

MIND THE GAP

Several of the techniques we use take advantage of the fact that our brains are designed to fill in the gaps in our understanding of the world around us. We are experts at filling in the gaps. All stories are full of gaps, which facilitate their telling in short time frames.[2] Without the gaps a story would take as long to tell as the experience it tells about. We fill in the gaps to make sense for ourselves of the story. Film works because we fill in the many gaps necessary to create a continuous experience.

These gaps have been called points of indeterminacy, formally defined as any site in a story at which the attributes of an object, situation, or character are underdetermined or underdescribed. Every interpretation of a story centers around these points of indeterminacy,[3] which inspire us to fill in the gaps with what matters to us, with what increases our sense of value and purpose.

It is through these gaps in the story that we enrich it, that we insert our own details, our own associations, and make it personal. Gaps in a story not only demand additional effort from the reader/listener, but enable him or her to see something extra, to make new connections, to add richness to the story.[4] Bridging these gaps and filling the holes in the narrative is what readers/listeners do continually as they absorb a story and come to an understanding and interpretation of it. The reader/listener mobilizes his or her already available knowledge of the world to supplement and make sense of what has been left unsaid. Words activate so many semantic/neuronal networks that we have our whole lived experience available at our fingertips for adding meaning to what is being perceived.

We do this when we look at the world. When we are faced with a set of circumstances, we create a story that binds them together. Stories emerge and elaborate themselves through the interaction between minds and gaps.

The Role of the Brain

Holes and gaps are inherent in stories, for a good story provides a structure from which our imagination can improvise. Filling these holes and gaps in an interpretive way is part of the everyday activity of the brain.[5] Exploring how we do this is part of the everyday activity of psychotherapy. In the well-known (in neurology circles) Charles Bonnet syndrome, people who are blind, or nearly so, have full visual experiences looking out a window, for example, in the dark and seeing things that other people cannot. The receiver of a story similarly automatically fills in indeterminacies and "concretizes" the referred-to objects, scenarios, and characters so that they seem to be "fully determined."[6] These points of indeterminacy stimulate rather than demand completion from our existing store of knowledge.[7]

Compensating for gaps and holes is what our brains do well. What parts of the brain are involved in filling these gaps? Raymond Mar, who studies story, wrote a comprehensive review of the neuroscience in 2004.[8] He notes that researchers Frith and Frith from University College London point to the medial prefrontal cortex, the paracingulate cortex, and the temporo-parietal junction, which is located at the superior and posterior portion of the superior temporal sulcus near the superior temporal gyrus.[9] These are important areas for the comprehension of story. Less consistent activation occurs in the temporal poles and the amygdalae. This circuit is connected to another, which manages spatial relations and includes hippocampal regions,[10] along with parietal and medial occipital areas, and the posterior cingulate cortex.[11]

The default network, about which we have already written, is composed of stable sub-networks, which flexibly couple and uncouple with one another, based upon task demands (episodic memory tasks, for example, versus spatial memory tasks). Recall of events and recall of places (spatial memory) share a common medial temporal lobe–based area that is activated during these tasks with recall of events recruiting additional prefrontal components when needed.[12]

Virtue and colleagues used functional magnetic resonance imaging to study how people listen to and understand short stories that implicitly or explicitly contain references to events outside the stories. They wanted to study how we make inferences about what is happening in the story when we have to rely on information not present in the story. They observed distinct patterns of increased fMRI signals for implied over explicit events at two critical points during the stories: (1) within the right superior temporal gyrus when a verb in the text implied that an inference was needed; and (2) within the left superior temporal gyrus at the point at which participants needed to generate an inference to understand the story (called the coherence break).[13]

Virtue and colleagues examined fMRI signals at these two critical points separately for people with high working memory capacity (i.e., those who were most likely to make inferences during text comprehension). These participants showed greater activation of the fMRI signals for implied rather than for explicit events in the left inferior frontal gyrus compared to people with low working memory capacity. Their study provided evidence that areas within the superior temporal gyrus and inferior frontal gyrus are very active when people make inferences, even during ongoing story comprehension which is already using many cognitive processes. They suggested that the right hemisphere's superior temporal gyrus was particularly involved during early inference making, while the left hemisphere's superior temporal gyrus was particularly involved during later inference making, all in the process of story comprehension.[14]

Their results are supported by others comparing comprehension in normal controls and patient groups, such as by cognition researcher Tiziana Zalla,[15] and Debora Burin and her colleagues from Baylor University School of Medicine in Houston, Texas,[16] The relevance of this comes from human relationships being like stories (or being stories), full of gaps and holes, that require us to fill them in. Our success in this filling process makes all the difference for how well our relationships function or how poorly. Story comprehension ability seems associated with one's ability to manage relationships.

Gaps Make Room for Healing

To understand a story is to interpret it, to place a meaning and a purpose upon it. The more indeterminate a story is, the greater the number of meanings and purposes that can be imposed upon it. Interpretation has been called a complex meeting point of the horizon of the story and that of the reader/listener.[17] Stories, written or oral, can carry multiple meanings and do not lead to what Gadamer calls a perfect fusion of horizons or a resolution of all indeterminacies.[18] "One text is potentially capable of several different realizations, and no reading can ever exhaust the full potential, for each individual reader will fill in the gaps in his own way, thereby excluding the various other possibilities; as he reads, he will make his own decisions about how the gap is to be filled."[19]

It is in this gappiness that narrative healing functions. The stories we tell to self and others are inherently full of gaps and indeterminacies. Changing one's story involves filling the gaps differently. Skeptics of our approach sometimes remark on how impossible it is to change the events of our lives. We counter with the idea that we can change which events are in foreground and which are in background. We can change the ways we connect events, the ways we fill the gaps between events, and the spin we put on those events. As we explore our lives with the same techniques we use to explore fiction, an almost infinite array of possibilities begin to appear. We read our lives in a never-ending hermeneutic circle, which entails a feedback circle between content and how we interpret that content.

Here's an example. Lewis saw Karen, who was unhappy with terrible low back pain and chronic ulcerative colitis.

Technique
•—•—•
THE "ILLNESS" NARRATIVE

When someone comes with a presenting physical complaint, there is usually a story that comes with it. We usually begin by asking about the person's life around the time that the illness started. Sometimes the correlations just pour out because the person had never considered that his or her life related to the maladies of the physical body. At other times, it's slower going.

My first question, was, "When did your back pain begin?"

"Shortly after I got married."

Technique
•—•—•
FOLLOW THE CLIENT'S LEAD

Like Perseus following Ariadne's string, we pursue the connections given to us by the client. However, we should begin with the least number of assumptions or ideas. My minimal set of assumptions is that lives and illnesses are connected and that healing through dialogue is always possible. We try to follow what the client tells us and to ask questions that will make this description come alive in story form. We let our theories about the illness arise from what the client says and not from any preconceived notions about the client or about the illness.

Karen did more than answer the time question. She linked the pain to an event—getting married. Asking questions now about her marriage makes sense.

"How long ago was that?"

"Six years."

"And how has your marriage been?"

"It's been a struggle."

"Are you happy"

"I, I . . . don't know."

"If you had to guess, what would you say?"

"I'd say, 'no.'"

"Tell me a story from your marriage that would help me to understand in what way you're not happy."

Technique
•—•—•
AVOID THE QUESTION, "WHY?"

We never, or hardly ever, ask, "Why?" Not because we don't want to know why, as we certainly do. The problem is more in the socialized response to the question "Why?" In a medical setting, the question elicits a reductionist response, and in a psychotherapeutic setting, it tends to send people into an entangled quandary of how to assign value to past life events in order to determine which one is more directly weighted in this outcome. Those kinds of assignations of value are largely arbitrary and in any case impossible to determine quickly.

Questions such as: "Tell me a story of when this came to be true for you," "Tell me a story of how you came to understand this," or "Tell me a story about . . . that would help me understand how you came to think this way" provide an effective way of getting a story that contains a metaphor.

We're already well on the way to developing a potential metaphor like "bending over backward to serve others" or "the back-breaking work of taking care of others." Once these metaphors develop, they will help bring the client's awareness to the connection of her life with her pain. This also has the effect of allowing the client to begin to use language of self-efficacy—to see herself as an agent in her life and her choices as empowered ones, although possibly ineffective.

"Well . . . here's the first story that comes to mind. We went away on vacation to Marabella, Spain. I was with my husband, our two boys, and our two-year-old. Not once did anyone ask me what I wanted to do. Not once did anyone even ask me how I was feeling. Not even once did anyone offer to help me. My husband spent the whole time talking about himself, as did our two boys. He never offered to take care of the baby so I could do something. Nor did our sons. I spent the entire trip looking after the baby and listening to *him and his sons* talk about what they wanted to do and what they did. I was so annoyed by the time I returned home that I wanted to go away for my own vacation without them."

Technique
•—•—•
FOLLOWING HUNCHES
We engage in what grounded theorists call the constant comparative method, to continually hold stories next to each other, looking for similarities and differences, until a solid theme emerges.

I have an idea that the colitis and the back pain are related. Following this thread I next ask, "When did your colitis start?"

"Around when I graduated from high school."

"How long ago was that?"

"More than twenty years."

"That's a long time to be sick."

"It sure is."

"How old are you now?"

"Forty-seven."

"So that's almost thirty years."

"I guess you're right."

"That sounds very hard. At least you haven't had to have surgery. That's something very positive."

Technique

•—•—•

FIND THE POSITIVE AND INVITE POSITIVE SELF-REFLECTION

It is important to begin by honoring people's suffering, meeting them where they are. We then begin to look for something positive in the story to emphasize as part of an overall program to drive the conversation in an uplifting direction. The parallels from research on facilitating change include ideas from critical theory, participatory action research, appreciative inquiry, or peer empowered evaluation research. People in our mainstream, conventional world rarely take praise well. It runs against the grain of the critical commentary being silently made in their minds. We start praise early to get people used to the idea of positive self-talk.

"I suppose it is. I hadn't thought of that. I hadn't thought of it in that way."

"It's a really wonderful thing to have had colitis for almost thirty years and to have managed to avoid surgery. That's really great."

"I . . . I suppose it is. If you say so. I mean, I guess it is."

"Of course it is.

"Now, could you tell me a story about something that happened soon after you were diagnosed with colitis? Whatever comes to mind."

"I remember feeling terribly alone. I was away from home at college. I had no friends. It was bizarre. I was homesick even though I hated home. I wanted nothing more than to leave home, but once I was gone, I missed having a home. I didn't really know how to make friends. I remember going to a dance with my roommate, and I hadn't really had much experience with alcohol and I liked the taste. We were drinking those sweet girly drinks. At least, that's what I'd call them now. But then I was just having fun. And I think I was near passing out. I found myself in a bedroom with some guys undressing me. That's when my roommate burst through the door, screaming. She grabbed my wrist and pulled me out of there, half-dressed and all. I think they were afraid of her screams, afraid that someone in authority would hear. They let us leave. I felt so ashamed. I don't think I went anywhere else that entire year."

Technique
•—•—•
COLLECT MORE STORIES AND NOTE COMMON ELEMENTS

Once the stories start to come, collect several to provide multiple perspectives. I have learned from Native American elders that if you want to really understand someone, you must know all the stories that have ever been told about him or her and all the stories he or she has ever told. I can't hear every story, but I like to start a nice collection.

I proceeded to collect more vignettes about Karen's life, looking for similarities in the stories related to her back pain and to her colitis. On the vacation that described her marriage, she felt alone in the company of others, isolated. At the time her colitis began, she felt "terribly alone," without friends, homesick. We have a new idea of feeling ashamed, which didn't appear in the marriage story. I suspect that Karen felt isolated and alone in her shame. This is worth pursuing.

The themes of Karen's vignettes often centered on entering less than optimal relationships, jobs, situations, in relation to not believing that she deserved any better. I would call the plot "settling for less." We all know this plot. We have all been a part of this story at some time. Not only did Karen settle for less, but she was overburdened in doing so. Her story of getting trapped in the fraternity bedroom was a metaphor for her life and perhaps why it was one of the first stories she told. Her sense of life was that she was innocent and having fun, and before she knew it, she was trapped in a bad situation. It seemed that her story had changed when she got married, but the vacation was proof that this was not the case.

I don't know how people get the specific illnesses that they have. Sometimes it's logical, sometimes not. But the susceptibility for illness does seem to grow out of a story about how life should be lived. Susceptibility has logic. It makes sense within the story of the person's life. Some plots seem to wear down the body. The "settling for less" plot is one of those. So is the "overburdened" plot. Feeling overburdened and developing back pain makes a kind of poetic sense.

To get more stories, I reviewed Karen's memorable stories from childhood. She described her parents as a somewhat despotic bunch, who seemed to engage in random, unpredictable acts to humiliate Karen. The underlying message of their various dramas was very much "you're not good enough." Despite what Karen did in school, she never felt she was good enough to receive her father's full approval. Despite what Karen did at home, she perceived her mother as always finding fault with her. Karen was an only child and had no siblings with whom to share the blame. It fell solidly on her shoulders.

Our childhood stories set the stage for how we will see the world. They train us to a perspective and a mode of interpretation that few people challenge. Karen's stories were those of being an inferior person, of failing to "measure up," of failing to please the important people in her life. The voices inside her head were those of her parents—her mother and her father. Whatever she chose to do, they criticized her. Whatever she did, it was not good enough.

I recognized that despite her attempts to please and to be contrite as a child, she was also very angry: angry that she hadn't been better protected, angry that she hadn't received the praise she deserved, angry that she didn't really live in a loving environment as she believed she should have.

> **Technique**
> •—•—•
> ## COCONSTRUCT A SHARED META-NARRATIVE
> ## (STORY ABOUT STORIES)
>
> Plot orders our experience and gives form to our narratives.[20] It brings together what would be separate and heterogeneous elements and organizes them into our experience and understanding of time, enabling us to make sense out of the events of our lives. Plot is composed of a series of discrete incidents. It takes an infinite succession of sequential "Nows" and organizes them into a manageable chunk.

From small stories we begin to construct a larger narrative, the story of a person's life. It's a richly complicated story, not easily reduced into one single plot or theme. Nevertheless, it can be useful to play with the idea of the story as having one plot, one theme, just to highlight the problem on which we are currently working.

As I got to know Karen better, I became more aware of the anger and resentment smoldering beneath the surface. At first she seemed sweet and yielding, but when one got to know her, the anger was barely contained, held in check just beneath the surface and always threatening to erupt. I began to become more aware of the equally poetic quality of colitis as a fire smoldering within. This metaphor aptly described the Karen I was getting to know.

These sorts of almost whimsical linkages are easy to dismiss, even mock, from the framework of conventional medicine, and yet they make a narrative sense. They fit within a novelistic sense of life. They make sense within a plot and a story even if we can't provide a physiological mechanism. However, I once gave my students in a class on multicultural healing a series of life stories of women who had cancer. The students were able to correctly identify those patients who had relapses with only the story to guide them. They didn't know how they made the correct classifications. It just felt "right." I'm not sure how we can make this more "scientific" except to show repeatedly that we do make accurate predictions, even if we don't know how.

That is perhaps the fundamental error of contemporary scientific culture, that we have lost our capacity to intuitively grasp a whole without knowing how we come to understand this. We do have enormous powers of reason that defy logical thought. Malcolm Gladwell made this obvious in his book *Blink,* as he told story after story of people who made incredibly complex judgments in the blink of an eye, using mental processes that they couldn't begin to grasp. Because we can't explain these gestalts in linear, rational logic, we dismiss them, yet Gladwell showed over and over how accurate and important they are.[21] I believe we have the same perceptive ability for life stories about illness.

To summarize Karen's plot: A woman moving through life who has come to settle for less than she wants, to feel ashamed of herself (her intellect, her naïveté), to be isolated and alone, and to smolder inside, to be angry and not express it directly, to let it emerge in more subtle, more passive ways, all the while feeling trapped in a situation she cannot escape. The metaphors for this included her image of herself on the bed in the fraternity room and vacationing at the beach with the family, but very alone. Karen agreed with my shorthand description: "settling for less, and sticking with it."

How do we "overthrow" this? How do we create a competing narrative, then allow the main character, Karen, to slide over into this different story? We take advantage of the "gaps," of the indeterminacies that allow other interpretations to be made. Remembering that we never unlearn stories, but that they slip into oblivion as we continually rehearse a new story, what new story should we rehearse? We need a story that transforms "not good enough" into "just fine." We need a story that promotes the direct expression of emotion and refuses to stay put in unworkable situations.

Stories are, of course, constructed by the people who are telling them. The next step, then, is to explore the characters that repeatedly turn up in Karen's stories.

Technique
•—•—•
IDENTIFY THE CHARACTERS
IN THE CLIENT'S LIFE STORIES

We need to identify the characters and the roles that repeatedly recur in the stories we are hearing. Given enough stories it's readily evident what roles recur. Here are some shorthand questions:

- Name some people in your life who have opposed or attempted to thwart your plans.
- Name some people in your life who have helped or supported you.
- Who do you imagine to be judging you or evaluating you in your life?
- Who are your favorite heroes and villains?
- If you were going on an adventure, who would you want as your trusty sidekick?

These questions aim to identify actual characters and their roles and ideal characters. The ideal characters begin to move us toward new stories that could be constructed. They give us some sense of who the person wants to be and who could oppose them to give them even more strength as a character through being a worthy opponent.

Karen named her husband and parents as people who opposed or thwarted her plans.

Karen surprisingly said that her colitis and her back pain were both her enemies and her supporters.

She imagined "Society" continually evaluating her and finding her wanting. When I asked who they were, she replied, "Everyone." I typically counter this type of overgeneralization logically by asking people to name everyone, which no one can do. This brought Karen's awareness to her having invented "Society" from a number of sources about good and bad, right and wrong, elite and nonelite, and so on. Her sources included the Methodist Church, Ann Landers, her parents, and more. Bringing people's awareness to the specific characters they imagine to be judging them can be liberating, for this audience almost always exists in their minds and not actively in the external world around them.

When asked about her hero, Karen named Annie Oakley, from the musical, *Annie Get Your Gun,* and from multiple movies. Annie didn't take any crap from any man. I mentioned to Karen how Annie Oakley reminded me of the statue of Molly Stark in Wilmington, Vermont. Molly was the wife of General Stark, credited with being the winning general at the Battle of Bennington, one of the turning points in the American Revolutionary War. In her statue she stands firmly with a baby in one arm and a rifle in the other. "That's my kind of girl," Karen said. Karen's favorite villain was Poison Ivy, from one of the Batman movies. "She's also my kind of girl—uppity, in control, takes charge, doesn't take shit."

Technique
•—•—•
CONTINUE TO DEVELOP THE NARRATIVE
Identifying high points, low points, and turning points in the life narrative advances the creation of a new story.

Karen identified the low point in her life. She said it was the vacation in Spain. She described her high point as graduating with her master's degree in physical therapy, which surprised me, since we hadn't gotten around to talking about her educational history. This detail lay buried until I asked specifically for something positive. Her turning point came when she went back to school to get her master's degree, even though her husband and all other family members strongly discouraged her doing so.

Now we had what we needed to begin playing with changing her story.

> ### Technique
> •—•—•
> #### BEGINNING TO BUILD A COUNTER-NARRATIVE
>
> We work to construct counter-narratives—stories that lead to the opposite conclusions from those that form the dominant plot. This is a time when we want to engage the client's imagination. We sometimes use guided imagery to assist in exploration, along with storytelling.

I sought counter-narratives that would strengthen Karen's sense of agency and capability, the sense she had when she succeeded at school. I gave a relaxation/induction in which I emphasized the idea that Karen was adequate. I talked about nature and its adequacy, about feeling secure within nature, and similar images. I asked her to imagine a new identity in which she was able to see herself as capable of refusing to shoulder other people's burdens and to express her anger directly and openly.

We also used role-play to practice expressing these traits to various family members. Just letting her husband be in charge hadn't improved the colitis. I wondered if taking charge and expressing her anger in an initially shocking and unsettling manner to others in her house would be associated with improvement. Could she change her identity narrative to "I'm a person who doesn't have to carry everyone else's burdens. I have a right to be treated equally and with respect and to have whatever feelings I have and to express them."

> ### Technique
> •—•—•
> #### CREATING A CHANGE STORY
>
> The next part of our work was to begin to create a story of change. To do this, we use a version of the Six Part Story, developed by Mooli Lahad.[22] To be asked to create a story can be intimidating. The six part story is a useful outline that includes the narrative markers

that are needed to create a story that outlines a journey from where the person is currently to where he or she wants to be.

In this exercise we imagine going on a journey from where we are (or our low point, sometimes) to where we wish to be (or to our high point).

- We need a hero (us, or a critter representing us).
- We need a place where the story starts.
- We need an obstacle, which can include a villain.
- We need resources or assets, which can include helpers, supporters, guardian angels, power animals, and so on.
- We need an attitude or mood for the hero (here we sometimes find it useful to wonder what the sound track might be like for a certain moment in the story, the color scheme, the lighting, the kinds of things in the scenario that add detail).
- We need a goal—what is the hero seeking? We can dress it up through exaggerating it to superhuman detail or keep things realistic. We can merge the client with the ideal hero to make a bigger-than-life protagonist.

I used the six-part story technique to encourage Karen to tell a story about how she got from the vacation in Spain to graduating from university with her master's degree. I encouraged her to embellish the story as much as possible.

Technique
•—•—•
HAVE PEOPLE TELL STORIES THREE WAYS

It's hard for us in this culture to sing our own praise song. So sometimes we use a process, asking our client first to tell a story about himself or herself in the first person, next, tell the same story in the third person, and then tell the same story, still in the third person, but transform everyone to animals.

Karen used puppets and told a story about a Raccoon, who was beaten down by the other animals in the forest. These other animals, especially the Bear, the Fox, and the Dragon, demanded that the Raccoon wait on them hand and paw, serving them tea at all times of day, bringing their food to them in their dens, sweeping the forest floor clean so that dirt never collected on their paws. The Raccoon obeyed them, but secretly longed to escape the forest and attend the university to become a scholar raccoon. She saved her pennies in secret, keeping them in a hollow area of an old oak tree. An Owl, who approved of higher education, helped guard them for her. When Raccoon had enough pennies, she approached Horse, which was quite scary for her, because horses are large and sometimes kick first before getting the whole story.

"Horse," said Raccoon. "I need help getting to the city. Would you take me?"

"Why in the world would you want to go to the city?" said Horse.

"I'm going to go to university and become a learned raccoon," she said.

"Does Owl approve?" asked Horse.

"Owl does," she said, "and she sent me to you."

"If Owl approves, I'll do it," said Horse. "Have Owl come around and talk to me, and you be here tomorrow morning at dawn, for I'm taking the master of the farm to the city and I'll go right past the university. You can ride on the back of the carriage." Raccoon excitedly went home to tell Owl, who visited Horse that very evening, and explained why this was important, all the while munching on barn mice.

Raccoon rode to the university on the back of the carriage and kept going every day despite the criticism of the other animals in the forest, who made fun of her and ridiculed her for being uppity and neglecting her duties and thinking she was better than anyone else. Raccoon persevered and, to the amazement of all the other animals, got her degree in the least possible time, making all A's. Raccoon felt so proud of herself.

Karen enjoyed telling this story, letting herself be represented by

Raccoon, and could allow herself to feel a pride in her accomplishments that she couldn't feel when she told the story with herself as the first person narrator.

Narrative approaches to healing are often playful. Brian Boyd writes that "The appeal of the cognitive play in art makes art as compulsive for us as play, enticing us to forgo mental rest for mental stimulation that helps us to learn and overlearn key cognitive skills, especially our capacity to produce and process information patterns. Art entices us to engage our attention and activate our minds in ways that we find most pleasing."[23]

This describes our attitude toward healing. We approach it with the sense that we are playing, that the work is fun, that we can enjoy ourselves as we are learning. During this play we learn and overlearn key cognitive skills that may have been underlearned and underused by people who are suffering. Through the play of narrative healing, we learn to recognize new patterns that we couldn't see before.

Over the course of sixteen weeks, Karen's back pain and colitis improved greatly. We continued to refine her life story to one that was progressively more satisfying. She formed stronger relationships with women friends to create a support network for resisting the criticism and humiliation she experienced from her husband and parents. Would she stay with her husband? That was yet to be determined, but what mattered was the dramatic improvement in her back pain and colitis. The conflict was exiting her body and entering into the social dimension where it belonged. Her body was no longer the battleground.

6

Creating New Stories, *Imagining* Transformation

If my mind can conceive it, and my heart can believe it—
then I can achieve it.

MUHAMMAD ALI, *THE SOUL OF A BUTTERFLY:*
REFLECTIONS ON LIFE'S JOURNEY

Imagination is not just an artifact. We have no faculties that are present in us merely for entertainment. All of our human abilities appear to be critical to survival, and it is reasonable to suppose that imagination, which gives us the ability to create new realities and experiment with what is, is a practical faculty designed to help us across that hurdle to human transformation, fear of change. In some senses our work is to learn how to engage our imaginations in the construction of a new reality.

Anthropologist and social neuroscientist Charles Whitehead, who researches consciousness in London, says, "We may be capable of 'purely' verbal thought and linear reasoning, but fantasies and dreams, the bulk of what buzzes around our minds each day and night, resemble embodied virtual reality experiences."[1]

Healing requires us to enter into that virtual reality and change it.

We do that through hypnosis, through guided imagery, through dialogue, through drama therapy, through ceremony and ritual, through whatever means are available to us.

How is this storied approach to understanding the past different from other psychologies? It eliminates a slew of unnecessary theories and concepts. It evens the playing ground. We don't so much need experts because we are all experts in story. We run stories all the time in our simulations of the world to help us decide how to behave and how to get our way. We don't need to construct "things" inside our minds to explain our behavior. We can do what people have been doing for thousands of years and look for the story that explains a person's beliefs and desires. This has been called folk psychology, for it is what all everyday folk do everywhere unless they have had psychological training and have learned to speak in code about "things" that can't be touched, seen, or heard, "things" like complexes, archetypes, ids, odds, and superegos. Stories suffice and stories are accessible to everyone. The stories that we are still living from our past are very much alive and being continually retold by us silently and to everyone around us. Find those stories, and what actually happened so long ago in the past ceases to matter. It's unimportant. Only the story as it is now being told and now being lived matters. It's quite a transition, from seeing ourselves as defective to seeing ourselves as living or enacting defective stories. It's so much easier to change the software than the hardware!

Here's a story about a person with chronic pain whose stories were outside of her awareness. She came to me for help with pain in the context of family doctor. I brought Barbara to the work with her so that both of us were working with her in the same session. Nancy had chronic sciatica and back pain. We used Cherokee bodywork (our form of osteopathic manipulation) on her upper back and sciatic area. When progress seems difficult in the ordinary world, we try to find an altered state of consciousness in which to work (using a variety of techniques). In Nancy's case we used guided imagery. We often do guided imagery in combination with movement or bodywork.

Technique
•—•—•
ACTIVATING THE PROBLEM STORY

We use guided imagery to aid the person's ability to relax and to set the stage for a dialogue with the sources of problematic stories.

I began by saying: "We're going to explore the world of the mind, which is a hard world to find, but one that everyone knows. We paradoxically go inward to get to this world, which is quite large, perhaps as large as the entire universe. I want to assure you that we are perfectly safe here. You can relax, and I will stay alert for you. I will be aware of our surroundings. You can take this time to explore your inner world.

"I've learned to start these processes for myself by directing my attention to my breathing and watching myself breathe. Whenever I do that, I realize that I am always breathing faster than I really need to be doing. I can always slow down my breathing just a bit. When that happens, my heart takes a cue and slows down, too. When my heart slows down, my blood pressure falls just a bit, and my nervous system goes off red alert.

"So I want to encourage you to simply watch yourself breathe, to relax a bit of the tension in your shoulders and jaw, to slow down. Perhaps you were rushing to get here, perhaps it's been a hectic day until now, and you've reached that place where you can really let go and slow down.

"Slowly a landscape will gradually form around you, and there will be a path and that path will lead to a place in which we can encounter some of the people from your past or even from the distant past who told you stories that you believed about the world. We're going to look for those people and those stories, to encounter those beings who have formed your life, who have provided you with the stories that tell you how to live and what to think. And then, when you're ready, you can speak freely to us about whatever comes into your mind."

The images that arose related to feeling inferior and saying yes to everyone. Suddenly, Nancy associated to being raped at age seven. She told the story. She was seven years old and playing happily with her friends on bicycles in the summer. A sixteen-year-old boy, whom she had known all of her life as the gardener's son, came by on his bike and invited her to come see something. She happily came along. He unzipped his jeans and showed her his penis. She had brothers and a father and had seen that before. What she hadn't seen was an erection, which he proceeded to have, to her surprise. He asked her to lie down and she did. He pulled off her panties and proceeded to put his penis into her vagina, which hurt very much. When he was finished, he threatened to beat her up if she ever told and promised to give her caramel ice cream next time he saw her at the ice cream shop. She agreed. He made her rearrange herself properly and rode off on his bicycle.

She stumbled, crying, back to her friends. They wanted to know what he had shown her, but she just cried and said she wanted to go home. At home, she just cried. Her vagina hurt. She tried to make it feel better, to no avail. Her irritated mother asked her why she was crying. She said, "I don't know." Her mother told her to stop crying if she didn't have a good reason.

Nancy was stuck. She had a good reason to cry and couldn't tell. She was trapped in a double bind. She wasn't allowed to feel what she felt unless she explained herself, and she couldn't explain herself under fear of reprisal. I believe these kinds of double binds make us sick or crazy.

Another plot was revealed—that Nancy couldn't refuse to do what others asked. She had grown up in a story that valued women for serving others, even at considerable personal cost. Some form of female martyrdom was valued and even celebrated by her family. A good woman sacrificed her own needs in the name of fulfilling the needs of others.

This is a common, dominant story of many societies. An Afghanistan veteran told me a story of having to watch helplessly when a woman of that society put her hand on the shoulder of her husband who was having a particularly angry argument with another man. She supposed the woman feared they would come to blows, and her husband would be the worse for it since the other man was larger and more muscular than her husband. Nevertheless, the two men united in beating the woman senseless. As she lay bleeding on the ground, they returned to their argument with each other. The veteran's story was about how deeply wounding it had been to watch this and to be under orders not to intervene on the woman's behalf.

Nancy grew up in a milder version of this kind of family and story about gender and gender relationships. Her plot line was "never say no; figure out how to give the person what they want." She couldn't say no and run from the sixteen-year-old (maybe she actually couldn't have anyway, for he might have run after her, but maybe her running and screaming would have scared him away), she couldn't say no to her mother and continue to cry, she couldn't say no to the order to be silent. She couldn't say no in any number of other situations in which she found herself over the years.

The "weight" she carried on her back increased and increased until I mused that she did everything with a sixty pound pack on her back full of all the unsaid "No's" and rocks dropped inside by the people she believed she had to please. I wondered if she might want to take off that pack.

All the while Barbara and I continued using somatic techniques to encourage muscle relaxation. We believe that combining physical therapies with imagery and talk makes for a synergistically powerful combination. Conventional practice often separates touch therapies from talk therapies, but our work emerges from Cherokee practice, which did not have the philosophy of mind and body as separate, distinct entities.

We believe mind exists in the quantum world in which everything is possible. Focusing our attention is equivalent to taking a measurement. When we focus we force mind into one state. When we go into a trancelike state, we move closer to the undifferentiated quantum world in which all possibilities exist at once. In the Lakota idea of the *nagi*, the swarm of every story that has shaped us, the stories and tellers are superimposed upon each other, all contained within each moment. When we relax our hold on how the world is "supposed to be," change is facilitated.

Nancy practiced stretching and shaking off her backpack. She imagined tossing the heavy rocks aside. I suggested she imagine her mother doing what she would have wanted her mother to do. She readily took to this suggestion and began to narrate a story in which her mother had comforted her for crying and held her, gently encouraging her to tell her about what had made her cry. She imagined slowly coming to believe that her mother could protect her from the sixteen-year-old and telling her mother what had happened. She imagined her family confronting his family and a reconciliation happening. Interestingly, she never imagined the boy's being arrested or put in jail. What mattered most to her in the imagery was that he should apologize, not that he be punished. She imagined his apologizing and his family making amends to her family.

This imagery coupled with the osteopathic work was accompanied by resolution of her back pain and sciatica. She said she felt amazingly better. We speculated that perhaps she could avoid chronic pain by refusing to accept more rocks in her backpack. She could keep other people and their problems off her back. This led her to tell us a story about someone who was currently "stabbing her in the back." She provided us with a rich collection of back pain metaphors. She began to brainstorm about how she could extricate herself from the business relationship she had with this woman. "I don't need to be involved in her organization," she said. "It's not serving my higher good, and it's really just a pain in my back (and behind). I really can just let her go."

Nancy did not need much more in the way of extrication of story; now she needed coaching to implement her new story—that she could say no and that she didn't have to do for everyone else. She could practice being unabashedly selfish. The ensuing work over time consisted of helping her to implement her newly modified identity story. Her back pain became an early warning signal that she was beginning to carry too many stones for too many other people. She learned to take stock of the imbalances in her social relationships whenever her back or her sciatica started to ache. When she made changes, the pain was relieved.

This approach can be much shorter and more cost effective than conventional medicine. If the pain goes away with interventions such as these, we don't need as many X-rays, CT scans, or MRIs. We didn't need a long course of physical therapy. We didn't need pain medications. Nancy's initial treatment took four hours. Her subsequent treatment averaged less than one hour per month for one year.

The political element in our work with many clients such as Nancy consists of the recognition of dominant cultural social stories that aren't aesthetic and don't work. Of course, the romance narratives appear to be aesthetic at first, for they make very entertaining movies and fairy tales, but further exploration of their actual effects when implemented reveal how ineffective they are. The martyr woman narrative is more under social criticism, but still exists insidiously and blatantly in areas of our culture. Feminism continues its ongoing critique of these stories. What matters is that we appreciate how often the dominant social system frames the behaviors and lives that are labeled psychopathological and even encourages them and profits from them.

DISCERNING TRAITS FROM STORIES

What a difficult transition we are trying to make! We are saying that people are fundamentally fine. Suffering arises from the stories that flow through people, that people faithfully reproduce, and that are enacted by people. People are not the cause of suffering. Stories are the cause of suffering. Change the story, and we change the suffering.

Discussing these character templates as stories we have embraced and are performing is so much less threatening than discussing our own foibles and probably more accurate, too. The reigning psychological theory assumes psychological traits and personality characteristics that are stable over time. If we are misbehaving or behaving in dysfunctional ways, it's because of our character flaws or personality difficulties or disorders. In this indigenous-derived narrative approach we are presenting, our difficulties arise from performing stories in situations in which those stories do not work or are not appropriate. Nothing is wrong with us.

We don't "have" personality in the sense of a thing that lives within us. In that same sense, we don't "have" psychological traits. We "have" stories that we are enacting in an embodied manner. We have characters or roles that we assume to match the situations in which we find ourselves. When our story brain and our error detector brain are off, we may enact roles that don't fit the situation. Then some might say we have personality disorders. The concept of personality sounds so difficult to change. The literature is full of articles about how hard it is to "treat" personality disorders. To say that someone has a character or a role that isn't quite matching the play in which he or she finds himself or herself is much less personally insulting. It's more playful and novel and therefore inviting of engagement and dialogue, which leads to change. We tell people that perhaps they have stories and characters that are less than adequate for the task at hand. Perhaps they need to learn new stories and find new characters. By focusing upon the characters in these stories as templates to guide our behavior, we can have sophisticated discussions without feeling threatened or attacked. We can examine the pros and cons of particular characters we may be performing without feeling inadequate or humiliated. We can have spirited conversations about what better characters or stories we might use without feeling personally criticized at all. Those stories can change, and when the stories change, our behavior and social interactions change. These changes lead to subsequent physiological changes.

Technique
•—•—•
EXTERNALIZING A ROLE

Allowing people to create distance between themselves and something that appears to them to be an innate trait allows them to have a sense that there is a natural dialogue to be had with this element and also that they have power in the situation—to speak, to ask for something different, to reject the influence of that character, should they be so inclined.

Melissa came to see Barbara for some therapy, as she said, "to get over my procrastination." She arrived nearly forty minutes late for her appointment and was ambivalent about being there. Intrigued by the row of puppets, small figurines, action figures, stuffed toys, and various other items, she asked about the kind of work we do. Barbara gave her some examples, and she decided she would like to try doing some of the "art stuff." They didn't have much time, so Barbara invited her to look at all the figures and see if any one of them "felt" like her procrastination.

"This won't work!" Melissa said.

"Well, we don't have to do this," Barbara replied.

"Well, I want to! But are you sure you're allowed to do this? Is this therapy? I mean, is that license real?"

Barbara reassured her. Alternating between being intrigued and proclaiming her certainty that it wouldn't work, Melissa finally selected a panda bear puppet. Offered choices, Melissa asked Barbara to wear the puppet for her. They began a conversation and to play. Melissa supplied some details of what she did when she procrastinated.

"I want you to go away!" Melissa told her Procrastination.

The Procrastination Panda snuggled closer and replied, "But I'm so nice and snuggly and comforting! I'm a great place to be! I'm soft and warm, and I don't make demands!"

"I know, but I really need you to let me go."

"Awww, but when I'm with you we get to hide in the corner and sleep and smoke weed all day! It's sure better than thinking about stressful life and dealing with a difficult mother."

"Well, I probably should cut back . . . Oh! This is too silly."

They wrapped up the session and spoke briefly about some other things that were bothering Melissa. Melissa said she didn't really know if she wanted therapy, and Barbara said that was fine, and she was welcome to just drop by. They then agreed to end the session. Barbara did not expect to see her back. A couple of weeks later, though, she got a phone message.

"It's me, Melissa! I still think that therapy is not for me, but I have to tell you, I can't get that Panda out of my mind. I keep thinking about the Panda, and, like, talking to him. I realized, if I am telling a stuffed Panda that I need him to leave me alone, I'm not in good shape. I got a job. I'm the night manager at Taco Bell." It doesn't often happen quite this way, but it was an example to us of how truly engaging and powerful it can be to negotiate in this way with our different selves.

HEALING AS THEATER

Once we identify our stories, we can begin to wonder if they work or not. If not, then why not and how would we improve them? Whitehead helps us again here. He wrote, "Thought is theatre . . . real, embodied theatre. . . . In imagination we rehearse and explore social scenarios and actor–audience interactions, and if we observe our own thoughts, we may note how often we are present in our minds, as performing actor and/or responding audience."[2] To do healing work requires a commitment to being theatrical, to performing with another, to engaging in an ongoing drama, thereby influencing it to change.

Here's an example of improving on a story that's not working well with the help of theater. Louise's migraines began in earnest after a car accident in 2001 in which her face was hit and her neck injured. Before then she had the occasional migraine, but nothing she couldn't manage. I wondered what had changed with the car accident. Her first association was to how helpless she felt. She had been a passenger in a taxicab. The entire event was over before she could register it as happening. That particularly terrified her.

> **Technique**
> •—•—•
> ## DETERMINE WHEN THE PROBLEM BEGAN AND
> ## WHAT HAPPENED AROUND THAT TIME
> We ask about important life events that occurred around the time a problem began. We think of a 20 percent time window so that if the problem began ten years ago, we would explore up to twelve years past. Of course, that's just a quick guideline.

I asked about the context of this life event. I learned that Louise was a middle child, always feeling like an extra in her family. She'd been married for thirty-two years and had two children. One had autism and gave her many reasons to have headaches in the metaphorical sense, compounded every time he was kicked out of school, not to mention his other tangles with authority. Beyond that her bosses at work gave her headaches.

We continued to explore the details of her life to extricate the stories that were involved. Louise revealed that the majority of her relatives had died. Other close connections had moved away. She felt she was doing her best to meet all her challenges head-on, but her migraines persisted anyway. The story she told herself was disbelief that migraines had become a problem. "This is crazy," she said. She said, "I'm not supposed to be like this."

Louise's story was that she was standing on shaky ground, floating around, not feeling particularly grounded. She had stopped moving. The pain could happen if she moved incorrectly. She was kicking herself because she didn't want to be stuck in her tracks. She said she'd been trying to find a new job since she had gotten her previous one more than sixteen years ago. She had done a lot of physical labor on her apartment to put in new floors and walls, but she felt that this work had exposed her to harmful toxins.

I asked if migraines were related to feeling alone in the world? She agreed that her greatest need was for a sense of connectedness. She thought about that and realized that her lack of family was both liberating and lonely. This surprised her. Logically, she felt like most of the time she had a good handle on everything but also that life was feeling overwhelming, just like her migraines did. She felt like she had a rope around her ankle.

"I was looking for an art studio space. I really want a workspace for my art. That's still at the top of my list. It's all about making art for me and preferably in relation to other people." She wondered if she could pull off even a part of these things, because she was sixty-one, but said that she had to try or die. I wondered how she might communicate her optimism to her migraines.

She remarked that she had become timid, like a little mouse, after the accident. She wouldn't speak out and tried to blend into the environment, but she didn't really have any other ideas about her migraines. When this happens guided imagery is often a useful next step.

Technique

•—•—•

EXTERNALIZATION OF A PROBLEM

If a client seems stuck, I find it particularly helpful to ask the problem itself to tell its story. I use guided imagery to help the client personify the problem and dialogue with it.

After a relaxation process/trance induction, I asked Louise if Migraine could speak directly to us. She assented and it did. Here is what Migraine said:

"After the accident I was in my heyday. After one to two years, it got harder to keep that going. She even took medicine to suppress me."

"How did you overcome that?" I asked.

"I redoubled my efforts to get her attention," said Migraine.

"What do you want to tell Louise?" I asked.

Migraine responded, "You're so busy. You never let me speak. You have a lot of pain, and you never let it out. All your physical symptoms are nothing. You have a big boulder of pain from lifetimes of everyone you have ever seen or met. You'd better let me speak, 'cause your head isn't big enough to hold all the boulders I make. The boulders are only getting bigger if you don't change. You're very timid. You need to be center stage more. You can't be as small as you'd like to be. How many years do you think you have left? Nobody's there for you the way you want them to be. You have to stand up for yourself."

I asked Migraine: "Would you be willing to relax or even leave if she really heard you and acknowledged you and made the changes in her life that you've recommended? You don't like the way she's being in the world, but what if she could change?"

"Then I might leave her alone," Migraine said. "I don't know if I'm willing to leave her, because I've been with her most of her life, but I would be willing to go back to the way I was before her accident."

"That would be a big improvement for her," I said.

"But first she's got to make those changes," replied Migraine.

"So let's summarize," I said. "She has to become more visible, she has to stand up for herself, she has to get that studio space that she's wanted forever, and she has to do her art. She has to slow down and take more time to breathe, create more space in her life and her head. A studio would do that, wouldn't it?"

"That would all work," Migraine responded. "I'd be willing to stand down if even a big part of that happened."

"Can you and she remain in discussions?" I asked. "If Louise were willing to change, could your ferocity be managed?"

"I'm ready to lighten up as soon as she shows she means it."

"Are you ready now?"

"I don't think so, because she seems to want me around. She hasn't made any changes yet. She's going to have to fly. She has to be willing to be the star of her own script. She'd have to put me in my place. She shrinks. She slips away. She'd have to get really big. She might get a guru complex."

"What else?"

"She has young, dark moods. Some were her mother's. She sat outside and cried. Her closets were full of dark moods. At age twenty-one, she learned to call it depression. Then she ran away from that. She did things to not feel that darkness. Her story is about fertile conditions."

We continued the dialogue until the behavioral steps were clear for what Louise needed to do to lessen her migraines. In my experience when people follow the advice they receive from their problem during guided imagery, they usually get good results. The problem, as with any behavioral activation, is for them to actually do these things. Action produces results. Procrastination does not. As Louise began to implement the instructions from Migraine, her headaches lessened. Further coaching was needed over time for her to make these behavioral changes in her life, and this is often one of my important functions—coaching, witnessing, reminding, praising, and cheering on the changes.

People need to hear their story told out loud. When we hear ourselves speak our story to an audience, we gain a new perspective on "how it sounds." I prefer to do this work in a group setting, because people can be moved more powerfully when the audience enlarges. However, this can also be effective in the individual setting.

Technique
•—•—•
ENGAGE GROUP WORK

We believe a healing group is a necessary accompaniment to any individual sessions people do with us, even though not everyone will come, because opportunities emerge in interaction with other people that are not possible alone. For example, we can enact the results of a guided imagery using other members of the group to play the various characters encountered. The change that can come from such an enactment can be inspiring.

In the context of a healing group, Louise constructed a short play about her migraines. The play included her older brother and her younger sister, both of whom had died. It included her husband and two children. The younger child was the one with autism who had given her many headaches over the years. She described a series of endless little plays in which she was timid and shy and finally could take no more and erupted, leaving people flabbergasted at her behavior. She wanted to change this pattern.

Technique

•—•—•

MOVE INTO PERFORMANCE

In scripting short plays (theater of the illness), we have to convince people to let go of the idea that they have to "do it right" and be exactly correct. What's fabulous about theater is that a short description suffices for people to play the characters in our lives. Consistent with theater and improvisation, when people relax and follow their impulse, the results are more perfect than if the play had been scripted. When we immerse ourselves in someone's story about his or her family or life, we understand it on a nonverbal, energetic level that we can rarely articulate, but can enact. As with any good clowning, we tell people, "always say yes." Whatever someone does in the play, add to it. That keeps the energy moving forward. At times we make masks for people to wear to play these characters, ranging from the simplest form of paper plates colored with crayons to plaster masks, elaborately decorated.

Louise cast the following characters:

Shy Sheila, played by a stuffed animal of the Church Mouse.
Big, visible Sheila, played by Coconut Bliss or Cocoa Bliss.
Migraine, played by Meryl Streep.
A character emerged to negotiate with Migraine, whom she called

Chai Lady. This character was subservient, a pretend yogi, anonymous, faceless, and served people to make them happy. "There's something exquisite about pouring a perfect cup of chai," Louise said.

The Dark Prince, a devilish youth, her younger son with autism.

Her mother, Queen of the Dark Woods, who was perpetually disapproving of her.

Her grandfather who died when she was ten years old.

Her sixth-grade teacher, who terrified her.

Members of the group volunteered to play each of these characters for Louise, who first explained what she knew or thought about them, and then, got to sit back and watch as the characters interacted. The play was an improvisational piece in which Big Sheila emerged as the powerful character to take on Migraine and change the usual plot that everyone expected. Big Sheila slowly turned into Big Louise; this meant emerging and becoming visible, as Migraine had instructed.

Louise was able to watch the person playing her character negotiate the minefield of old relationships and emerge victoriously strong and powerful. This was further inspiration for making the changes she needed to make in her life. In sixteen weeks Louise was able to reduce her migraines to virtually zero. During those sixteen weeks she came to a healing group and to an individual session once a week. This is within what is practical and doable in the general practice setting.

INTERCONNECTION OF PERSONAL, PROFESSIONAL, AND POLITICAL

What we do is determined in partnership with the client(s) with whom we work, so what emerges is different every time. Roberts discusses how practice is an emergent, self-organizing, relational activity, which is what makes a practice guideline manual so difficult to write.[3] We agree with him when he says that self, practice, and context are intertwined and that the traditional boundaries regarded as separating what is perceived as personal, professional, and political are challenged and discovered to be more permeable and interconnected.

In Lana's case the personal, professional, and political were clearly intertwined to begin with. She had grown up as the only daughter in a family of males, all of whom were or would become police officers. She, too, aspired to join the force and worked her way up to detective, senior grade, through a combination of skill and affirmative action policies for women. Her husband, however, lost his job and found a new job in another city, so she was forced to transfer departments if she wished to continue living with him on a daily basis and do police work.

Her new job was not as pleasing as her previous one had been. She viewed the chief of police as a bully and slowly discovered that he was also unethical—taking bribes on the side and losing evidence for a fee. The rank and file officers followed his example, making her feel disoriented, as if she were in a movie. Life is often stranger than fiction, she told herself.

Unfortunately for her attitudes toward women officers in her new department were equally dismal. Women "should be seen and not heard." She found herself bearing the brunt of sexist humor and practical jokes. Other officers felt free to keep money that had been seized, and some were selling confiscated drugs. Her sense of social justice and "right and wrong" was deeply affronted.

She resolved to bring up her concerns with the chief, but in a non-adversarial manner. She correctly realized that direct confrontation would be a career-ending move. As it was when she met with the chief, he insisted that the meeting be in his office, kept her waiting for an hour, arrived in full dress uniform with all of his medals, and sat behind his big, cluttered desk to address her from afar. He was not interested in her observations or concerns and made that clear. Everything was fine from his point of view.

This created a crisis for Lana. Within her story about correct behavior, she had to "blow the whistle" on her boss and her "corrupt colleagues." She had no choice less she be forced to revise her view of her own character. Paradoxically, she also fully understood that the repercussions for doing so would be severe. Police departments do not tolerate stool pigeons. She was going to be ostracized. As I listened to her description of this moment in her life, I thought of Jesus in the garden of Gethsemane. Her words pulled me back into that past moment in which she wrestled with her conceptions of right and wrong and decided to make the difficult choice. It was admirable and heroic.

We all prefer to think of ourselves as this moral. Having made this choice, she proceeded to collect evidence against her colleagues, and when she had enough, she presented it to the regional authorities. Indictments followed, but not before she was predictably crucified and put on administrative leave without pay. At that moment she both sued the force and hurt her back. Her lawsuit and her back smoldered along with the result of her experiencing progressively greater levels of pain. Through a series of draconian events that can only be recounted in horror movies, she descended into the Hades of investigations, counter-investigations, and scandals. Eventually an out arose for her—to take a disability retirement for her back pain and injuries. This was her choice—to cancel the lawsuit and take what disability would give her.

When I saw her, she was nursing her considerable wounds—to reputation, dignity, back, self-concept, and relationship. She and her husband were divorcing, which she believed to be the direct result of the stress of her pain and lawsuit. She felt like the world had fallen down around her in pieces. Our task was to rescue her sinking ship.

In developed countries the majority of people watch movies and some even read novels. We frequently imagine ourselves as characters in these movies and novels. There are a limited number of strategies and plots, and the characters we encounter in these movies and novels embody most of them. We can use these characters to shed light on our own strategies and plots.

> **Technique**
> •—•—•
> ## PUBLIC HEROES PUT TO WORK, PART I
> Elicit a public character (one that several of us could view and understand) that embodies the role that the client is performing in her life dramas in the present time. It could be a celebrity, a political figure, a character from a movie, play, novel, or short story, a cartoon, or a comic book.

I began by asking Lana what character she imagined herself to be in her interactions with the police department. Immediately she answered, "Mrs. Peel of the *Avengers*." In her interactions with her supervisors in the police department, she emulated Emma Peel.

That's important information. As desirable as Emma Peel was, she existed within an imaginary world of espionage and probably couldn't have survived without her trusty sidekick, Steed. Lana did not have a Steed character, and she didn't have the imaginary world of espionage and privilege accorded to Emma Peel. She felt perpetually disappointed in her interactions with the upper echelons, in part because of her feeling that Mrs. Peel would have done it better. She had unrealistic expectations of what was possible based upon her strategy for how to manage her situation. She hadn't consciously adapted an Emma Peel strategy, but, rather, her strategy most closely resembled what Emma Peel would have chosen. As romantic as this was, it wasn't working in her actual world. Emma Peel always escaped unscathed from her adventures. Lana did not.

Lana had failed to perform the "grace under pressure" strategy of Mrs. Peel, who was unfazed by crisis after crisis, managing to perpetually sport a glib, tongue-in-cheek reply. I brought her lack of a Steed character to her attention. She had expected herself to perform Mrs. Peel in a way that even Mrs. Peel had not done. She was by herself without someone to watch her back. No wonder she had performed less well than she had expected.

Lana's identification with Mrs. Peel touched me deeply. When I was younger, I eagerly anticipated every episode of the *Avengers*. Mrs. Peel and Steed were so cool in the way in which they managed every crisis, even life-threatening situations, with wit, high fashion, and aplomb. Looking backward I now realize how unrealistic their portrayal was. I doubt anyone could manage so many dire situations and remain unaffected. These characters were our collective social construction of how people should act under pressure (especially English people). They became templates into which we endeavored to insert ourselves. When we couldn't measure up, like Lana, we demeaned ourselves. We never stopped to consider that no one could meet these standards. In our cultural context, Emma Peel was larger than life, a symbol of cool, calm, and collected under stress, and one that no living being could actually emulate.

Lana's identification with Mrs. Peel immediately communicated to me a strong hypothesis for the nature of her "story-world" mismatch. Performing Mrs. Peel in any hierarchical employment situation simply wasn't possible and could only produce friction and probably worse. A new character template was needed.

Technique
•—•—•
PUBLIC HEROES PUT TO WORK, PART II
Look for some alternate public characters. Ask how they would play that same role/situation.

When I posed this question to Lana, she answered, "Ms. Frizzle of the Magic School Bus or Buddha." They represent two other, very different strategies for interacting in the plot. I wondered with her if perhaps we could consider how these other characters could manage her situation. Of course, when we look at these characters, we see that the alternatives do not involve the kind of conflict in which Lana had found herself. Neither Ms. Frizzle nor Buddha did direct conflict. They were not warriors in the way of Mrs. Peel. For both of these characters, the strategy involved escaping the conflict rather than engaging it.

When I brought this to Lana's awareness, she understood. She had already decided to leave law enforcement. She had decided to study massage therapy to become a healer. I posed the question to her to consider how Ms. Frizzle or Buddha would make that transition. Right away she had an answer. "Ms. Frizzle would just get into her bus and fly away," she said. Buddha would implacably shrug his shoulders and ignore the din of noise that was the upper echelons of the police. Both strategies involved exit from the field of conflict. I encouraged her to practice being Ms. Frizzle or Buddha and release Mrs. Peel.

Working in this way gives us access to a powerful shorthand. Jung might have called these characters archetypes. I resist that characterization, because archetypes sound too universal and terribly difficult to change. When we think about internal characters who come from stories we have heard, lived, or invented, we are less defensive, because the problem is not us as a core human being but a story we have absorbed, often unknowingly. We live in a culture in which stories abound. Durkheim wrote about collective representations. These are ideas created by all of us together and made real by our practice of these ideas. An example is money, which is really just paper, but we make it valuable by saying it is. Stories are the glue that keep cultures together and inform us about how to behave in our culture. Within these stories are roles and strategies, which synthesize many complex ideas. When we identify with one of these stories or roles, we grab hold of a meaning that is more than we can say in words. We connect to these characters in a way that transcends logic and rational discussion. We capture the many stories that surround these characters and define them. However, to say these characters are universal and unchanging diminishes the incredible creativity and complexity of cultures and individuals, limiting the amazing creativity and diversity of options and roles we find in the world's many stories.

When we imagine ourselves as one of these characters, we can do things and behave in ways that we might not be able to do otherwise. Amazingly, we are not often aware of whom we are emulating until someone asks us as I did Lana. We must also wonder about the extent to which our communities support us to live the characters. Without the permission of the community, we cannot change our character. Lana's supervisors were not about to permit her to change.

We humans easily become overcommitted to roles and strategies that don't work. Ori and Rom Brafman have written eloquently about this in the book *Sway*.[4] Apparently, it's hard for us to let go once we have invested considerable time and effort, even if everyone else can see that what we are attempting will never work. Lana had invested time and effort into becoming a certain kind of policewoman, which wasn't going to be possible where she found herself. The ethical standards she had set for herself were so far above the bar that her superiors were not going to let her get away with being that pure. They had invested in their pragmatic way of thinking for too long, so they were prepared to vigorously oppose her. Continuing to push against them could only increase her suffering and manifest in the symptoms she was experiencing. Her "self-world interface" was excessively frictional. Her only option was to exit.

I had another set of rich associations with Ms. Frizzle. I had spent hours with my children watching her Magic School Bus. Ms. Frizzle is the epitome of competence, magic, resourcefulness, and fun. She is an educator and a leader par excellence. She embodies a bit of the rebel because she makes secret (from the administration) trips with the children that are both exhilarating and educational. She has both science and magic on her side. Ms. Frizzle was a potentially better template because she was able to do what she wanted without anyone in administration being the wiser. I suppose the parents of the children who journeyed with her simply believed that their children had vivid imaginations, since her trips were too impossible for ordinary people to believe (voyages to the sun, to distant planets, to the insides of the body, to the insides of volcanoes, to under the sea!).

If Lana performed the Ms. Frizzle character in her work, she could slide under the radar and continue to be wonderful, awesome, and transformative, but in a way that no one in authority noticed. The danger in performing Ms. Frizzle is the reality that not everyone can escape detection as well as she and not everyone can practice the same level of magic. Shrinking a school bus or turning it into a space ship or an undersea submarine is a level of competence few possess. If one identifies with the Ms. Frizzle template too thoroughly, one is doomed to disappointment.

Buddha was her other option. Buddha is the ultimate peaceful character, unfazed by anything, anyone, or any conflict. As she performs Buddha, she can be less affected by the antics of her superiors. She can reduce the degree to which their machinations affect her. She can become both more permeable and more impenetrable. Emulating Buddha can always help us, but even that could take us too far. Buddha has become larger than life. I doubt that any living person today could perform Buddha in the way that Buddha is now presented to us. The actual, living Buddha may have been more human and less perfect, but his contemporary image allows for none of that. Lana could also become disappointed in herself for not being able to become sufficiently Buddha-like to completely let the slings and arrows of her trials at work pass through her or pass her by.

For the remainder of the session and the next, I practiced with Lana imagining herself in her situation and confronting her troubles as either Ms. Frizzle or the Buddha. Emma Peel needed to go. That character wasn't possible any longer without a higher price than Lana was willing to pay. I asked Lana to write some short vignettes about how Ms. Frizzle or Buddha would handle some of the situations she would encounter in the coming week, trying out Ms. Frizzle and Buddha as templates for managing the work situation.

The characters with whom we identify become all the more powerful when we imagine them as embodied. We visualize them moving. We see them in action. We imagine ourselves acting as they would. Abstract concepts are harder to imagine than beings moving about in the world, interacting in ways we can understand. It's easier to imagine changing our behavior when we see ourselves donning the characters as we would a suit of clothes or a dress and then performing their role as we would if we were the actor hired to play them. We can more easily pretend to be them than we can pretend to have an abstract quality. The more we imagine ourselves acting as they would, the more we move toward an altered state of consciousness, which facilitates change and transformation.

Excessive seriousness about our roles and characters prevents us from changing. We become too attached to one specific strategy. Using public characters from our culturally shared stories allows us to be more playful and less serious. Once we have some characters and stories, we can begin to transform them. We had reached the time to move toward guided imagery to allow ideas to emerge from Lana's inner world.*

> ### Technique
> •—•—•
> ### *ENHANCE IMAGINATION*
> ### *THROUGH GUIDED IMAGERY*
>
> Imagination alters our usual state of consciousness. Any shift in awareness from our usual, habitual state of being can facilitate change. As early as 1969, Charles Tart wrote that "an altered state of consciousness for a given individual is one in which he clearly feels a qualitative shift in his pattern of mental functioning, that is he feels not just a quantitative shift, but also that some quality or qualities of his mental processes are different."[5] This shift is what we seek for change and transformation.

We began with relaxation—breathing slowly and deeply, meditating on the rainbow. "Rainbows appear at the end of a storm," I said.

---

*I use this term loosely to refer to what I don't understand—that place within where images emerge. I don't know exactly where it is or how it works, so it's mysterious but effective.

"Remember summers when the thunderstorms descend upon hills, and after an intense downpour, the rainbow appears. It's a symbol of transcendence and transformation," I said. "Rainbows have all the colors of light, continuous, though we see them as discrete. We can feel happy or sad when we see them—happy about the changes they signal or sad about what has been washed away. Rainbows announce new beginnings. The world has been cleansed and we are ready to start anew. Just like we are going to do now."

I continued with this theme of suggesting that the hard work was over. The storm was done. Now we could awaken to a brand new day in which the world was fresh and new. She was ready to end her conflict with the police department and with her husband and move on.

I invited Lana to allow a new story to emerge, a new way for her to approach the world. She could cross over the rainbow and emerge brand new. She could emerge as another character, as an animal, or as a new version of herself. Whatever was best for her would happen. She connected with a part of her who was an eagle and who could fly solo and majestically soar above the daily hassles of life. This eagle came to guide her into her new life. Eagles can fly alone as she was preparing to do. They can stay above the petty hassles of the Earth's surface. They can maintain their majesty above all else. Lana practiced seeing herself in this way.

Technique
•—•—•
ENHANCE IMAGINATION BY TELLING STORIES

A good story can come from anywhere, in any form. Traditional stories of all cultures offer enduring templates for life strategies, which is no wonder, since they have been tested, sometimes for centuries. The values communicated in traditional stories often place the community above the individual, emphasize cooperation over individual achievement, give elders and animals their due respect, and inculcate compassion and forgiveness. We often point to the Lakota virtues as an example of this—courage, strength, endurance, vision, compassion, forgiveness, kindness, love, protection, nurturing, and cooperation (paraphrased from multiple original sources). One can readily find a story to support these virtues. In this world of media storytelling, there is an abundance of stories being created that inspire transformation. It is a very good idea to know a few good stories so well that you can begin telling them at a moment's notice.

We allow ourselves liberty in the details of the story, as long as the energetic structure remains consistent with the point we are trying to make. Sometimes the right move is to tell the story as true to the way we learned it as possible. Sometimes, though, we insert elements of a person's life into the story and sometimes we spontaneously invent stories. In general, we look to tell a person a heroic story.

Over the coming weeks, I told Lana a variety of Eagle stories to reinforce her transformation. She was progressively relaxing and releasing her losing battle with the police force to move toward peacefulness and fulfillment in her life. One memorable story that I told her was that of Spotted Eagle and Black Crow. I have heard this story in many ways and versions. There is an Internet version that is reported to have been told by Makpiya Luta (Red Cloud), an Oglala Lakota.[6] In this story I liberally changed the details to appeal more to Lana and to facilitate her making the story her own.

A very long time ago before people had come on the Earth, there was Wanbli Gleska (Spotted Eagle) and Kangi Sapa (Black Crow). They were friends but, as it happened, were both in love with Zintkala Luta Win (Red Bird). Unfortunately for Black Crow, Red Bird liked Spotted Eagle best, which made Black Crow unhappy and jealous.

Black Crow proposed that they resolve this dilemma by staging a raid upon their nearby enemies. Whoever performed in the most honorable way and brought home the most trophies might impress Red Bird and win the rivalry.

"*Good idea,*" *said Spotted Eagle, and the two purified themselves in an* inipi *lodge. They got out their war medicine and their shields, painted their faces, and did all that warriors should do before a raid. Then they rode out against the enemy.*

The raid did not go well. The enemy was watchful, and the young warriors could not get near the herd. Not only did they fail to capture any trophies, they even lost their own weapons while trying to creep up on the enemy. Spotted Eagle and Black Crow had a hard time escaping because the enemy was searching for them everywhere. Spotted Eagle's wing was broken, perhaps even shattered. Flight was impossible. The two had to hide underwater in a lake and breathe through long, hollow reeds, which were sticking up above the surface. At least they were clever at hiding, and the enemy finally gave up the hunt.

Traveling on foot made the trip home a long one. Their moccasins were tattered, their feet bleeding. At last they came to a high cliff. "Let's go up there," said Black Crow, "and find out whether the enemy is following us." Clambering up, they looked over the countryside and saw that no one was on their trail. But on the ledge above them they spied an eagle's nest. Spotted Eagle greeted those eagles. While Spotted Eagle explained how they came to be there, Black Crow stealthily flew away leaving Spotted Eagle alone. Spotted Eagle was taken captive, which Black Crow thought the best. If Spotted Eagle had been lost, Red Bird and Black Crow could marry.

Spotted Eagle was left to confront the entire Eagle village and to explain why he and Black Crow were there. Black Crow returned to the village and announced that "Spotted Eagle had died a warrior's death." There was loud wailing throughout the village, because everybody had liked Spotted Eagle. Red Bird wailed the loudest of all, but in the end, because life must go on, her marriage to Black Crow took place.

Spotted Eagle, however, was not dead. The eagles got used to him, and the old eagles brought him food—rabbits, prairie dogs, and sage hens—which he shared with other eagles. Over time, the eagles came to trust Spotted Eagle and to welcome Spotted Eagle into their camp.

Spotted Eagle wondered if he would ever fly again. The wing had healed but had not been tested in flight. Instead of flying Spotted Eagle could find himself shattered on the ground. Spotted Eagle jumped from the nest. With a mighty flapping of wings, the wings finally broke his fall and Spotted Eagle landed safely, saying a prayer of thanks and promising a giveaway at the earliest possible moment.

Spotted Eagle returned to the village. The excitement was great, for the dead had come back to life. Spotted Eagle wouldn't tell anyone what had happened. "I escaped; that's all." Spotted Eagle bore the pain of Black Crow and Red Bird being married in silence. What had happened could not be changed. Strife and enmity would only weaken the people.

A year or so later, the enemy attacked the village, outnumbering our heroes tenfold. Spotted Eagle's band had no chance for victory. All they could do was fight a slow rear-guard action to give the aged, the women, and children time to escape across the river. Guarding their people this way, the handful of warriors fought bravely, charging the enemy again and again, forcing them to halt and regroup. Each time, they retreated a little, taking up a new position on a hill or across a gully. In this way they could save their families.

Showing the greatest courage, exposing their bodies freely, were Spotted Eagle and Black Crow. In the end they alone faced the enemy. Only one could escape. "Save yourself," Black Crow said. "I betrayed you. Now I will make recompense." Black Crow fought bravely while Spotted Eagle retreated across the river. Spotted Eagle was the only one to watch Black Crow's last fight. When Spotted Eagle joined the people across the river, the enemy did not follow them. "Your spouse died well," Spotted Eagle told Red Bird.

After some time had passed, Spotted Eagle married Red Bird. They lived happily ever after, and Spotted Eagle completed the giveaway to the Eagles. Spotted Eagle thanked them for surviving even as Black Crow had ultimately died.

I explained the point of my story to Lana. "You are like Spotted Eagle," I said. "You are at that point in your life in which the enemy is closing in and it feels like all is lost. Your wing is broken and you can't fly away. Yet you will find a new strategy and will prevail. You will make your way back into your world just as Spotted Eagle did and all will be well. This and other Eagle stories inspired Lana to complete her transformation of herself into someone who was a healer, who forgave others, who completed a massage therapy course and found herself in an entirely new profession with an entirely new community, feeling happy for perhaps the first time.

INSIGHTS FROM HOLLYWOOD

Mookie had taken his nickname from Spike Lee's movie, *Do the Right Thing*. The Mookie character in the movie delivered pizza in the 'hood. My Mookie lived a life of uncertain meaning in Vermont. He had grown up in New York City, but was a self-described "house negro." He said he ran with the "field negroes," but at his parents' displeasure. His mother was a social worker and his father an executive for a Manhattan bank. They spent summers on Cape Cod.

Technique

•—•—•

EXPLORING MOVIES AS CLUES

Asking the client which movies (or books, plays, stories, poems, etc.) will help me best understand him or her provides an amazing short-cut to enter the world of the client's stories, to understand the roles he or she is playing. Watching those movies and then asking about them demonstrates a genuine interest to the client.

I asked Mookie what two other movies would help me to under-stand him. He replied, *Friday* and *Boyz in the Hood*. I asked him what was special to him about these movies. He described the conflict between coming from money and being "of the hood." He described how most of his childhood friends were now dead or in prison. While he identified with the guys of the streets, he also expected his parents to take care of him, even though he was turning forty years old. He was bitter that they had not bankrolled a business for him, because they could afford to do so. He had developed an expertise in sound and video and wanted to open a store, but he had no way to develop it.

As I had not seen any of these movies, I promptly ordered them on Netflix and watched them. The theme seemed to be black men doing little in poor neighborhoods. I thought this was ironic given Mookie's wealthy origins. He seemed to have romanticized his image of "the ghetto black man" and aspired to be one, while at the same time resenting his parents for not helping him start a business. I thought probably he needed a new story. This was delicate ground, however, for he could interpret my questioning his story as evidence of racism.

At our next meeting, I told Mookie that I had watched the movies and had some questions for him. I observed that all the characters in the movies had little money, but he had grown up with parents who had more money. How had that worked? We talked about how hard Mookie had worked to be cool, including providing money for his friends from time to time. Yet, he felt he had never really succeeded. He was always marked by his status as a "house negro" among the "field negroes."

I asked Mookie what success would resemble. He described the high-end audio/video store he would own and manage, the custom systems he would install for the wealthy people of southern Vermont.

"How will you meet them?" I asked.

"I don't know," he replied. "They'll just come into my store because it's the best."

"How will you start your store?" I asked.

"I don't know," he said. "My fucking parents should have given me the money long ago."

"Why don't they?" I asked. I was thinking about Ice Cube's character in *Friday* whose parents wouldn't give him money either. Nor would Sal in *Do the Right Thing* give Mookie money before closing. Even the stories he admired involved parents and bosses not giving children money unless they earned it.

Over time we used these movies to explore the contradictions in Mookie's identity narrative. The characters he admired didn't accomplish much in these movies. I could imagine that his parents were bothered by his attraction to these ghetto black stories, when they probably saw themselves as having worked hard to provide a different experience for him, some of which he acknowledged and some of which he didn't. In the end of *Do the Right Thing,* Mookie loses his job when an angry mob of people destroys the pizza place where he worked. My Mookie hadn't developed the skills to interact with people who could potentially be his financial partners for a high-end audio/video store.

At the end of *Do the Right Thing,* Mookie's girlfriend screams at him, "get yourself a fucking life, because the one you've got isn't working." I remarked upon how this Mookie's girlfriend was saying the same thing to him. Despite his ambitions Mookie was working as a cook at the local Wendy's—not quite the situation to which he aspired, but similar to his hero characters, who either delivered pizza or were unemployed—which also happened to him frequently. My Mookie's girlfriend was frustrated by his high ambitions and his lowly income. She wanted to see more cash coming across the threshold every two weeks. This was a perpetual source of conflict between them.

Technique
• — • — •
REFLECT THE CLIENTS' STORIES BACK TO THEM

Use the clients' own stories (the stories they use to explain their identity to me) to show them how these stories aren't working. Offer them opportunities to craft a story that could work better. Humor always makes the job go better.

Immediately I began thinking of movies with characters that could offset Mookie's heroes. I was drawn to some of Eddie Murphy's characters, particular Beverly Hills Cop, in which he is so smooth that he could attract money to start a business. Of course in that movie, Eddie Murphy's character doesn't want money to start a business; he just wants to be a successful cop, but the imagery works. He has the people skills so that he could attract capital if he wanted. I shared that with Mookie.

My Mookie didn't like Eddie Murphy for exactly the reasons I proposed him. "What's wrong with his character?" I said.

"He's too smooth. He's not raw enough. He could have never come from the 'hood."

"Could you have come from the 'hood?" I asked.

Mookie was hesitant. "Maybe," he finally ventured.

"So you're not really sure?" I asked.

"No, I'm not," he said. "I think the boys just tolerated me because I supplied them with money for cigarettes and booze."

"So you feel inadequate at 'hoodiness?" I asked.

"Yes," he sighed. "I was never really part of the crew."

"That was kind of your dream," I said.

"It was," he admitted. "And yet, I didn't want to get killed or go to prison, so I really wasn't a good candidate for what I was trying to achieve."

"So how is this working for you now?" I asked. "Is being a boy from the 'hood getting you where you want to go?"

"Not really," he said.

"I'm guessing your parents don't really trust doing business with a boy from the 'hood. They want someone a little smoother, a little more reassuring about taking care of money, a little less edgy."

"Maybe," he admitted.

"So maybe it's time for a new movie," I said. "You don't really like Eddie Murphy, so there must be some other character in whom your parents would want to invest. How about Sidney Poitier?"

"No way," he said.

"Martin Luther King?"

"Maybe him."

"Tough job to fill," I added, "and maybe a little dangerous."

Over the course of a few weeks and some joint sessions with his girlfriend, Mookie and I were able to find a movie character who could be a template for his new strategy for dealing with the world. We came up with the black rugby player from *Invictus,* the Clint Eastwood movie about the 1995 South African rugby team who galvanized national unity by winning the World Cup. Mookie could identify with that team's black player. He could begin to imagine himself as a success differently from his previous roles/strategies. Over time we rehearsed his performance of that role.

Part of his study for his character was to go to Chamber of Commerce meetings and to meet the wealthier people of his town who might come to his imagined store (or invest in it). He patterned himself after his character, who traveled into white neighborhoods and taught young people how to play rugby. Through this process he radically changed into a man who inspired confidence and trust. He seemed solid in a way that he never had. Over time, Mookie was able to revise his story and actually gain his parents' trust and confidence to such an extent that they invested in his store. Mookie was not that different on the inside, but his outside demeanor had radically shifted. People saw him extremely differently because he presented himself like a successful professional rugby champion from South Africa and not a down and out black man from the 'hood. The change was remarkable and made all the difference.

7
Magical Potions, Alchemical Solutions

The true alchemists do not change lead into gold; they change the world into words.

WILLIAM H. GASS, *A TEMPLE OF TEXTS*

Efforts to facilitate healing are dominated by our contemporary culture's magic potion story: that the right external substance can solve our problems quickly and effortlessly. Stories of magic potions range from tales of a plant growing in the high mountains of Tibet, which will cure an otherwise incurable illness, to our search for the psychedelic that will make us enlightened (the current most popular candidate is ayahuasca from the Peruvian Amazon), to essiac tea to cure cancer, to narcotics for pain relief, and on. The power of substance, though, can never be separated from the beliefs and expectations of the people who take the substances and from the relationships they have with the people who give them the substances. The power of substance comes in part from the stories that surround the substance and the contexts in which those stories are told. We propose that this is equally true for biologically active substances as for inert ones (placebos).

Human beings have been seeking magic elixirs for as long as

recorded history exists. The Spaniard Ponce de Leon tramped around Florida seeking the "fountain of youth," the potion that would make him eternally young. Today's television infomercials equally promise to quickly remove our woes with whatever product is being showcased.

Of course, substances can be powerful, but the power of a substance also derives in part from being embedded in the story we tell ourselves about its power. We are well aware of the powerful substances that can immediately alter our physiology (cocaine, heroin, alcohol, etc.). However, the quest for the external substance that can make us well is another very ancient story. The placebo effect, the nocebo effect, and the art of stimulating self-healing all reside in this complex arena that surrounds the giving of a medicine. The term *placebo* describes simulated medical treatments, that is, interventions that lack pharmacological or physiological properties that lead to specific efficacy in treating a specific patient's condition. The term *placebo effect* focuses on the various measurable phenomena that result from the expectation that a treatment will be effective.[1] Contemporary research is focusing upon how patient expectations (beliefs, or the stories that we have about treatments, treatment environments, and our illness) and the quality of healer-patient communication can influence the efficacy of any intervention—something that can become much more obvious with an inert intervention.[2]

Luckily, neuroscience is bringing the placebo effect to a new level of respectability, by showing that placebo response is associated with brain changes. Pain researchers are particularly intrigued with placebo. Our relationship to pain is complicated. Studies have shown that the amount of pain we perceive subjectively is related to the amount of pain we expect to have.[3] Pain can seem to travel through our bodies and disappear and reappear mysteriously. X-rays and MRIs don't necessarily reflect our experience. Analgesia, when the body does not feel pain, can occur in puzzling circumstances. There is much that is mysterious about pain.

Dr. Lauren Atlas from the National Center for Complementary

Medicine and Dr. Tor Wager from the University of Colorado's Center for Neuroscience conducted formal meta-analyses of twenty-five neuroimaging studies of "placebo analgesia" (when the body does not feel pain as the result of placebo) and expectancy-based pain modulation (when perceived pain changes based on our expectation). They found that placebo effects and expectations for reduced pain both elicited reliable reductions in brain activity associated with pain processing, even during painful stimulation in those brain areas (including the dorsal anterior cingulate cortex, the thalamus, and the insula). They also observed consistent reductions of brain activity during painful stimulation in the amygdalae and striatum, regions involved in studies of emotion and valuation of experience.

What this means is that the placebo response has the strongest effects on brain regions commonly associated with pain but also on those regions associated with emotion and with assigning a value to an experience. They also found brain regions that showed reliable increases in activation when people expected reduced pain. These regions included the prefrontal cortex (including dorsolateral, ventromedial, and orbitofrontal cortices), the midbrain surrounding the periaqueductal gray, and the rostral anterior cingulate. These are areas that have figured significantly in the preceding pages because they are intimately involved in the story-producing brain.

RECLAIMING SELF-HEALING

How do we maximize healing within a world of magic potion stories? Can we reclaim and capitalize upon the placebo effect, which Herbert Benson called the self-healing response? Could it still work if we recognized that it was our mind and our relationships and the context of the healing environment that was working and not the substance? Do we need to rely upon a substance to mobilize our beliefs?

Here is a small part of an allegory from the *British Medical Journal* that highlights our critique of the magic potions story:

Once upon a time in a green and pleasant land there lived a Gatekeeper and a Wizard. The Wizard lived in a great white castle above a town. In this castle he had a marvelous crystal ball that could tell him why people were poorly. He would then use one of his powerful magic potions to make them better again. The Wizard was a very clever man. The Gatekeeper lived in a big house next to the entrance of the castle. His job was to decide who was poorly enough to need to see the Wizard and open the gate into the castle for them. The Gatekeeper was also very clever, and he too had magic potions to make poorly people better. After all, the Wizard and the Gatekeeper had both gone to the same school for wizards, although they had learnt different sorts of magical powers after leaving it.[4]

Though this allegory was meant to speak to the relationship between the general practitioner and the specialist, it implicitly reveals our devotion to magic potions and the wizards who provide them, and our expectations that these are what cure us. The story diminishes the idea that we heal each other. It also presents the opposite idea from what we are proposing—transforming the metaphor of wizards with magical powers and potions to the idea that we work together collaboratively in nonhierarchical ways to create healing without privileged experts who have great powers or know all.

These are our collective fantasies—the magic potion or amulet or object (the Holy Grail, the ring in *Lord of the Rings*) that changes everything without our having to change ourselves or our stories. When science replaced religion as the state sanctioned belief system, then science held the key to the magic of transformation.

SEARCHING FOR THE MAGIC PILL

The story of one family's search for the magic pill can inform us. I met Charles, the sixteen-year-old son of Karen, in Augusta, Maine. Charles was part Penobscot, French Canadian, and Scottish (on his father's side). Charles and his mother believed that his problems began when his father committed suicide while Charles was in kindergarten. Since then his teachers and his mother described his becoming increasingly oppositional. When he set fire to his classroom, he was admitted to the psychiatric hospital, beginning a years' long search for the correct diagnosis and medication.

We can wonder how the symptoms make sense within the overall collection of stories in which Charles was embedded. We don't assume that one story can explain it all—meaning the biomedical narrative, which said that Charles was misbehaving because of a brain disorder, which could be diagnosed and treated with medication. Though Karen knew that the onset of Charles' problems occurred after his dad's suicide, she could take that line of thought no further. She just wanted to know what was wrong with Charles' brain, and she wanted a medicine to fix it. She wished someone had given Charles' father the proper diagnosis and medication. If they had, she said, he would be here today helping her take care of Charles. I told her that I was certain we could accomplish something as we worked together.

Technique
•—•—•
CREATING POSITIVE EXPECTATIONS

We take great care to create a landscape of positive expectations. Something will work because of something we try. We always work to open up the imagination to possible positive futures.

Charles was the younger of two children of Karen and Charles, Sr. The pregnancy was unexpected and Karen was sick throughout. She smoked cigarettes and was anemic. Charles had gastroesophageal reflux disease during his first year of life. He had frequent ear infections and drainage tubes were placed into his eardrums (tympanoplasty). He was born with a "tied tongue," which was eventually clipped, but led to difficulties in his talking clearly as a young child. His tonsils and adenoids were removed before he was eighteen months old. His undeveloped right orbital sinus led to a surgical reconstruction. He received all A's in kindergarten through the end of second grade. His school performance declined in third grade after the suicide to mostly C's and D's.

From third grade to tenth grade, Charles experienced a litany of hospitalizations and medication switches. He got progressively worse despite all treatment. He carried an impressive array of diagnoses, including attention deficit-hyperactivity disorder, bipolar disorder, types I and II, and "Not Otherwise Specified," bipolar spectrum disorder, oppositional-defiant disorder, conduct disorder, schizo-affective disorder; borderline personality disorder; childhood schizophrenia; depression, anxiety disorder, and more. Each hospitalization resulted in a new diagnosis. He had been tried on multiple drugs within every medication class, with limited results and the inevitable side effects. His prescriptions ranged from antidepressants (bupropion, SSRIs, SNRIs, tricyclics, and even monoamine oxidase inhibitors) to antipsychotics (haloperidol, olanzapine, aripiprazole, risperidone, quetiapine, clozapine, and ziprasidone). He had been tried on a variety of anticonvulsant drugs (valproic acid, lamotrigine, topiramate, carbamazepine, and oxycarbazepine). He had been tried on benzodiazepines, buspirone, gabapentin, pregabalin, and more. His low frustration tolerance got lower. His anger came more easily and frequently. He broke things and made holes in the walls of his room. He gave away toys to his friends. He broke windows. He bit himself in front of his mother to irritate her. Once he tried to put his head through a wall. He climbed down out of his window and ran away. He stole cigarettes and money from his mother. He had friends at his house continually. By age twelve he had taken control of the house, keeping company with seventeen- and eighteen-year-old boys. By age thirteen he was sexually active. He was put on probation for hitting a peer in the eye. Karen said she gave in to all of his demands because of his pain over his father's death.

When Karen found a boyfriend, Charles fought with him. This led to his driving away in the boyfriend's car, getting charged with grand theft auto, and being convicted of driving without a license, driving under the influence, and possession of marijuana. Charles was placed on probation. At that time he justified all his behaviors. He said he enjoyed being aggressive and hurting people. He perceived himself as good sometimes and evil at other times. At the anniversary of his father's suicide, Charles gave himself cigarette burns. He couldn't explain why. At that time he was placed in juvenile detention, and the psychiatrist described him as hypomanic with irritability, fighting, emotional lability, attention difficulties, and easy distractibility.

Life changed Charles. At age fifteen Charles both fell in love and found a mentor whom he could respect in his probation officer. Charles's PO was tough. He had played professional football for two seasons before his knee was shattered beyond repair. He had run with gangs as a youth. He still had gang tattoos. His biceps were massive. For seemingly inexplicable reasons, the PO took an interest in Charles, who appreciated and responded to that interest. At the same time, Charles met a sixteen-year-old girl who stayed with him virtually every minute.

They were an unlikely couple. She was quiet and retiring. Though she dressed "emo," she was an A student, clearly bored with school and her life. Charles was possibly her excitement, but she was Christian and objected to anything resembling criminal behavior. For equally inscrutable (to me) reasons, Charles obeyed her when she told him what to do. She was able to soothe him. They began going everywhere together. Charles visibly relaxed. A level of tension disappeared. Though I worried what would happen if they broke up, they didn't. Nor did his new PO abandon him, even when he came off probation. His whole demeanor shifted.

Suddenly a combination of medications was declared as "working." Charles had been on all these same medications before, and they had not worked then. The combination of bupropion, lamotrigine, and aripiprazole was declared effective even in relatively small doses. Charles's mother praised me, since I was the one managing his medications. All I had done was to reduce doses of medications he was already taking. Charles's mother, however, was convinced that I had brilliantly found the right combination of each dose relative to the other. I was glad the medication had "worked," but I knew it wasn't me. I was more appreciative of the PO and the girlfriend. However, I didn't query his mother's understanding.

Did the medication combination help? Possibly. Had it been tried before without effect? Definitely. Was the change in life situation what really mattered, or was it the combination of change of life situation and medication? We can't ever know because we can't separate the belief in the medication from the medication. But that set up a dilemma. If we reduced the medication when everyone believed Charles's change happened because of the medication, perhaps Charles would deteriorate. My strategy, nevertheless, was to slowly reduce the medication, using a rationale that everyone accepted, that over time, Charles' own body would learn to do for itself what the medication was doing.

I don't know if this is so. I do know that the body can learn to duplicate the effects of a medication after having only received one dose when a placebo is subsequently given. So, in the sense that the body can learn to duplicate the physiological effects of a medication when the person thinks he or she is receiving that medication (but isn't), I am correct that the body can learn to do for itself what the medication is doing.

Over two years Charles and his girlfriend stayed together, and he began a process of rapprochement with his mother. He remained connected with his former PO. Two years later he was off all medication and doing well. My story about Charles's body figuring out how to produce the chemicals that the medication provided was accepted. We had a graduation ceremony for Charles's body when the last of his medications was eliminated. I still receive communications from Charles from time to time, and he continues to do well. He and everyone else in his life still believe his transformation was the direct result of my psychiatric genius, though I know it was not!

Technique

• — • — •

WORKING WITHIN THE TREATMENT NARRATIVE:
"YES AND . . ."

Because the family narrative was medication based, we worked within their treatment narrative. The other interventions occurred on the side and through fortunate life circumstances. We don't argue; we say "yes, and," as we look for ways to enhance the existing narrative.

This case also exemplifies the beauty of the universe to provide! Without his girlfriend and enlightened PO, Charles would not have had such a good outcome.

Enter Sleeping Beauty: Biting into a poisonous apple puts her to sleep, the spell having been weakened from lethal to soporific through spiritual intervention, until her own true love kisses her. What is rarely noticed is how rural her situation was and how rare visitors were. The kiss, in this case, becomes another type of magic, a step forward, since it requires interpersonal contact, though minimal, since Sleeping Beauty does not even know the person who kisses her. Nevertheless, at least the Sleeping Beauty story brings into the equation a reliance on relationship (the kiss of the beloved) to effect the change.

QUEST FOR THE HOLY GRAIL

The Story of the Grail, by Chrétien de Troyes, is a potential metaphor for the quest for the externally powerful object, though hidden within the story is how the quest (perhaps for anything) carries the potential for transformation. Written in the second half of the twelfth century, this poem tells the story of Perceval, a teenager raised in the forests of Wales by his mother. By chance he stumbles upon the Holy Grail in a castle that disappears around him. Despite his mother's objections, he is inspired to head to King Arthur's court, where a young girl predicts greatness for him. Perceval's father had died, which limited his being able to become a knight. Nevertheless, that was what he wanted. He was taunted by Sir Kay, but amazed everyone by killing a knight who had been troubling King Arthur and taking his vermilion armor.

Perceval finds the Grail, but doesn't realize its significance. He awakens in an empty field, the Grail Castle having disappeared around him. Realizing his error he wanders the countryside in hope of finding it again. In this process he rescues and falls in love with the young princess Blanchefleur and trains under the experienced Gournemant. After being raised in a forest by his mother, he now discovers the ways of the world—knights, kings, the pleasures of love, and the pain of combat. Naive at first, he slowly adapts to this world, yet never really fits. He continues his search and eventually finds the Fisher King, who invites him to stay at his castle. While there he witnesses young men and women carrying magnificent objects from one chamber to another, passing before him at each course of the meal. First comes a young man carrying a bleeding lance, then two boys carrying candelabras. Finally, a beautiful young girl emerges bearing an elaborately decorated *graal,* or "grail," which contains a single Mass wafer, which miraculously sustains the Fisher King despite his wounds.

The Grail story is the story of sacred objects, those items through which we contact or communicate with the supernatural realm; it also brings to attention a dialectic about the degree to which we give power to objects (and potions!) or give power to ourselves and our intentions. The grail in *Perceval* has the power to heal, so it may be seen as a mystical or holy object.

Eventually Perceval meets a hermit, his uncle, who instructs him in the ways of the spirit and teaches him about the Grail. The Fisher King dies, and Perceval ascends to his throne. After seven peaceful years, Perceval goes to live as a hermit in the woods, where he dies shortly after. He takes the Grail, the lance, and the silver plate with him to Heaven.

The story also illustrates the power of the journey, through which our vision turns inward and we find what we uniquely bring to bear on the quest for the object. We cannot dismiss the power of the quest. This is demonstrated by a study from Ontario that found better outcomes when people had to travel from Toronto to Thunder Bay for radiation therapy for cancer (due to the machines breaking in Toronto) than was found for those who stayed in Toronto and did not have to travel.

PLACEBO RESEARCH AND THE QUEST FOR THE MAGIC POTION

What interests us about placebo research is how people can heal themselves with inert substances that stimulate their faith in the possibility of getting well. Is this our bridge from the Holy Grail to collaborative healing? How to stimulate the inner healing capacities of human beings is the important question. We use whatever we can find to do that—from hypnosis to working within the person's beliefs, which medical anthropologist Arthur Kleinman calls working within the patient's treatment narrative.

What do we know about the activation of the self-healing (placebo) response? As an example we know that most of the effect of antidepressants comes from the self-healing response. In various published studies, the placebo response rate varies from 25 percent to 60 percent for groups of patients with major depressive disorder.[5] Using the Freedom of Information Act, Irving Kirsch, a psychologist at the University of Connecticut, and his colleagues obtained the results from all studies of antidepressants that had been reported to the U.S. Food and Drug Administration (FDA) (all trials must be reported whether or not they are published). They found that antidepressants are no more effective than placebo at any level of depression. At the most severe end of the spectrum of depression, placebos worked less well, giving the illusion that antidepressants were more effective.[6] However, in neuroimaging studies of depression, when placebos worked, the activation of brain regions was indistinguishable from that seen with active drug treatment.[7]

Resolution of depression with placebo is associated with increases in metabolism (brain activity) in the prefrontal cortex, anterior cingulate cortex, premotor cortex, parietal cortex, posterior insular cortex, and the posterior cingulate cortex. Decreases in metabolic activity were seen in the subgenual cingulate cortex, the parahippocampus, and thalamus. The regions of change overlapped those seen in people who improved while receiving the drug, fluoxetine, which makes sense if fluoxetine is no different from placebo in depression. Fluoxetine, however, was associated with some additional brain changes (which may be unrelated to depression) in the brainstem, striatum, anterior insular cortex, and hippocampus.[8]

Even if the biology of an illness is well understood, a host of factors make the typical course of the illness different for everyone who has it. People differ in their individual resistance, resilience, and genetics. HIV infection is no exception.[9] Before the development of effective treatments, some infected individuals survived fifteen or more years, while others had a rapid demise. In 1989 Dr. Beth Chan and Lewis had the opportunity to study the extent to which patients' faith in a treatment influences its efficacy. The study included 140 men, who were requesting an alternative therapy for AIDS at an AIDS treatment center in San Francisco. The treatment consisted of repeated injections of typhoid vaccine. Patients were interviewed before entry into the protocol and at intervals of every two months for two years. The patients' "faith in treatment" was assessed at each contact. Clinic physicians made weekly ratings of the patients' sense of subjective improvement. CD4 cell count and white blood cell count were measured at each visit.

Patients initially responded very positively, but the positive response fell off among most of the patients. However, twenty patients continued to respond, seemingly to the vaccine, at the end of one year and two years. These were the ones who had and continued to have a high "faith in treatment." We concluded that faith in treatment had an impact on the course of AIDS and that faith may be important, regardless of the efficacy of a treatment. Faith may be a mediating variable, which renders biologically inert treatments highly effective for those who believe in them.

Similarly, nonbiological prognostic factors contribute to the variable prognosis of psychiatric disorders. Especially in psychiatry, the difficulties in assessing a treatment's usefulness are compounded by the limitations of the way we make diagnoses (which seem rather arbitrary and not necessarily linked to biology) and our lack of knowledge regarding the causes of most psychiatric disorders.[10]

Studies have searched for characteristics of people who are strong placebo responders, linking it to traits such as "agreeableness," "ego-resilience," and "novelty-seeking."[11] Molecular biologist, Kathryn Hall, in Harvard University's placebo laboratory, has been studying a gene that encodes the enzyme catechol-O-methyltransferase (COMT), which breaks down catecholamines—a family of compounds that includes the neurotransmitters dopamine and epinephrine. In pain studies people who inherited two copies of the "val" form of the gene reported feeling less pain than those with two of the "met" form. If the "met-met" types sense pain more acutely, Hall thought they might also be more sensitive to the pain relief of the placebo effect. Placebo response has been linked to activity of the mesocortical-seeking system, which involves dopamine and projects into the prefrontal cortex.

Two forms of COMT exist—"met" and "val." The "val" form metabolizes dopamine three to four times faster than the "met" form. The slower form allows dopamine to linger in the receptor, resulting in greater relief of pain, regardless of whether the treatment is active or placebo. People diagnosed with irritable bowel syndrome (IBS) respond to sham acupuncture treatment (needles only appear to penetrate the skin). However, people with the "met-met" form of the gene have pain relief that is 50 points higher than people with the "val-val" form on a 500-point scale of severity. As expected, people with only one allele ("met-val") fell in the middle.[12]

Psychologist Tomas Furmark of Uppsala University in Sweden and colleagues reported that a variant of a gene involved in regulating serotonin production predicted which people with social anxiety disorder symptoms responded most strongly to a sugar pill.[13] Yet for this disorder, Furmark has found no link between COMT and placebo response.

These kinds of studies represent an effort to eliminate placebo responders from drug trials by the pharmaceutical companies so that they will have an easier time of showing whether the drugs work. A common procedure already in use is to have a two-week lead-in period in which everyone gets a placebo and those who respond are eliminated from the study. Then the study commences with those who remain. The criticism of this line of work comes from the idea that the same factors that drive placebo response may also drive drug response. In addition, it seems like cheating on the part of the drug companies. In clinical practice physicians have to treat all comers. We are interested in how well a drug works for everyone, not just placebo nonresponders.

Speaking for this other perspective, Dr. Luana Colloca and colleagues at the National Center for Complementary and Alternative Medicine in Bethesda, Maryland, said:

Recent findings on placebo research corroborate the evidence that the placebo effect represents a promising model to shed new light on the brain-mind-body interactions. In particular, this research has partially elucidated the role of how patients' expectations and the quality of physician-patient communication can influence the efficacy of interventions and overall clinical outcomes. Accordingly, the study of the placebo effect should be incorporated in the core clinical practice curriculum of all health practitioners. While the growing knowledge of the placebo effect points to it as an irreducible primary reality of the medical sciences, an ethical analysis aimed at avoiding the misuse of placebos is needed, while maximizing the opportunity for beneficial placebo effects.[14]

This perspective is quite opposite those of the pharmaceutical companies.

PLACEBO SURGERY RESEARCH

Surgery can also be a placebo. The first report we could find that addressed surgery as placebo appeared in the *Journal of the American Medical Association* in 1961.[15] Harvard University professor Henry Beecham, who had previously been studying placebos for nonsurgical indications, wrote a paper in which he reviewed fifteen studies with a total of 1,082 patients, which showed that 35.2 percent ± 2.2 percent of patients in pain had a satisfactory response to a placebo. In introducing the idea of surgery as placebo, Dr. Beecham cited a 1959 and 1960 study by Leonard Cobb, a Seattle cardiologist, who performed a randomized, controlled trial of a procedure then commonly used for angina, the internal mammary artery ligation, in which two arteries in the chest were tied to increase blood flow to the heart.[16] As *New York Times* journalist Margaret Talbot says, in her comprehensive review of the placebo in medicine, "90 percent of patients reported that it helped—but when Cobb compared it with placebo surgery in which he made incisions but did not tie off the arteries, the sham operations proved just as successful. The procedure was soon abandoned."[17]

J. Bruce Moseley, an orthopedic surgeon at the Houston V.A. Hospital, recruited ten middle-aged men for a study of arthroscopic surgery for knee arthritis.[18] Two of the men would undergo arthroscopic surgery in which the knee joint is scraped and rinsed, three would have rinsing alone without scraping, and five would have sham surgery. They would go to the operating room, be draped and anesthetized and would receive the same incisions as the active surgery cases. The surgeon received his instructions only after the patient was completely prepared for the surgery. Six months after surgery, all ten patients reported less pain. All were pleased with the results of the operation. The physicians performing the postoperative assessment and the patients remained unaware of which treatment had been provided. Patients who received the placebo surgery reported equally decreased frequency, intensity, and duration of knee pain as those receiving the actual surgery. Both groups thought the procedure was worthwhile and would recommend it to family and friends.

In an interview with the *New York Times,* Nelda Wray, one of the physicians involved in the study, said: "The bigger and more dramatic the patient perceives the intervention to be, the bigger the placebo effect. Big pills are more effective than small pills, injections have more effect than pills and surgery has the most effect of all."[19]

Next these researchers proceeded to a larger study with 180 patients.[20] Participants were randomized into three groups according to the severity of osteoarthritis (grade 1, 2, or 3; grade 4, 5, or 6; and grade 7 or 8). After the patient was in the operating suite, the surgeon was handed the envelope. Participants were randomly assigned to arthroscopic debridement, arthroscopic lavage alone, or the placebo procedure. Dr. Moseley performed all the operations. Patients in the debridement group or the lavage group received standard general anesthesia with endotracheal intubation. Patients in the placebo group received a short-acting intravenous tranquilizer and an opioid and spontaneously breathed oxygen-enriched air.

To control for patients in the placebo group possibly not having total amnesia for the procedure, a standard arthroscopic debridement procedure was simulated.

After the knee was prepped and draped, three 1-cm incisions were made in the skin. The surgeon asked for all instruments and manipulated the knee as if arthroscopy were being performed. Saline was splashed to simulate the sounds of lavage. No instrument entered the portals for arthroscopy. The patient was kept in the operating room for the amount of time required for a debridement. Patients spent the night after the procedure in the hospital. Their nurses were unaware of the treatment-group assignment. Postoperatively, there were two minor complications and no deaths. Incisional erythema developed in one patient, who was given antibiotics. In a second patient, calf swelling developed in the leg that had undergone surgery; venography was negative for thrombosis. In no case did a complication necessitate the breaking of the randomization code. Postoperative care was delivered according to a protocol specifying that all patients should receive the same walking aids, graduated exercise program, and analgesics. The use of analgesics after surgery was monitored; during the two-year follow-up period, the amount used was similar in the three groups.[21]

The pain outcomes, before and after the procedure, were the same for the three groups. Similar results were found for the bending-moving subscale of the Arthritis Impact Measurement Scale.The unanswered question is whether it's possible to gain the results of placebo surgery without having placebo surgery. Can we gain the benefits of the ceremony of surgery without performing the ceremony?

These studies have had an impact on the world of surgery, which used to hold to a principle that surgery was real and placebo imaginary. Surgery has come around to recognizing the power of sham or placebo surgery. By 2003 a study of fetal stem cell transplantation into the substantia nigra for the treatment of Parkinson's disease used a placebo control group, finding that the stem cells performed no better than placebo (though both helped).[22] Prior to that a vigorous debate had taken place in the *New England Journal of Medicine* about the ethics of placebo surgery.[23]

PLACEBO POWER, PAST AND PRESENT

Speaking of the drugs of his day, Oliver Wendell Holmes observed in 1860, "I firmly believe that if the whole materia medica [medical drugs], *as now used,* could be sunk to the bottom of the sea, it would be all the better for mankind, and all the worse for the fishes."[24] Some *were* effective—like cinchona bark for malaria, foxglove for heart failure, cowpox vaccine for smallpox, and poppies for pain—but these ventured into the overlap of allopathic medicine with herbal medicine, historically the medicine of the people, and largely tested over a great deal of time.

In 1955 Harvard researcher Henry Beecher concluded that 30 to 40 percent of any treated group would respond to a placebo.[25] More recent studies on pain, depression, some heart diseases, gastric ulcers, and irritable bowel syndrome have raised that estimate to 50 to 60 percent of subjects and sometimes even more. Placebo effects sometimes exceed those of the active drug, but there is a bias against publishing these kinds of studies.

The power of the placebo effect in randomized clinical trials appears to actually be increasing, thereby contributing to problems of demonstrating statistically reliable effects of treatments that directly target biological mechanisms.[26] To the bane of biological researchers, it may be that no treatment fully works without belief, expectation, and emotion. In one review of the placebo tests in twelve randomized controlled trials for burning mouth syndrome, treatment with placebos produced an average response that was 72 percent as large as the response to active drugs.[27] Overall, the placebo effect is impactful in the acute treatment of migraine attacks with analgesics; studies show average placebo response of 25 percent for headache relief, which is similar to a response of 30 percent seen in the treatment with triptans, the active drug used to treat migraines.[28] For neuropathic pain 45 percent to 62 percent of the effect of active medications was attributable to the placebo response.[29]

In the summer of 2000, the share price of a British biotech company called Peptide Therapeutics dropped 33 percent after it was revealed that its new allergy vaccine was only as effective as a placebo. During the trials on food-allergy patients, a company spokesman had reported delightedly, 75 percent had improved to the point where they could tolerate foods they'd never been able to eat before. But when the control group data came in, so had 75 percent of the subjects taking inert tablets.

In a recent study on VEGF, a genetically engineered heart drug, announced with much fanfare by its manufacturer, Genentech, the placebo actually performed better. Two months after their treatments, patients who had gotten low doses of VEGF could walk twenty-six seconds longer on a treadmill, those who had gotten high doses could walk thirty-two seconds longer, and those who had gotten a placebo could walk forty-two seconds longer.

Clinicians have described placebo effects among Parkinson's disease patients for decades.[30] More expensive medications work better than less expensive ones, controlling for the biological activity of the medication.[31] To the surprise of many in the scientific community, placebo surgery for Parkinson's disease has shown significant benefit.[32] Previously, conventional wisdom would not expect a placebo effect to occur in a disease for which the neurobiological basis is so well understood. Nevertheless, these and other studies have shown the capacity for strong placebo effects within this patient population. Neuroimaging studies show that placebos stimulate the release of dopamine in the nigrostriatal tract of patients with Parkinson's disease (where the dopamine-containing neurons have largely died), and single-cell recording studies show that placebos can increase the activity of the remaining dopamine-containing neurons in this area. Apparently expectation of effect can induce neurochemical changes—in this case disease-specific nigrostriatal dopamine release.

ATTITUDES AND RESPONSES TO PLACEBOS

Some people are not happy to hear that they have been given a placebo. "Once we did a PMS study where we treated people for a month with placebo and then told people who'd responded what they'd been on," says Karen Weihs, a psychiatrist at George Washington University. "And as it turns out, it's a very difficult thing to confront somebody with. Some people feel insulted, or silly. You're telling them it's all in their mind."[33] On the other hand, in one study that openly offered placebo to treat irritable bowel syndrome, where everyone knew they were taking placebo, patients were so satisfied that they asked for prescriptions for the sugar pills to continue taking them.[34]

People vary in their relationships to their own suffering. We would never tell anyone that a phenomenon was "in their mind" or "just in their mind." We hope to awaken them rather to the possibilities of their power to mitigate their own mind/body reactions.

Having positive expectations before treatment is associated with having a more positive response to inactive treatments, which is thought to be through the brain reward or seeking circuitry.[35] The strength with which people seek seems to reflect their responsiveness to placebo, which varies among individuals. Furthermore, the response to placebo is affected by previous experience. A stronger placebo response can be conditioned or learned. The degree of analgesia induced by an inert substance is increased if people have had prior experience with an effective treatment, possibly increasing their expectation that another treatment will work.[36] Even the expectancy of benefit can be changed just by providing information about a medication during a study, which influences outcomes.[37]

Sometimes, patients respond to doses of medication that are well under what we expect is necessary for a therapeutic response. In clinical practice we need to take advantage of these "nonspecific or contextual effects," because in many conditions, the response to the inert substance is very close to the "drug effect," as occurs in the treatment of neuropathic pain.[38] Placebo effects even occur in progressive and degenerative diseases, including multiple sclerosis and epilepsy.[39] We don't actually know how to design a study that eliminates these human and contextual and expectation factors (placebo) from treatment.[40] These contextual effects are a very important aspect of ceremony and ritual as well and have been part of healing since time immemorial.

The Nocebo Effect

The belief in inert substances, however, can backfire. Dr. Kimberly Tippens and colleagues at the Helfgott Research Institute of the National College of Natural Medicine in Portland, Oregon, studied the role of expectancy in the placebo effect of an inactive dietary supplement given to 114 obese adults with metabolic syndrome.[41] In the study the participants were given lifestyle education. One group then received an inert capsule that they were told had an active weight loss ingredient. A second group was told that there was a 50 percent chance that they had received the active supplement, but all received the inert substance instead. The third group was not given any capsules. Unfortunately, the participants who received the capsules began to doubt their own agency in weight loss and began to turn toward dietary supplements! Those *not* taking the capsules, however, developed a higher sense of self-efficacy and took charge of their own health.[42]

Inert supplements appear to have negative effects through diminishing people's sense of self-efficacy. We have seen a similar phenomenon among people relying upon opiates for pain—their sense of self-efficacy is diminished and their reliance upon pills increases.

A number of authors have suggested the term *nocebo* (Latin for "I shall harm") to describe adverse effects from biologically inactive interventions or treatments. Physician Walter Kennedy first described this effect in 1961, noting unpleasant, undesirable, or harmful results from an inactive treatment.[43] He termed this the *nocebo effect*. The nocebo phenomena is a concept that allows us to extrapolate the occurrence of adverse effects with the use of active substances; in this way the patient starts to take a medication and relates adverse effects that are not necessarily common for that drug. Billions of dollars have been spent in research trying to describe the biological activity of drugs. What if no drug or treatment is exempt from the effects of expectations and the doctor-patient relationship (relational medicine), both for the benefit and for the detriment of the patient?[44]

The nocebo effect may turn out to be as important as the placebo effect. The way we inform patients about possible side effects of drugs and treatment may induce nocebo effects, such as anxiousness, mistrust, and lack of relationship or contact, which may aggravate symptoms and thus outperform, in part or in total, the effect of, for example, analgesic drugs.[45] Similar mechanisms are proposed to explain the nocebo effect as the placebo effect: expectation, conditioning, and anticipatory anxiety.[46] Patients can expect that medications or treatments will fail to work. Previous experience can contribute to that expectation. When we suggest that medications or treatments will fail to work, we induce anticipatory anxiety, which activates two independent pathways: the cholecystokinin system and the hypothalamaic-pituitary-adrenal axis.[47] The activation of each of them is related to the occurrence of negative effects after the administration of an active medication and remaining doubts about the possible attenuation of the nocebo effect from the inhibition of these pathways.

Here is where the practice of hypnosis and the understanding of persuasive communication become important. We need to know if we are persuading people to improve or to get worse. Most people tend to experience more severe symptoms if the clinical encounter or setting fosters mistrust, anxiousness, and lack of continuity.[48]

THE ROLE OF EXPECTATIONS IN EXPLAINING THE PLACEBO EFFECT

Cinnamon Stetler at Furman University in South Carolina asked why good adherence to a placebo treatment is reliably associated with health benefits. This has been found for beta-blockers with cardiac disease, among other conditions. In these studies adherence was more important than whether or not the patient was taking a drug or placebo. In Stetler's model initial expectations are proposed to shape adherence to treatment. She told her seventy-two participants that her intention was to study physical activity and memory. Participants were asked to increase their physical activity by 35 percent for two weeks (in this case exercise was the placebo treatment). She measured whether or not people actually adhered to increasing their physical activity by having them wear pedometers.

She assessed people's expectations and short-term memory (free recall) before and after physical activity. People's expectations of the study results did predict whether or not they undertook the expected physical activity, though whether or not they continued to exercise did not predict whether or not they expected their memory to improve. However, if they believed that their memory would improve through physical activity, they indeed showed better memory, even after the study ruled out other factors. Furthermore, the more the participants expected to improve, the better their memory. The group concluded that it is possible that actually exercising contributed to stronger expectations and therefore good results, but they couldn't say that the actual exercise had an effect. Therefore, they deduced that placebo was at work, as it was the belief that produced the results.[49]

Pain is again a good example, as it is also modulated by psychological, social, and contextual factors, which are even more powerful than anyone expected. Pain is not just a symptom we treat but an experience that can even be rewarding in some cases. All these factors can modify the person's response to analgesic drugs. Pain can activate reward mechanisms when experienced within contexts that have special positive meaning.[50] A positive therapeutic context induces positive expectations, which activate the dorsolateral prefrontal cortex (DLPFC), the rostral anterior cingulate cortex (rACC), and the periaqueductal gray area (PAG). This is an inhibitory pain-modulating network. Positive expectations engender greater levels of pain relief.

Negative expectations activate cholecystokinin, which facilitates pain transmission, thereby increasing the subjective experience of pain.[51] They also activate the hypothalamic-pituitary-adrenal axis, which increases anticipatory anxiety, also known to increase pain. They change dopamine activity in the nucleus accumbens (where the cell bodies live for major dopamine-containing nerve tracts that relate to pleasure and reward) and deactivate the mu-opioid receptors, which respond to the opioids that the body itself produces. Thus, placebos are actually not biologically inactive, though their substance may be. Again, we see how much we want to try to separate pure biological activity from the context and relationship in which something is done.

In one study patients were given remifentanil for pain reduction. When they believed they were receiving the actual drug, the dorsolateral prefrontal cortex (DLPFC) and the anterior cingulate cortex (ACC) were activated and the pain reduction was more than double what they experienced when they were told they were receiving saline (even though they were receiving a drug). When they expected they would be receiving nothing, the hippocampus was activated and the pain relief was minimal.

PLACEBO AND THE HEALING RELATIONSHIP

The complexity of the placebo response is increasingly noted in scientific research. *New York Times* writer Margaret Talbot reported on a clinic that researches psychotropic medications. The clinicians are at pains to discern the impact of placebo, not only from the drug, but also from the physical and even systemic environments. Concerned that the friendliness of the clinic staff was impacting results, the workers were issued a directive to wear lab coats when in contact with study participants, to assist in creating a formal distance, and in one case, a staff member was counseled that her ability to empathically communicate with people involved in the experiment was a disadvantage, as it might provide a therapeutic experience that could skew the results.[52]

Talbot's article ponders the failure of current health care, which seeks to get more bang for the physician buck paid. What if part of the placebo effect is the effect of someone listening to us? Perhaps it is the committed and hopeful attention that is communicated that helps us recover or feel better? Researchers on clinical studies are invested in retaining participants, so they may be more generous with their time and care and more enthusiastic about the treatment being tested than they would be in ordinary clinical practice. Placebos may provide an important context to believe that somebody is at last in league with us against our illness.

These studies bring us to the realization that most of the elements of placebo healing happen in the context of the doctor-patient relationship. Better relationships produce more powerful placebo responses. This phenomenon is well known in the psychotherapy outcome research, where the quality of the therapist-patient relationship explains about two-thirds of the effectiveness of the treatment. It would seem that this phenomenon exists in all medicine. This belies the idea that health care providers are interchangeable, although many administrators hold that one doctor should be equivalent to another and that continuity of care should not matter.

Placebo arises out of the context of the healing relationship and the expectations for that context fuel the placebo response.[53] New approaches to placebo research are defining placebo as the effect of the meeting between the doctor and the patient and the context in which a specific treatment is given.[54] One of the first studies to demonstrate the importance of the relationship in medical treatment was that of British general practitioner-researcher K. B. Thomas at the University of Southampton.[55] He studied 200 patients with what we now call "medically unexplained symptoms" (MUS). The term is used in reference to patients who suffer but for whom we can make no diagnosis. He randomly assigned these individuals to one of four groups: (1) a consultation in which the doctor made every effort to be positive and either (a) provided a treatment or (b) did not; (2) a consultation in which the doctor made every effort to be neutral and (a) provided a treatment or (b) did not. Two weeks later the patients were much happier with the positive consultation than the neutral one, but whether or not a treatment was given didn't matter: 64 percent of people receiving a positive consultation got better regardless of treatment or not, while only 39 percent of those receiving the neutral consultation improved; 53 percent of those treated got better compared with 50 percent of those not treated.[56]

Thomas later wrote in the *Lancet:* "The placebo effect in general practice is the power of the doctor alone to make the patient feel better, irrespective of medication. It is one of the most important factors in the consultation, yet generally it is neglected, unrecognized, and untaught. A better appreciation of this power would change doctors' attitudes to the consultation and would result in the making of less illness, the prescribing of less medication, and a better understanding by the patient of his or her condition."[57] In the introduction to his 1987 study, he wrote, "The doctor himself is a powerful therapeutic agent; he is the placebo and his influence is felt to a greater or lesser extent at every consultation."[58]

Dr. Frede Olesen, Head of the Research Unit for General Practice at the University of Aarhus in Denmark, writes that there are three obstacles to doctors' ability to make more effective use of the placebo effect.[59] He says that doctors neglect the power and usefulness of the placebo effect because they have been indoctrinated to view the placebo as inert—a fake pill that doesn't do anything—or as something that is even deceptive. Doctors do not like to think of themselves as "merely" placebo physicians. They want to do "real" treatments. Yet, the goal of ensuring maximum symptom relief is gained both as a result of specific treatment with known biological efficacy and a host of other, nonspecific, context-mediated factors, including the impact of the interpersonal encounter between the doctor and the patient. Dr. Olesen suggests replacing the term *placebo effect* with *context-mediated effect*.

The second obstacle is the lack of clarity and precision with respect to where context should, or should not, be used as a relevant treatment modality. Obviously, context-mediated factors diminish in relation to biological factors in severe trauma, cancer, and emergencies such as myocardial infarctions. However, there are exceptions. The hypnotherapist-obstetrician David Cheek, with whom I (Lewis) learned hypnosis, was fond of telling how he used hypnosis during emergencies while he was mobilizing the medical interventions. He claimed to have stopped postpartum hemorrhages using hypnosis before he had time to administer the drugs necessary to do so. I have had similar experiences in my obstetrical career. In almost forty years of experience with acute care medicine, I have used the influence of my role as doctor and the power of suggestion to aid emergency situations. I do not see a dichotomy between context-driven factors and biological factors. Both are helpful and can be used simultaneously.

However, emergencies are not the main focus of general practice, which focuses on alleviating symptoms, many of which do not have obvious causes. As Olesen said, "Symptoms are complex. They are influenced by cultural and personal factors and appear as the result of conscious and nonconscious emotional and cognitive processing of cerebrally perceived signals. Symptoms may include pain, nausea, tiredness, dizziness, anxiety, depression, and other conditions in which the cerebral cortex plays an essential role in the expression of the disease."[60] We may or may not be able to locate a diseased organ or physiological process to treat with evidence-based drugs and procedures, but our primary focus is to treat the patient who experiences these symptoms. The physician-clown, Patch Adams, is quoted as saying, "Treat the illness, you win some, you lose some; treat the patient, you always win."[61] Often we treat symptoms without being able to identify the presence of a specific disease.[62] In general practice it has been estimated that 40 to 60 percent of patients lack firm diagnoses.[63] Symptoms are strongly modulated by the patient's expectations and beliefs and the clinical context surrounding the specific treatment. Essential components of the total context are the doctor's attitude, especially his or her communication skills, the doctor–patient relationship, the way the doctor applies therapeutic procedures or rituals, and, ultimately, the doctor's ability to create trust.[64]

The third obstacle is a severe lack of research in cerebral processes and how these can be manipulated. Over the past twenty years, much empirical research has shown impressive symptom-modulating effects, not only from placebo pills, but also from the context surrounding the encounter between patient and therapist (including therapists practicing complementary and alternative procedures, for example, acupuncture).[65] Biological processes in the brain are strongly influenced by a variety of contextual factors.[66]

We know that drugs influence the brain, but now we are learning that the context and the relationship also influence brain processes and thereby the experienced symptoms just as much, or possibly even more, than medications. "Doctors may actively modulate the total context surrounding the encounter with the patient."[67] This opens the door for relational medicine—that the quality and duration of the relationship with the patient is equally important if not more so than the efficacy of the medication administered.

Another line of research can help us understand the potential physiological power of a good doctor–patient relationship. Dr. Greg Stevens and colleagues at Princeton University's Neuroscience Institute have studied what happens in the brains of storytellers and listeners using functional magnetic resonance imaging.[68] They asked speakers to tell real life stories from their personal life while their brains were being imaged. Then they played recordings of those stories to listeners. They found that the speaker's brain activity is coupled in location and time with the listener's brain activity. This coupling vanishes when participants fail to communicate, as when the speakers spoke a language the listeners did not understand. Thus, the same areas in the brains of the speakers lit up in the listeners with a short delay. Moreover, they also found areas that lit up in anticipation of what the speaker would say. They connected the extent of neural coupling to a quantitative measure of story comprehension and found that the greater the anticipatory speaker-listener coupling, the greater the understanding.[69]

We could speak about coherence between brains and even speculate about auditory mirror neurons so that people develop empathy for each other through the telling and hearing of stories. Brains convey information in this fashion, but what is essential for understanding the power of the doctor–patient relationship is that this coupling between people produces powerful effects in the brain. This is what placebo research has been lacking—the understanding that life experience and interpersonal interactions change our brains.

To summarize, in our medical culture, even in placebo research, we have focused on the thing ("the placebo") instead of the situation. The term is unfortunate. We should speak about the aspects of treatment that influence it beyond the biological impact of what we are doing. In much of our work, these nonspecifics are the healing. When we ask spirits for help, we can't explain their impact in the same way that we can a drug. They are part of the situation, as is the quality of the relationships for all concerned, the intent and energy of all involved, the beliefs and expectations of everyone (not just the person who is suffering), and so much more. Healing is disguised in the placebo response.

UNRAVELING THE MYTH OF PHYSICAL PAIN

It's not easy to make the transition from believing in drugs to believing in relationship, self, spirit, and more. We use hypnosis, the power of suggestion, and any other technique we can imagine to inspire people to believe that they can heal. Here's a story.

Paul believed he had a bad back. "My pain is from degenerative changes in my back. It can't get better. Bones don't regenerate." As I continued the discussion, Paul had more to say. He was getting agitated. "You can see my pain on the X-ray; I've got four bad disks." Paul had the usual dominant culture story: pain is valid if the X-ray is abnormal; pain is invalid if the X-ray is normal. Exercise, including walking, has been shown to improve back pain. I asked Paul if he was doing that.

"I can't exercise or walk; it makes my pain worse."

"What about yoga?" I asked. "Have you done any of that?"

"How's yoga going to help me," he said. "My pain is real."

Here is where we extract the belief (ending) from the story (in this case, a short vignette of a clinical encounter). The culturally dominant idea is that real pain is physical or mechanical and must be treated by physical or mechanical means (surgery, etc.), though pills are acceptable to relieve it. Imaginary pain is the opposite and can be treated by meditation, yoga, and the like. Of course, research doesn't support this distinction, but it is the dominant story of our culture.

But doctors contribute to this cultural myth, despite their supposed dedication to science. Here's a typical scene of an orthopedist talking to a patient. The patient is sitting and the orthopedist is standing next to an impressive X-ray viewing box, pointing vaguely, and saying "Here's where your pain comes from. Look at the degeneration in your joint. That's bone rubbing on bone." Of course, the patient can't read X-rays, so he doesn't understand what he's seeing. Nevertheless, the authority of having physical evidence and of the specialist pointing to it makes the story absolutely true. Then the orthopedist says, "Your pain is not going to get better; you're just going to have to learn to live with it until it gets bad enough that we can replace your joint." Again, we have reinforcement of the passive position, the position of being patient for the process to get worse and worse until replacing the joint can be justified. This is one of our dominant cultural narratives.

I replayed this conversation for Paul, and he confirmed that his encounter with his orthopedist had been essentially the same. The outcome of that encounter was to put Paul on oxycodone, a narcotic pain reliever. The doctor had progressively increased Paul's dose until he was on a massive dose (over 600 milligrams), which is 450 milligrams more than the maximal recommended amount for non-cancer pain. It is enough to put a moose to sleep.

The alternate conversation, which all patients with pain dread, is for the specialist to say, "I can't find anything to explain your pain; it must be all in your head." The implicit belief here is that pain in the head is imaginary and that real pain must be in the body. Of course, the pain literature is full of the appreciation that all pain perception occurs in the brain. Nerves from the periphery of the body are sending messages to the brain to let it know that something unpleasant (potentially damaging to tissue) is happening, and the brain interprets this as pain. Then we respond to make the pain stop, by removing our hand from something hot or limping in such a way as to reduce the sensation coming from the hip. All pain is in the brain, which is of course linked to conscious awareness. All pain is perception.

Mostly physicians don't address this reality but write prescriptions and don't take the time to talk about other therapies with their patients. Writing prescriptions is quick and easy and fits within a six-minute office visit. Even talking about other therapies, not to mention doing them, takes much longer. But then when we listen to what physicians tell each other about chronic pain, we hear statements like the following, which one doctor said about a patient we shared, "He's just drug seeking." Of course, this same doctor had introduced the patient to the drugs that the patient was now seeking and had increased them to the point that the doctor now was uncomfortable. Now that the patient was addicted, of course he was drug seeking.

Another doctor said about a shared patient, "She doesn't really have pain because her sensations are so out of proportion to the X-ray findings and the exam." That doctor had missed the body of literature showing that pain is not correlated with findings on X-rays or physical examination.[70] Minimal findings can be associated with maximal pain and vice versa.

A doctor referring me a new patient said, "This one needs to see a psychiatrist instead of me." I would have said that "this person needs both medical care and attention to the emotional and social aspects of his pain." A team can provide that. People seem to need more than one provider to feel that their needs are being met. This makes sense, since families have more than one adult—two parents, grandparents, aunts, and uncles.

I also think it is important that members of the team share skills. Family physicians should have some psychotherapeutic skills and do some psychotherapy, though they can't provide this function for everyone. By doing some psychotherapeutic work (narrative CBT, hypnosis, family therapy, etc.), family doctors gain the skills to be more helpful in any appointment. They become more convincing at making referrals to other team members for this kind of work. We need a team, and we need to cross-train so that each of us has some skills at doing what the other does.

Without this approach in which we enter into the emotional and social lives of our clients, we roll our eyes when we see the names of chronic pain patients on the schedule and tune out before entering the room. Paul described the transition from interested to vacant eyes as painful for him. Suddenly he was no longer interesting, no longer someone the doctor wanted to see. He was someone to refer and eliminate.

Paul, like all of our clients, was searching for something—comfort, love, security, belonging. Paul was seeking relief from pain. In Panksepp's affective neuroethological perspective, this seeking is mediated by the mesolimbic dopamine system, which is a general purpose appetitive foraging system (which he calls the SEEKING system). We are motivated to seek. This helps animals to become acquainted with the diverse configurations and rewards existing in their environments, and thereby establish realistic and adaptive expectations and strategies for finding safety. This system also participates in protecting animals against the vicissitudes of their world (punishing contingencies) by promoting the seeking of safety.[71]

Paul had been saturated in the cultural stories about pain and how it is mechanical and can only be treated with opiates. He expected his pain to progressively get worse, so it did. He didn't have a mental model (which we construct from hearing stories) about non-pharmacological activities being helpful for reducing pain. So I started telling him stories about research on pain, without specifically directing the information at him and telling him what he should do.

Studying Pain

The experience of pain can now be studied thanks to fMRI technology.[72] Our subjective sensory experiences are heavily shaped by interactions between expectations and incoming sensory information. A mental representation of an impending sensory event can significantly shape neural processes that underlie the formulation of the actual sensory experience. The more pain we expect to feel, the more pain we will actually feel, and when we expect less pain than we are actually going to receive, we experience less pain. We also experience pain differently depending on whether we expect the pain to continue. Research has shown that if we expect the pain to continue, we retroactively feel more pain, and if the pain is likely to stop, we retroactively feel less pain.[73]

In one experiment participants were primed to anticipate amounts of pain that were different than they were actually likely to experience.[74] Tetsuo Koyama and his team of neurobiologists from Wake Forest School of Medicine found that as the magnitude of expected pain increased, activation increased in the thalamus, insula, prefrontal cortex, anterior cingulate cortex (ACC), and other brain regions. Pain-intensity-related brain activation areas overlap partially with expectation-related areas, including the anterior insula and the anterior cingulate cortex. Expectations of decreased pain powerfully reduced both the subjective experience of pain and the activation of pain-related brain regions, including the primary somatosensory cortex, the insular cortex, and the anterior cingulate cortex.[75]

Paul overheard Barbara giving a talk about pain where she told the participants that the literature is clear that long-term use of opiates (more than six months) actually increases pain, a phenomenon called opiate-induced hyperalgesia, where the brain recruits more areas to feel pain, so the patient wants more opiate, and the cycle continues.[76] For this reason coming off opiates can be associated with improvement in pain. Research from 2014, by Matthew Lieberman and Naomi Eisenberger, neuroscientists from University of California Los Angeles, corroborates early 1981 findings by researcher Jaak Panksepp, that the pain treated best by opiates is the pain of social distress, loneliness, and isolation, which uses the same common pathway through the rostral anterior cingulate cortex that is used by pain from the periphery of the body.[77] Our pain patients, however, tend to focus on the injury site and the drugs, but leave out their isolation and loneliness.

One morning we drove past a car whose front end was deformed around a telephone pole, which had broken and fallen onto the roof of the car. It appeared to be a single car accident. It seemed to us that someone had fallen asleep, as there was no other way to explain that accident. Later we learned it was Paul, who had indeed fallen asleep at the wheel, unsurprisingly, given his extreme dose of oxycodone. He was miraculously minimally injured, probably because he was so relaxed.

The accident was a wake-up call for Paul, with the power to make our research-related stories become very meaningful to him. Over a mere two weeks, Paul progressively and aggressively cut his large dose of oxycodone down to only 60 milligrams per day. He wanted to report to me that what Barbara had said was right. He was actually feeling less pain. He was preparing to eliminate all opiates.

He had also realized that the opiates were interfering with his relating to other people. Without the high dose, he found himself craving more contact. He began working with Barbara to help reestablish social relationships. The more he did that, the less his back pain became. Paul became a living testament for us on how long-term opiates do not reduce the level of pain experienced, and, in fact, make it worse.

Healing often involves changing expectations for what is possible, changing the story people have about their pain, which, in the process, increases resiliency, adaptability, and sometimes leads to transformation. Paul changed his story about pain. He no longer believed that opiates were necessary to control his pain. However, a number of life events may have led him to be open to this story. His wife had recently, unexpectedly left him, and moved West, saying that living with him was like living with a person sleepwalking. His recent car accident had a sobering effect. His school performance had been suffering from his excessive sleepiness. Maybe he had heard the story about opiates making chronic pain worse before. Maybe this time he heard it differently because of his life experiences. Maybe we have to hear a story several times before it sinks into us, before it impresses us to make change. Maybe we provided a safe holding space for him to experiment in relation to our ongoing practice of being nonjudgmental. All these factors may have played a role.

Our patients are seeking comfort, relief from distress, happiness, or even just a change in state. Their injuries initiate journeys that take on mythic proportions. More important than the seeking of the magic potion is the process of change that comes from learning to manage pain.

8

Our Bodies: Makers of Meaning

Movement is the unifying bond between the mind and body.
DEANE JUHAN, *JOB'S BODY*

Our body constitutes our main evidence as to our real, personal participation in a state of affairs where so much remains contingent.

ROGER GRAINGER,
THEATRE AND ENCOUNTER

One day as I sat by a sacred fire, waiting while Lewis* was "out on the hill," Tom came to talk to me. I had been sitting by the fire since Lewis had gone out. It was a short *hanbleceya* (vision quest)—only two nights before he and the other dancers went into the arbor. It was my first Sundance, and apart from a two-hour break in the middle of the night, I had elected to stay up, keeping vigil. The fire had been lit the day before when the group went out, and would stay lit until they came back. It wasn't usual to have a woman support a man, but it had been

---

*Barbara is the "I" voice through this chapter.

allowed because we were such close friends, and Lewis had asked specially, and we didn't know any of the other people in the community.

We were visitors, in a valley in the Columbia River Gorge. "High Altitude Prairie" they called it. In the daytime the temperatures were over a hundred, and at night they dropped to below zero. I had been relieved of my 2 a.m. to 8 a.m. kitchen shift to support Lewis while he sat out. They say that the supporter feels the cravings of his or her partner who is fasting on the hill, and I had spent the night with a pleasant longing for a cigar, the occasional wish for another blanket, and the strong need for coffee to resist sleeping. I sat on a log, painting in my sketchbook with coffee grounds. They had allowed my sketchbook, but not paint, but between the mud and the coffee I was well off for pigment.

During the day and night, people had dropped by to tell me things. Lewis's advice to me had been, "Listen—don't ask questions, listen to what you are told." So I did. I sat and practiced songs and "painted," and from time to time, people would drop by to sit and talk. I learned a lot that weekend, with teachers so gentle and kind that I barely knew I was learning.

Tom told me many things, but one struck me in connection with the work I do. He told me that in his view, we are spirit beings that come to Earth to walk in a human body. Before we take on an earthly existence, we choose a life, one we think we can manage. We walk on the Earth, as humans, and feel and experience what it is like to have our spiritual selves tempered by this clumsy, impermanent vessel of instantiation. Sometimes we take on more than we are really ready for, and that is when we look to Creator and the spirits for help with the world.

THE BODY AND THE WORLD

It is our bodies that require us to feel, to experience, to engage in community, interact with others as part of the interconnectedness of everything, and so to suffer. No wonder we resist letting them do their part in helping us heal. The quiet energy in walking, sitting, or moving gently with t'ai chi are belied by the intensity we feel at that moment when we engage with our physical selves. Movement, dance, or playing with physical metaphor can seem overwhelming.

Many of us have the sense that our bodies do not belong only to us, but that we share ownership with cultural and philosophical ideas of physical reality, with expert opinion on height, weight, shoe size. We read constant criticism of our physical form in magazines and on websites. We must make the best of our "imperfect" physical selves, decide if we are shaped like apples or pears, tubular or muscular, whether we are under- or over-developed, too muscular or not muscular enough. The "correct" appearance eludes us in so many ways. Our bodies are fought over by advertising from fashion, sports, and food. They are the location of punishment, violence, captivity. Good physical appearance is a sign of our health, our success, our ability to negotiate the world, self-discipline, and possibilities for the future. If we look physically distressed, it is a sign of our lassitude, our failure to measure up to the standards of the day. Our bodies remind us of our inadequacy. We feel hopeless.

Let's consider how we move in the world. What movements do we make in the course of a day? Often these are surprisingly restricted—stand up, sit down, lie down, maybe reach for something on a shelf or open a door, perhaps lift a bag of groceries, almost always emphasizing our dominant hand and foot. We sometimes find ourselves restricted in the movements we perform in our dance of life in a way that echoes the restrictions we feel in our bodies. We hurt more when we are anxious or tired, we favor injuries, and we form our bodies and our movements around these wounds. The connective tissue of our wounded body becomes like a favorite coat.

We carry blocks, pains, and tensions, and stumble about in the unfamiliar reality of corporeal existence. We block our bodies' sensations. We do not find our bodies a safe place to be. Once I took a woman with depression to a gym after hours. We were alone. With lots of love and some dancing, she worked her way over to the treadmill. When she finally stood on the exercise machine, she cried. As she began to walk, she discovered that every time she raised her arms, she was moved to tears. It took weeks for her to be able to stretch her thoracic spine without crying.

We all know how to live in our bodies in a healthy way, but we are bound in cultural and familial stories of thinness, fatness, fitness, six-pack abs, and in bodies defined by a culture that might not be ours. Bodies become the location for acts of resistance against our myriad bosses, against those who disdain us, against the norm, the ideal, the expectation that we reach the unattainable. We envy those who seem to find it easy, who groom their obedient bodies until they are the very definition of the social norm, who seem not to be dismayed by the multiple forces of expectation. We also envy those who find their bodies a comfortable place to live, somehow free from the pressures of appearance.

But our bodies are not mere containers. Recent work on brain plasticity deeply engages us in the idea that we are not fixed; it is impossible to draw a hard boundary between our physical selves and the world. No longer fixed by the boundary of the skin, we can understand ourselves to be permeable, changeable, responsive to the thoughts in our minds. Quantum physics tells us that our bodies are arbitrary and useful merely so that we can be found within this great unified energy field. Some representation of individuality exists in this idea. Human intimacy occurs at the local level, when we touch, one on one. The profound connection exists in community. This might be easier to understand when you are hungry or hurt and tired, and it doesn't seem as if there is space to plug in to the great energy source of oneness. For many of our clients, it is easier to participate in the great field of unity than it is to exist in a relationship with another person, negotiating day-to-day existence.

One way to better understand the difficulties of negotiating life is to consider anxiety. The state of change is the condition that gives rise to anxiety. Anxiety is the feeling we get when, either by our own efforts or because of external forces, change is happening. Anxiety is a necessary human feeling. It helps us learn about our environment and alerts us that things might be different. We probably will not ever get rid of anxiety, nor should we. How we respond to anxiety, though, is under our control, and we can certainly lower anxiety or stop it from escalating. We need only exert the amount of anxiety necessary in a given situation.

We tend to respond to anxiety by giving it a negative spin. Because the feeling is uncomfortable, we presume that it signals something bad. Most of us work really hard to avoid feeling anxious, although ironically our strategies can result in an increase rather than a decrease. Anxiety signals to us that there are unknown aspects in our changing situation. Anxiety changes the shape of our bodies and the way we move them. Toxins build up, memory slows, cortisol is produced, and fat gathers around our middles. Cytokines give us flulike symptoms and mysterious aches and pains travel around our bodies. We often employ short-term solutions to ease the feeling in a moment rather than thinking of how to lessen the feeling long term. Raising a glass may numb the feeling, but research and action often provide the necessary ingredients to truly control the anxiety. Substance use, risk-taking, and long-range financial planning are all part of the same group of strategies—lowering anxiety.

On the other hand, it is possible that the outcome of the new situation will be in fact very good. What if we take a minute and imagine that even though there might be tension, the ultimate outcome might be positive? What if we rewrite anxiety as the feeling of adventure? It changes the dance. In order to change our lives, however, we must pass through the anxiety to the new understanding, the new way of being that waits on the other side.

GAINING A NEW LANGUAGE

The body is a site of knowledge and a force in memory, as our container/recorder and decoder of experience, undeniably connected to the meaning we make of the life we live. For therapeutic purposes the new avenues for embodied connection give rise to a need for a new language to express them. How are we going to speak to our bodies? How will they talk to us? As we gain more understanding of the way the body holds meaning for us, it becomes urgent that we consult our bodies to help us understand ourselves. Stories arise from the body, and are their way of speaking to us.

We live in an explosion of understanding about mind/body connections. Nuclear imaging, electrical measurement, X-rays, and other tools are connecting us with our bodies in ways we have never before imagined. Suddenly we can see where our brains light up when we dance, when we move, or when we meditate. We can look at the Dalai Lama's brain and see the differences. "There," we are told, "there's the place in his brain that is different, that makes him happier than us." For some these new images are the inspiration they need to understand the connection, something to *see* that can show a change. "If you meditate," we can say, "you will be able to make your brain look more like this one, the happy one."

When we learn, our whole body pitches in to help us absorb the lesson. The experiences of life shape our endocrine system, our organs, our brains, our skin. We learn how to "be" fully and holistically. Then we perform what we have learned. For days, weeks, years, decades, we repeat the performance. Over time some of our ways are successful, while others no longer work in a given situation, or appear not to generalize to life as we get older. Sometimes we resist this understanding, even in the face of mounting evidence that we are not only failing to manage a given situation, but even that we are creating more chaos around us by holding on to our behavior. Eventually, though, even in these cases, we consider making a change. The next question, then, is how? When we do want to change a way of being, we have to consider how to make this change in the same kind of holistic way in which it was formed. We cannot just make a change by talking about it; we need to act it out with our bodies, to create a new performance.

Many of the people who come to see us manifest the frustrations and challenges of life in symptoms of physical suffering. One of my clients was Alan. I had met Alan in our chronic pain group, and after a year in the group, he had decided that he would like a few one-on-one meetings. Alan was turning fifty. He hadn't worked for a long time. In addition to his chronic back pain, he suffered from type 2 diabetes, headaches, and neuropathy. After years in the construction industry, he had accepted that his pain meant he could no longer work. He walked with difficulty and slowly shut his body down. He told stories of unexplained aches, wandering pain, sudden bursts of energy like a shock to the nerves.

He had run the gauntlet of professionals who had been unable to determine what might be causing his pain. Now, he felt abandoned. He recounted the moment when the specialist finally told him he could do no more, avoiding eye contact and mumbling, not quite confronting Alan with his suspicion that he was somehow making this all up, that he was malingering and complaining to obtain drugs. He told us of the sense of abandonment and fear that pervaded that last meeting, as he was cast off, unfixed, an embarrassment to the practice and profession. He felt blamed, ridiculed. And whether consciously or not, he complied. He treated himself unkindly, remonstrating against his aches and pains, adding to the other stresses on his body. His body became the enemy, and he was literally at war with his physical self.

To our bodies we are severe and unforgiving. In our self-talk we scold and reprimand and speak angrily to the offending body part. Alan's conviction that he was fated to die in pain was profound. His task as he saw it was to try to be comfortable until the inevitable end. It had already cost him his marriage, and he was deteriorating quickly, relying on opiates to be comfortable and asking for more opiates as time went by and nothing changed. He talked often about his conviction that the antidote to his suffering as an embodied soul was mysterious, beyond his reach, and futile. Activity itself was suffering. If he could live without any at all it would make him happy. He said he found it nearly impossible to express his feelings about his situation and generally resorted to derisive language and cursing. He said he knew he could work on his anger, but he was not open to alternatives. A pill would make him feel better. He himself could not change.

In the chronic pain group Alan had found people who shared his experiences and felt similarly about their pain. He had benefited from the education offered and was beginning to accept that narcotics would not in fact decrease his pain, that in fact they could increase it through narcotic-induced hyperalgesia, a function of narcotic use, where the brain recruits extra brain areas to feel pain. In the group he had been exposed to motivating videos, stories of people who had made a comeback from chronic pain and disability. He had received information on the profound benefits offered by lifestyle changes, especially exercise.

I often have many ideas that I want to enthusiastically share with clients, but have learned that they don't always want to hear them. Besides asking the question, "What are we going to do together?" I also now ask, "What are you prepared to do to make the changes you want?" Often people will say that they will do anything, but once we start discussing more specifics, it turns out that the list of things they are actually prepared to do is quite small. I wanted to help Alan become kinder to himself, to change his language and speak to his injured body with more compassion. I thought that if he could, he would begin to be able to work to recover some of the abilities he had lost due to inactivity. I wanted him to consider that by working with the stories he was telling himself, we could begin to find a shift in his self-perception.

I started, though, by inviting him to rock.

Technique
•—•—•
BEGINNING TO MOVE

Inviting a client to begin moving as an exploration is not always easy. For many the idea of engaging with their physical body in such a way that they move it volitionally goes against everything they have been told about the pain in their bodies. For some, years of caution and fear have translated into moving as little as possible. Over time that contributes to awkwardness and difficulty with any physical movement, resulting in slow walking and standing, in turn leading to muscle atrophy, weight gain, and the attendant problems. The most important guide is to start where they are.

In Alan's case my intuition was that rocking was the appropriate motion for him. I had a rocking chair, an old sliding rocker that I had found abandoned. Its motion was so soothing that I fixed it up and began using it in my practice. After fixing me with a glare, waiting to see if I had some ulterior motive or was secretly making fun of him, he agreed to sit down in the rocker and began sliding back and forth.

Soon, he closed his eyes and began speaking. He told me how his relationship with his father was suffering. His dad needed help, and he was unable to provide much. His dad was a lean, ferociously independent French Canadian, and he scoffed at the idea that his son was physically unable to help him. Both men took offence. It was adding to Alan's pain. We let the idea sit in the air. I had no immediate solution or advice. We tend to believe that advice is for the advisor, not the advisee. It's usually redundant and almost always resented.

That day by the fire, Tom had told me that if you offer your tobacco to an elder, which is the polite way to ask for help or to ask a question, they might ponder for some time before answering. I experiment with this idea, with relieving myself of the burden of having to answer a question as soon as it is asked. So I had no immediate answer for Alan. Finally, he laughed and said, as if it were a complete novelty to think, "I guess I could talk to him."

I continued to work with Alan, always with movements that he found pleasing—dancing, rocking, some simple stretches, or the smooth movement of t'ai chi, which he found particularly soothing. Along with that we talked about communication. Gradually, Alan began experimenting with ways to express his needs and his feelings. Slowly, he began to wonder if he couldn't take more pleasure in his body. He began to lose weight, not, he said, because it was a good idea, but because it felt better to move. His self-reported aches and pains diminished, and he began to experience more good days.

ENTRANCE INTO
CULTURAL HEALING STORIES

Wherever we are we encounter speechless experience—those things that happen to people that cannot be put into words. They cannot be narrated. Edward Shorter has written about the templates that cultures develop for the expression of suffering that cannot otherwise be articulated.[1] Without these cultural templates, people suffer with no path toward resolution. Suffering that is not narrated cannot be expressed. We need a story into which to insert our misery. Cultures provide such stories. Some cultures have stories that are more compatible with healing, others, less.

North American mainstream culture seems to resound with stories for the expression of that which cannot be articulated, but they do not progress toward healing and transformation. These stories emphasize chronic disease for which there is little hope of improvement. At the end of the nineteenth century, paralysis provided that template. In the late twentieth century, fatigue became the operative template. Today, we have a new term: "medically unexplained symptoms." These become diagnosed in a variety of ways, such as chronic Lyme disease, fibromyalgia, chronic musculoskeletal pain syndromes, chronic fatigue syndrome, and more.

In these stories a heroic and valiant patient keeps butting heads against a recalcitrant medical system, looking for the few doctors who can understand his or her symptoms (these doctors are then often persecuted by the mainstream) and provide the radical, unconventional treatment needed to resolve the problem, which is often very expensive and often incomplete because the patient came too late to reap the full benefit.

Shorter describes how cultural stories define which classifications of suffering are legitimate and which are illegitimate. No one wants to have an illegitimate illness. In our work we find it most helpful to avoid the categorization of some types of suffering as trivial and others as valid. Suffering is suffering. Those who suffer do not suffer less when they are told that their suffering is "imaginary."

Shorter invokes the unconscious mind as a mediator between suffering and the legitimate expressions of suffering. We would prefer to say that this mediation is simply outside of conscious awareness, without requiring imaginary structures that cannot be found in the brain. So much is outside of our awareness so much of the time. Becoming aware is a heroic journey.

Many stories live in our bodies and are not yet ready to be put into story form. Every ache and pain has its own story, and every situation we find ourselves in, where our emotions are aroused, can be understood to live in our bodies. The more we can get to know these stories, the better we can get to know the things that are troubling us and begin a conversation with them. Sometimes these stories are told *only* at this embodied level. They never become fully articulated, but are worked entirely metaphorically. When we let the stories express themselves in images, sounds, and colors, we find their energetic dynamics and they can begin to make sense.

THE EMBODIED STORIES

The stories that we tell ourselves repeatedly are embodied phenomena. Our illness stories animate the ill body. When we tell these stories, to others or silently, we have physiological reactions as if we were right there inside the story and it were happening in the here and now. Even language arises from our bodies and represents a metaphor for our internal biological events. The language we use in talking about our bodies is complex. For some, physical pain is literally unspeakable. Sometimes, the pain and suffering that cannot be articulated or understood can speak better through a directly embodied approach.

More than that we are embedded in stories that inscribe their own marks on our physical being. Pains and hurts we acquire, as well as moments of joy, and social and cultural events and forces provide their own meaning to events in our lives. The little physical "me" in the flux of all these forces can be overwhelmed.

Rafael is a husband and father. He has lived with chronic pain for years now and has failed every test he has been offered that might elicit the cause. Now he is intensely frustrated because he's unable to do the work he used to do as a skilled tradesman. It has affected his temperament and is affecting his life. He's coming to see me because he doesn't like the way he is in the world. He has become angry and defensive, and he's barking at his wife and young daughter.

He is designated a person with a "mystery illness," someone whose symptoms defy diagnosis and about whom opinions begin to form in the community that there might be something psychological going on. Rafael still suffers from his fall from grace. An easygoing man, he has failed in multiple attempts to impress his wife with his ability to manage his world. Thanks to his condition, she has taken over more of the family duties and he feels "ordered around," underestimated, disenfranchised. Rafael fights back with a bad temper and a desire to simply avoid the conflict by becoming increasingly solitary.

We have been working on appropriate expressions of needs, on his reclaiming space in the relationship, on testing limits and rediscovering his abilities. As I listened to him, I learned that his work in life had been to build stone walls. We began to explore the character of the "wall builder." When the Wall Builder took on a life of his own, Rafael acknowledged that one of his other personas, who didn't get enough time, was a jolly bearded man who might be mistaken for Santa Claus! Rafael had an inner character who liked to make people happy.

Around this time Rafael surprised me one day when he volunteered to try "some of that movement stuff" I had been talking about.

Technique

•—•—•

MOVING

We start slowly with simple dynamics, encouraging people to become aware of their different levels of energy, to play with moving, high or low, smooth or staccato, heavy and light. We explore the nature of standing still and the nature of beginning to move, taking that first step. We play catch to build flexibility and spontaneity. In his book, *Free Play,* Nachmanovitch makes a connection between the spontaneity of improvisation and life. Improvisation teaches us to be responsive not reactive, to approach life with a "yes, and" attitude. We can improve life management, Nachmanovitch argues, when we can move between life's shades rapidly and playfully. Play helps us rehearse different stories, integrate information, and try out ways of being. It helps us shift domains of action and rehearse roles.[2]

Drama therapist David Read Johnson uses a method of embodied work called "developmental transformations," where the therapist and client engage in a form of play with each other. Johnson considers this an embodied practice that takes place in the play space.[3] He endows the body with philosophical meaning. To Johnson, the body is a function of our experience, and is what puts us in life—as he says, "It is the reason we can be found."[4] To him a critical aspect of developmental transformations is the constantly moving body. Through observing his clients' practices of embodiment, Johnson deduces their level of *disembodiment,* which he sees as a critical diagnostic element in his evaluation of their healing resources. The ability to embody is, to Johnson, a sign of good health and a means to good health. He cites four conditions of embodiment that are explored during the course of play: body as other (as you see me) occurs during "surface play," body as persona (individual) during "personal play," body as desire (as an instrument in goal achievement) during "intimate play," and body as presence (the body when it is simply allowed to be) during "deep play." In the therapeutic journeying of developmental transformations, the work flows through these states of embodiment, with the therapist aware of the resistances that present themselves in each of these physical conditions.[5]

With Rafael, I began with improvised movement. We started with some simple exercises, games where we threw a ball around. Rafael felt the different tones in his body—quick and slow, heavy and light, nimble and awkward. I threw the ball quickly and slowly, up high and down low. We moved on to having conversations with me chasing him, playing with the distance between us and the response he felt to that. What is too close? What is too far? All the while we talked. We played games where we had to respond while we had the ball then pass the ball as soon as possible.

Our lives are literally written in our bodies. To change we need to change the active practical aspects of our lives. Change is physically uncomfortable; it feels strange, like writing with the "wrong" hand. Overcoming that feeling of strangeness defines the therapeutic experience.

In Rafael's case, once he was comfortable with moving, we began to explore the energy of the Wall Builder, as well as the energies of other internal characters. By now, along with the Wall Builder and Santa, Rafael had discovered Jazz, a man who liked to move. Jazz had been dancing during our sessions, reporting on the "free" life he could be living.

Technique
•—•—•
MOVE FROM FEELING INTO IMAGERY

We use colors and shapes to give meaning to the dynamics of different movements. Rather than probing any kind of psychoanalytical meaning, we engage at the surface level, looking at the way people use space, how they keep pace, their rhythm and changes in energy. We look at how they move to create the negative space around them. Usually when people move, it helps to regulate their heart;

it begins to bring their feelings into order, to create a sense of peace, even if there is not yet understanding.

As a first exercise in our exploration of Wall Builder, we built a wall (of puppets, each "stone" representing someone in Rafael's life) and he practiced knocking it apart. This simple exercise reduced him to tears. Next, we moved into the Dance of the Wall Builder.

Rafael moved ponderously around the room, eventually coming to a standstill.

"What would it take to move that feeling to one of lightness?"

Rafael experimented with gentle differences. He moved his body, not worrying about the words, just seeing what happened when he changed the energy from the outside in.

"I feel locked in." Rafael suddenly looked up. "That's how I feel with my wife!"

We played with that metaphor, imagining the lock and then the key that might open it. He repeated a simple gesture of opening and began to make a connection. The feeling that he got when locking the door began to become more understandable, and he moved back and forth, in a dance of locking and unlocking, feeling the energy shift in his body.

The next week he reported that he was able to use the memory of that exercise to shift his own energy when he began to feel locked. In his mind he moved swiftly to "unlock." His wife had noticed a change. It wasn't perfect, he stressed, but it was a little better. He was trying to bring out Santa at dinnertime.

Rafael continued to explore. The ponderous Wall Builder filled him with longing, sadness, and heaviness. As he came to understand more about this character, he renamed that energy the Bear. In further explorations he named other energies he feels at different times—the Swan, the Goat, the Twisted Swallow. Something about naming them led to a further stage of clarification.

Technique

•—•—•

TURN PATTERNS INTO CHARACTERS

The different associations and actions involved in behaviors can be usefully considered as patterns that can be given their own identities. By giving an identity to the pattern, we turn it into a character. Then clients can engage with the character at a distance from themselves.

In Rafael's case, by understanding the Bear's needs, he could identify an unexplored element of his own needs. Sometimes it is easier for a person to allow a character to state what he or she needs than it is to state personal needs. Rafael could then find a way to allow the Bear to have some of his needs met. Rafael realized that the Bear wanted to be "somewhere else." He liked to be alone, to sleep, to breathe, to be in a dream state. Rafael began to "feed the Bear." Instead of waiting until his frustration peaked, he took himself off for a walk through the fields, to give the Bear some time alone.

Rafael began keeping a journal where he wrote down conversations between himself, the Bear, the Swan, and the Goat. Rather than always resisting the Bear's need for dream time, he began to understand that he had condemned this in himself, tried to avoid it, and become resentful and grumpy. He agreed to conduct an experiment, to see if it might improve things to give the Bear a little of what he wanted. He could not live in the dream world, but he could certainly be more accepting of the Bear and build some dream time into his day. He began creating times and places for brief meditations, smudging, taking a picture, and finding this helpful.

In embodied work we learn to "listen" to the impulses of our bodies. We "feel" our bodies wanting to move a certain way. We gather and project impulses. We charge our bodies with characterizations and roles. A physical block or property invites us to loosen it or contain it or to form a shape, using it as its impulse or center. We intuit and ascribe meaning to these impulses and the ways of movement and shape in which they guide us. This approach arouses curiosity about how this relates to the way we construct meaning for ourselves in the sense of modern psychology.

There are traditions of embodied discovery. Feminist literature has long considered the impact of prescriptions on the bodies of women. Butoh dance theorists talk about discovering selves by following the impulses of the body.[6] Keri Brandt uses the way women communicate with horses to consider the connection between such communication and "embodied subjectivity."[7] Some work is giving increasing value to a discussion of proprioception, the way we "know" our bodies, the body's complex contribution to development of ourselves, and of the way we interact with the world.[8]

UNDERSTANDING THE MIND/BODY CONNECTION

Ideas of embodied mind refer to a "new" understanding that our mind and bodies cannot be seen as separate entities.[9] The idea has certainly arisen in recent literature that there is some value in therapies that involve working physically with this possibly fundamental aspect of our meaning-making structure. Various somatic therapies are becoming recognized for their effectiveness, and techniques that have long been part of the therapeutic toolbox are gaining credibility. Role-play, "sculpts" (taking a pose that represents a feeling), improvisation, movement and dance, ceremony—all these techniques are welcomed again in the therapist's office.

Action Therapy, a recent book written by Wiener and Oxford for the American Psychological Association (APA), provides instructions for even the most conventional therapists on how to use creative embodiment in their practice, to help "accommodate those who are visual or kinaesthetic processors, provide sense-based recall of experience, provide a different perspective on the issue at hand, assist in the understanding of 'intangibles,' provide a method for experimentation with new roles and behaviors, and a means of approaching problems indirectly, through metaphor, which can assist in expressing difficult concepts and formalizing client's transitions (through ceremony)."[10]

Dance is one such "action method," which I used with Sharon, a client who came to me after the death of her mother in a traffic accident.

Technique
• — • — •
DANCE WITH A FEELING

Some clients are not ready to articulate their suffering in words, and it may be some time before they are. Movement work can allow them to begin to connect with the "something" that they are experiencing at a safe distance, which they control. We invite them to locate a sensation in their body and begin to physically explore it, without worrying about definitions and words. Or we suggest that they write down any colors, images, that they may find. If they are ready, we try writing a poem with the images that emerge and see if it connects to them.

Though very young, Sharon left home very early and fell into the trap of substance use. She had recently been to jail for carrying drugs for her girlfriend. She told me at first that she never knew when she felt anything and didn't recognize her emotions. She had deeply conflicted feelings about her mother, who did not protect her from abuse by her uncle. Sharon came to me from a halfway house, a step down from jail so that she could work with her maintenance and recovery programs.

I told Sharon that it was not necessary to name her feelings or to know much about them, that we could just move. Sharon found a movement, repetitive. She began to allow it to travel through her body. I invited her to begin a dialogue with the feeling, through the movements of her body, to allow the different rhythms to play off against each other, to feel a correspondence in her body parts. I invited her to let me know, or not, if she saw colors, or shapes, or heard sounds or words. Or to just move.

This is a way we can use to explore the map of Sharon's consciousness. The elusive fragments and images are like marks on a page, which can eventually be connected with a story, a pathway through life's events that arrives at a destination of meaning. It will take some time before the pieces of life come together to make meaning for Sharon, and my role is to support her journey toward this.

Psychologist Eugene Gendlin must be mentioned here, for his work in "Focusing," a way to explore feelings nonverbally, although he may not have been the originator of the idea that feelings can be elusive and may not be readily available to conscious awareness. Suffering speaks in metaphors, some more literal than others. Our minds can produce physical sufferings that are no less real than if we had broken a bone or suffered a lesion.[11]

More and more the mind/body connection is being recognized in medicine. It used to be hard to persuade people to think that way. Medicine took comfort in being able to provide physical solutions to physical problems. Now, as we turn to an increasingly mysterious set of ailments—wandering pain, unexplained fatigue, physical symptoms that come and go—we increasingly find that it is not so easy to map symptoms with corresponding solutions. The more we study twenty-first century ailments like stress and systemic exhaustion, the more we find people turning outside the canon to look for clues for how to provide relief to their clients.

One of the newest ways of understanding our bodies is to contemplate embodiment in the context of epigenetics. Life's experiences literally change our bodies. Structures in our brains change shape. Biochemical responses alter, depending on the way we respond to the world around us.

The language of embodiment seems to refer either to the literal, in terms of movement, or to the elusive nature of the body, in metaphorical terms. This latter is, of course, a function of technologies of perception. Creative arts therapist Daria Halprin suggests that we look to postures, sensations, and gestures as signs of our "history and current ways of being . . . [that indicate the] . . . themes and patterns of our life"—that is, as a literal metaphor for our psychology.[12] Trauma specialist Babette Rothschild writes about the importance of treating the body's encoded meanings in PTSD sufferers, and proposes a body that transcribes suffering in a complex way that we can reach for but that still eludes complete understanding.[13] Social and transcultural psychiatrist Lawrence Kirmayer, who has for many years discussed indigenous ideas of healing, remarks on the shamanic use of metaphor in healing, theorizing that the strong emotional and sensory relationship we have to the metaphor provides an energy of transformation.[14]

Technique
•—•—•
AUTHENTIC MOVEMENT

In this technique clients can explore the relationship between life events and their physical self. We start by inviting them to imagine an unfinished conversation, or a chronic pain, or chronic anxiety. Then we suggest: "Close your eyes and feel where it lives in the body. Make a sculpture of your body in the way it would be shaped if that feeling were in charge. Now move with that feeling, and sound the way that feeling would sound." "Authentic movement" is a term used by Mary Starks Whitehouse to describe this way of encouraging people to move as directed by interior guidance.[15]

I used this technique with another client, Alice, who is thirty-five years old and frustrated by her inability to "have a life of her own." With talent and a commitment to work, she has somehow never sustained her own living place, routine, or profession. She comes to see me as often as she can, frequently trying to stay longer than her appointment, disappointed if I can't see her outside of office hours. She often tells me that she is desperate for an appointment and then when I offer her one, she refuses it, saying she has something better to do. She is almost entirely unable to articulate her feelings, but says that she feels "stressed" whenever she is asked anything. She talks nonstop.

In one session, after letting her vent a little while, I invited her to breathe and to stop talking. We stood up. I said, "You have a rush of anxious thoughts. Close your eyes and feel where it is they occur in your body. Where in your body do you feel the same feeling as you do when you think those thoughts? Now, shape your body the way it would be if that feeling was in charge." Alice shaped her body into a "C," with her legs bent and her arms swinging loosely by her side. It seemed that this feeling was droopy, slack, not able to grip very hard, and could barely stand up. "Now move that feeling around the room," I suggested. Alice had done this before, and she knew the drill. She began moving around the room, turning from side to side, sometimes swinging her arms with the motion of her torso.

"Now, see if it has a sound. Maybe even a phrase." Alice let herself fall to the floor, her arms flopping, and began mumbling under her breath. She turned a somersault.

"Let the movement guide you. Let your body tell you what to do."

Alice danced with the feeling, swaying and jerking, lost in an interior world. She moved slowly, quickly, high up, low down, sometimes smoothly, sometimes with staccato motions.

When Alice started working with me, she barely moved, just looked at the ground and giggled. Even if she closed her eyes, or I left the room, she still didn't make a connection. But something in the process worked for her, and she kept at it. Now, when she moves the way her body wants her to, she feels some kind of peace. Alice now goes weekly to a local authentic movement group. She knows where all the dance possibilities are in her town, and drops in to the studio when she feels the need for some kinetic self-expression. With her dancing she has embodied exploration, release of energy, good deep breathing, and community.

EMBODIED STORYTELLING

We are looking at a new role for the centrality of our bodies in meaning-making. It has long been observed that the way we know our world begins with our physical exploration, moves on to symbolic representations and imagery, then finally to language. These were considered evolutionary steps, with language proceeding from reason, as a hierarchical pinnacle of meaning-making.[16] However, cognitive science professor Tom Ziemke, who studies the way our bodies are involved in meaning-making in our cognitive and emotional interface with the world, takes a more holistic approach. In his words we develop a "body schema," a system involving sensory (external) information, proprioception (sense of ourselves as embodied), and vestibular information (sense of ourselves in space).[17] We then use this schema to process information in the world in terms of the meaning it has for us as experienced by our physical selves.

Technique
•—•—•
PERFORMING LIFE IN A DIFFERENT WAY (A SMALL SOCIAL EXPERIMENT)

We suggest little experiments with different physical energies to help to inspire shifts. When we change the way we feel physically, we can change the way we are in the world. Of course these are small changes, but they introduce a new feeling into us and can begin to write a new "code" into our embodied selves. Small things—changing clothes, gait, observing facial expression and seeing if we can change it, changing our posture, carrying a lighter load, changing what we carry with us all day—these small things can offer a different perspective.

Sue Jennings's E.P.R. process (embodiment, projection, role) seems to support Ziemke's model of physical schema development. She agrees that our first developmental step in understanding our world is through our bodies, not in discrete stages, but in a continuum of meaning-making.[18] We do not leave behind physical exploration and move on to other sorts. Rather, we become very sophisticated at physical knowing. To Jennings this initial physical engagement creates our "body-self," a critical ground that we use as a foundation for our body image. We move on from there to a stage where we use things in the world as symbols of things that mean something to us (a typical example is to consider the use of a stuffed animal or blanket as a proto-mother). The final stage happens when we understand that our "selves" are fluid and under our control and that we can be flexible with our embodiment and undertake different roles.[19]

Some pathologies relate to the incapacity to maintain this flexibility, resulting in our inability to adapt our roles (or personas) to the situation, a situation that may have its ground in an early problem with the embodied or the projection stage. Therapists may work to help a person break out of this stasis and begin to be able to embody different roles.[20] The process of reembodying, or reenacting (or rerepresenting)—otherwise described as behavioral activation—is likely a reliving or awakening of those early meaning-making strategies. We can wonder if multilevel meaning is, in fact, made possible only through a *combination* of thought and embodied representation. This would work both ways—not only are our bodies involved in our meaning-makings, on conscious or unconscious levels (or perhaps both), but conceivably, in order to prompt changes in those meanings, it might be that the embodied approach is not just useful but necessary.

Rolf Zwaan has found that perception, motor language, and verbal language must work together to allow us to form abstract representations.[21] Apparently, we awaken our sensory system in specific ways by taking physical shapes that have meaning to us[22]—in other words we code experiences into our bodies, and by embodying we make meaning—and without our bodies, we cannot properly make abstract meaning.

Drama therapist Roger Grainger considers that not only are our bodies the experiencers, but they become our cultural inter-relaters, the means with which we engage all the conditions of culture. He comments: "Ideology . . . is inseparable from the bodily experience of persons."[23] Failing to consider this deeper nature of embodiment means that we relate to our bodies only as representations. According to him, "bodies, it seems, have difficulty in remaining themselves without becoming ideas."[24] He is suggesting that we have a culturally constructed body that can exist separately from our ideas about it, but that we tend away from knowing this embodied self as such.

In some ways he intuits this essential body based on his ideas about art and the artistic process. He suggests that our bodies process cultural ideas and then emit them as artifacts—literally as art. He suggests we think of art as the "sign language" of culture, with all signs emergent from our bodies. Presumably, then, what is left behind after we "throw off" the art is the embodied self, as a collection of experiences and meanings. It is this self in Grainger's terms that we must come to know. The work, "offers an experience that connects the past and future to the present through the embodied exploration of a moment in time. This examination of life as lived in space and time in turn gives us access to embodied truth."[25] Grainger believes that drama therapy gets its force from seeing individual concerns in this socio-cultural construction.

This leads us to the idea that emerges from an increasing understanding of the neuropsychology of narrative, that when we hear or tell stories, we engage virtually all the major areas of our brain.[26] Zwaan reports that, based on the way we move and look when we tell stories, our bodies are also strongly involved in narrative construction and that this physical and spatial dimension is critical to recall. We tell stories both verbally and physically, because the energy of the story is resident in our bodies. Grainger seems to pursue those same lines of thinking when he says that observations of our bodies "give our narratives the immediacy of experiences that precede thoughts. . . . Our body constitutes our main evidence as to our real, personal participation in a state of affairs where so much remains contingent."[27] Our bodies tell us the story of being there.

Technique
•—•—•
HEIGHTENING AWARENESS
OF EMBODIED STORYTELLING

Learn a story by heart! You can tell a story from your past or a story from literature. Practice telling this story to others. See how the gestures you use change as you tell it to different audiences. It can be a small story or a long story. Allow it to transform while it is being told. How does it change the way you relate to your own body?

This embodied storytelling was present when our client Ella undertook to tell history. Embodied storytelling in this case meant literally or metaphorically acting out events so as to discover more details about the subjective impact of trauma. This happened during a workshop where we explored suffering and trauma in embodied ways. It was a weeklong retreat in a remote part of Vermont. The clients had all experienced trauma and most were diagnosed with some kind of psychiatric disorder.

Ella was a woman who lived in remote northern Vermont. She identified as two-spirited and as a Métis woman, though she had little connection to her community. She had suffered from unbearable trauma as a child and had been beaten and assaulted. Now, she lived in a shelter some of the time or in a series of cars given to her by her brother who was a mechanic. She seldom spent a night inside. She had been diagnosed with PTSD, trauma, and dissociative identity disorder. She first asked us to promise that we were not trying to get rid of any of the personalities that inhabited her body. We created a ceremony to establish this boundary and to bless and purify the place where we would be working.

> ### Technique
> •—•—•
> #### SACRED PERFORMANCE AND CEREMONY
> We do this kind of work late in a workshop, when the group has had a chance to form. We work to create a space of radical acceptance, where we agree to accept whatever is asked of us by the writer/director and follow their lead in what happens. We treat the space as very sacred. Within that space anything can happen. We agree to go with whatever happens.

Ella asked me to go with her for the lunch hour. We wandered around the area, eventually finding a large empty dirt lot, where Ella found a bone. She had been trained as a tracker, and soon she had a group of bones gathered. This prompted memories in her of her childhood, and by the time we returned to the group, she had decided to work on the pain she suffered daily from many episodes in the past where her bones had been broken and not properly healed. Because of that she had many severe pains and issues with dislocation of joints and limbs.

> ### Technique
> •—•—•
> #### OFFER A STORY OUTLINE
> We usually start a storytelling by inviting people to come up with a hero, obstacles, helpers, the attitude of the hero, and the goal of the hero. We invite people to think of one illustrative scene and two possible endings. This takes away the panic that some people feel about creating a story. Some people worry that they will not be able to think of anything or have a belief that they are not creative. Having a story outline enables people to just fill in the blanks, without the pressure of creating a masterpiece. We invite people to rely on their intuition and to cultivate radical acceptance of their own ideas, not to question or judge them. Sometimes people will create

a scene using the energies or identities that they have worked with, and often they will portray the characters as animals.

Ella decided that the heroic character would be Coyote. She also decided that she would watch and invited me to be narrator. She cast Coyote, three animals who had committed the violence against her, and then three to stand as three of her broken body parts: the jaw bone, the rib bone, and the backbone. As people improvised the work, I narrated, following her suggestions.

Coyote, who in her story was male, suffered from unbearable pain because he had survived so much violence. Coyote's body had been broken in fights with a monster spirit who entered into the other animals in the community when they were vulnerable. Each time Coyote was pulverized by the animal possessed by the monster spirit, but each time one bone remained. Thanks to the spirit of rage, Coyote was able to fight back and Creator helped him to re-create himself from that one bone and thus come back to life. By the end of the story, there were many Coyotes living inside one body, each struggling for space. This explained the suffering, and the fact that many of Ella's bones slid in and out of place—they were vying for space with the other Coyote bodies.

Meanwhile, Ella/Coyote discovered as a revelation that there was yet another body, that of a stillborn baby, a child of rape. With the group's help, Ella was able to perform a ceremony where those bones were extracted, and properly put to rest. In this ceremony all the animals (the other workshop members) gathered together to carry the little body up to the stars. Ella had never been able to mourn for the stillborn child. When it was born, the midwife took it from her and wouldn't let her hold it, and she had always carried a lot of guilt because her feelings about the baby were complicated and unclear.

The discoveries Ella made during this exercise impacted her for many years, and she was finally able to sleep inside. As of writing she lives in a small cabin on the edge of a forest, where she happily contributes to a community garden. She is in a relationship that she enjoys. She has reconnected with community, and she has written her story, recognizing the multiple social forces that helped construct her as she was. She has bad days from time to time but is able to keep them at bay.

THE TRANSFORMATIVE VALUE
OF ROLE-PLAY

Drama therapy practitioners like Phil Jones consider that an individual's relationship with his or her body is fundamental to his or her identity and that it is through bodywork that transformation takes place. Jones believes that training and rehearsal in role-play allows us to overcome inhibitions and to open up our language of embodied communication. Taking on the physicality of another identity, either a person or other being, encourages us to explore and possibly expand our range of behaviors and feelings.[28] As therapist Richard Courtney suggests, using our bodies therapeutically allows us to reflect on an event by reconstituting it, more than just remembering it.[29]

More, our bodies can enter into another level of exploration through role-play of other characters, the coded physical language of metaphor. Linguistic cognitive scholars Lakoff and Johnson consider that embodied understanding is critical to the formation of abstract concepts, which to them are metaphorical. One of the ways we engage with metaphor is through storytelling and making and engaging in role-play.[30] The idea that there might be physiological benefit in the way we form our bodies contributes to the idea that it is of value to embody archetypes and other forms, and to enact ritual activities, in order to engage metaphorically with those realms of our consciousness and remake the meanings of events in our lives. Shaping our bodies has been attributed in other literatures to creating a kind of portal to another consciousness, akin to shape-shifting.[31]

All these ideas presuppose that changing the meaning in our bodies, changing our actions and performances, we can change the coded information on multiple levels and therefore change the state of our beings and allow for a release from suffering. By changing the meanings, we change the hurt, and we need our bodies to change the meanings. Embodiment through role-play is seen as a way to change meaning because it allows for the investigation of other ways of perceiving a situation and the embodied experience of that perception.

Technique
•—•—•
TELLING OUR OWN STORY:
WRITING OUT THE PARTS

Try writing out the parts you play in life. What parts are given to you? Which ones are forced upon you? Which ones do you reject? Are there ones that you think you "should" play? Invite one of the parts you play to take the lead in a heroic story. Write the story in the third person. Do this multiple times with multiple roles, and see what new perspectives emerge.

Technique
•—•—•
TELLING OUR OWN STORY:
PRACTICE TELLING THE STORY TO OTHERS

See how the gestures change as the story is heard by different audiences. It can be a small story or a long story. Allow it to transform while it is being told. See how it changes the way you relate to your own body.

When we work narratively, we activate the body by virtue of activating the mind and its meaning-making structures. To perform our illness, to embody a new reality, is to begin to encode that reality and those behavioral possibilities in our psyches. Movement can be more revealing and therefore more frightening than speaking, as we have not had time to process the information. When we articulate something by speaking, we have gone over the information until its meaning can be found in words. When we move we express ourselves in a different way. Our bodies allow us to experiment with self, with transformation and connection. We can attempt new realities, explore possible worlds.

Our bodies tell us stories. Physical presence is complicated. Our bodies exclaim and lash out. Every injury has a voice to add to the clamor. The stories that our bodies tell can be confoundingly different from the ones we understand with our minds. Our uneasy relationship with biology and the early predilection of therapies to make a firm separation between body and mind have created this rift. Our bodies reveal things we wish to keep hidden. Casual movements, ways of anchoring ourselves, how we touch the ground, our posture, the weight we carry, and how we carry it, are all revelatory.

To become aware we must step back, reflect, and tell our stories to others while listening all the while. Through repetitive cycles of reflection and retelling, we develop a meta-story about our story, which manifests as awareness. This is what happened with all the people described in this chapter. They developed awareness and changed their stories.

Conclusion

This book contains selected stories of healing interventions to illustrate some techniques that we use in our practice. We in no way have presented a comprehensive review of individual cases from start to finish, but rather select moments in treatment to illustrate techniques. Each encounter with a client is a new beginning, and our goal is to work collaboratively to help our clients discover for themselves the healing approaches that will work best for them. There are many pathways on the journey to change.

In writing this book, we aimed to show how we work with clients using narrative methods in a way that listens to the body, that takes into account the deeply healing value and importance of the fundamentally social nature of human experience and the human mind, and rests upon what is good about conventional practice. We use biologically active treatments in ways that are conventional, but we suggest that the over-reliance on pills is detrimental and that other healing work needs to be done as well to bring about recovery and change.

We do not accept the mind-body split. We approach the misery that manifests as physical with the same zest and methods as the misery that some say is psychological. As we are fond of letting people know, the anterior cingulate cortex can't always tell whether the source of pain is emotional or physical; it sees all pain as one. We work to help people activate their own self-healing mechanisms, through a commitment to food, sleep, and breath as medicines and through an exploration of multiple dimensions of human experience using dance, movement, story, enactment, and community. We advocate meditation, exercise, and journaling. We invite clients to contribute to the chart notes with any writing they wish.

We support the idea that the person is the expert on his or her own experience. In this book we have provided some useful tools, techniques, and ideas to inspire other clinicians and those who suffer to find new pathways toward recovery.

We often begin with the life story and are fond of the "Life Story Interview" of Dan McAdams from Northwestern University. This interview format can easily be adapted to one done by the client as a writing exercise or done with the client as an interview. It's helpful to the clinician to know people's high points, their low points, their turning points, times when they were heroic, and times when they overcame obstacles. It is equally helpful for each of us to gain such perspectives about ourselves. Just reflecting upon one's life story starts the healing process since it provides a historical perspective, a sense of identity that extends backward and potentially forward in time. Our goal is always to build more self-agency into that character.

We work to create a positive expectation in our clients, that they will improve and that something will work, no matter how long it takes. We firmly believe that change will happen so long as people keep coming and stay engaged in the dialogue, even if at times none of us have a clue what to do. It's through the ongoing dialogue that ideas emerge. We have observed that contemporary medicine and its practitioners more often take more advantage of the nocebo effect than the placebo. Patients are highly susceptible to negative suggestions, especially when it involves a severe disease or condition, and often it is the treating physician who provides the negative.

We invite our colleagues to monitor the words coming from their mouths. We advocate learning hypnosis if only to become aware of the barrage of negative suggestions that we spew forth to patients all day long. We invite us all to change the culture of health care from the office visit forward, to create the welcoming, nonjudgmental healing environment that people need to thrive. Our elders caution us against thinking that any of us own healing. Rather, they tell us, our job is to provide a safe space for healing to take place. That is what we work to do.

Much of the rationale for our work comes from neuroscience. The leap from the laboratory to the consulting room often offers ideas to inspire people to believe that they can change and recover. The idea of mind maps and remapping the mind is central to much of our work. Our minds are extraordinary worlds, as evidenced by our dreams. We are guided by inspirations from Mikhail Bakhtin, Hubert Hermans, and indigenous elders to think about our minds being occupied by avatars or characters that we construct to manage our relationships with actual people in our lives and some characters who are more extraordinary— God, Coyote, Moses, Allah, a variety of mythical beings, animal spirits, and many more. These inner characters become metaphors for heroic journeys that our clients are making toward recovery, and their stories can be related in the form of plays, writing, poems, and conversations.

We work with a process of negotiation with these avatars so as to minimize friction within the mind and then with mind–external world interface. Through these activities we aim to move the identity narrative toward one of greater self-agency and empowerment, which is what helps people to recover. When we mind map, we grant full ontological status to each of the avatars we encounter. This means that all the characters in our mind are granted full validity as independent beings. We find this works equally well for people with mental illness who hear voices as for the most tightly wound, conservative skeptics. This helps people build better theories of mind. The better we can represent our own and others' mental states, the easier it is for us to get around in the world. The more complete and empathetic our models of others are, the less friction we have with the social world around us.

As with all of Lewis's books, we draw on his understanding about healing from his indigenous background. In forty years as a physician, his focus has been to treat people instead of illnesses, to work within the patient's story about how the illness emerged and what will make it better, to form mutually rewarding and collaborative relationships with people and their communities, and to explore how healing can occur within this context. He understands that to heal we need community and that we may need to acknowledge our spiritual connections to nature and our ancestors, to reach out daily, and to acknowledge that faith and spiritual help are also key ingredients in healing.

Areas of the Brain Prominent in Understanding and Producing Story

Recent advances in neuroscientific research, especially those aided by functional magnetic resonance imaging (fMRI), provide a solid underpinning for the narrative work we are doing. Across a number of imaging studies on narrative comprehension, there is relatively good convergence of findings. Here are two summaries of the discoveries made so far, the first from the point of view of the areas of the brain and the second from the point of view of the specific functions of "storying," linking them to the brain areas that perform those functions.

WHAT ROLES DO PARTICULAR AREAS OF THE BRAIN PLAY?

When the current state of the imaging literature is considered along with lesion and patient research, it is possible to pinpoint some neural substrates of narrative processes and subprocesses. In the summary here, rarely activated structures are grouped in broader categories (e.g., subcortical activations), areas with no activations are omitted (e.g., medial temporal), and in some cases categories are collapsed to ease interpretation (e.g., middle temporal gyrus and sulcus).

Medial Prefrontal Cortex

Both comprehension and production are associated bilaterally with the medial prefrontal cortex. Based on the available imaging research, it appears that ordering and selection processes engage this area and are likely partially responsible for the shared activations observed. The medial prefrontal cortex is also likely responsible for sponsoring another narrative subprocess, namely theory of mind (the idea that other people have minds similar to ours and that we can infer their beliefs and desires from their behavior). There is theoretical support for the idea that mental inferencing plays a role in narrative processing and evidence for the engagement of this cortical area during theory-of-mind tasks.

Lateral Prefrontal Cortex

Lateral prefrontal activation for narrative understanding and expression appears largely right-hemispheric, corroborating studies of patients who have experienced damage in this area. This region of cortex, particularly the dorsolateral portion (Brodmann's areas 6 and 8), appears to be important for the ordering of events within a narrative. Consistent with this idea, other theorists have associated this area with cross-temporal ordering[1] and the working-memory processes that likely underlie this process.[2]

The lateral prefrontal cortex may also be involved in other working-memory functions, such as cue-maintenance for long-term memory retrieval. Although this region of cortex has been associated with episodic memory retrieval, the activations observed during narrative processes appear to be posterior to those associated with such retrievals.[3] Some evidence suggests that the motor cortex is also activated when we understand stories. Mental simulation of the actions depicted within the story may be responsible, particularly if the story is self-oriented. The fundamentally goal-centered nature of stories is a good match for the many goal-based functions attributed to the frontal lobes. These include (1) forming and executing plans for action, (2) keeping our goal in working memory, and (3) organizing speech, behavior, and logic in time.[4]

Increased activity in the lateral prefrontal cortex, the dorsal anterior cingulate cortex, the thalamus, and the cuneus is associated with increased activity in the executive control network regions and decreased activity in the default mode areas (story brain), including the ventromedial prefrontal cortex, the posterior cingulate cortex, and the insula.[5]

Temporo-parietal Region

Story comprehension and story production are associated bilaterally with a region at the juncture of the temporal and parietal lobes. Event-ordering activations are also found in this area, although there is no evidence from lesion work that this area is necessary for the successful execution of this process. Furthermore, some imaging researchers have concluded that temporal areas are not uniquely engaged during such tasks. A more likely candidate process for this region is the attribution of mental states. Along with the medial prefrontal cortex, the temporo-parietal junction is one of the most frequently identified cortical regions for mental inferencing.

The competing possibility that this area is responsible for basic language functions is rendered less likely when we compare the observed activations to those depicted in a meta-analysis of lower-level language processing.[6] Temporal lobe regions linked to simple semantic processing do not appear to overlap with those observed for story processes. It is possible, however, that the temporo-parietal junction is related to some aspect of sentence or cross-sentential processing, as others have theorized.[7]

This temporo-parietal junction area is crucial in understanding sentences and pictures. It is included in a common network that includes the middle and inferior frontal gyri, the parahippocampal-retrosplenial complex, the anterior and middle temporal gyri, and the inferior parietal lobe. A technique called DTI tractography allows us to see the white matter tracts that come from this temporo-parietal area and reveals a network reaching into the temporal pole, the ventral frontal pole, and the premotor cortex.

A significant correlation has been found between the density of this pathway and the imageability of sentences for individual subjects, suggesting a potential functional link between comprehension and the temporo-parietal connectivity strength. This may represent a "meaning" network that includes components of systems for semantic memory, embodied simulation, and visuospatial scene representation. This network substantially overlaps with the default mode or story network implicated as part of a core network of semantic representation, along with brain systems related to the formation of mental models and reasoning. These data are consistent with a model of real-world situational understanding that is highly embodied. The neural basis of this embodied understanding is not limited to sensorimotor systems, but extends to the highest levels of cognition, including autobiographical memory, scene analysis, mental model formation, reasoning, and theory of mind.[8]

Anterior Temporal Region including Temporal Poles

All of the story processes and subprocesses that have been examined are involved bilaterally with the anterior temporal lobes including the temporal pole (Brodmann's area 38). Although activations associated with ordering and selection are found here, no evidence from brain-damaged patients indicates that this region is necessary for such functions. In conjunction, temporal areas may not be uniquely involved with ordering according to the available imaging research. Conversely, lesion evidence demonstrating narrative comprehension impairments following damage to this area does exist, implying that the poles support some other necessary process.

Two likely candidates are theory of mind and the concatenation of sentences or propositions; both abilities have been associated with the temporal poles and appear necessary for story processing. Although no activations associated with narrative production fall directly within the polar region, production does appear to be related to areas just slightly posterior. As with the temporo-parietal region discussed above, comparison with a meta-analysis of language activations reveals that this area is not involved in simple language processing.[9]

Posterior Cingulate Cortex

Comprehension and production are associated bilaterally with the posterior cingulate, and this common activation is not attributable to selection or ordering processes. A variety of functions could lie within this area, as it has been tied to the association of new information with schemas or prior knowledge, visuospatial imagery, episodic retrieval, and the emotional modulation of memory processes. The latter three possibilities all seem congruent with the concept of autonoetic awareness, a self-experiencing of oneself in fictional stories, which likely involves imagery and episodic memory processes that are emotional in nature. This area may be directly involved in the simulation aspect of story processing, in which we imbue comprehension and production with realistic elements such as personal experience and related imagery.

Affective theory of mind, in contrast, involves a neural network comprising prefrontal cortical structures, as well as smaller regions in the posterior cingulate cortex and the basal ganglia.[10]

General Discussion

A number of brain structures are consistently activated during particular story processes. These brain areas appear to be unique to narrative processing, different from those identified for word and even sentence-level operations. Imaging studies that employ rigorously controlled stimuli and control conditions reveal that story-processing activations are not the same as those for sentence processing.[11] Many aphasics appear to have intact story level abilities despite gross syntactic impairments.[12] Both lines of evidence, imaging and patient, indicate the importance of right hemisphere areas in sharp contrast to the traditional portrayal of left lateralized language processes (i.e., Broca's and Werniche's areas). Lastly, when compared to a recent review of the imaging literature, it is clear that the full pattern of activation for narrative processes differs from those for attention, imagery, word recognition and production, working memory, episodic encoding and retrieval, and semantic retrieval.[13]

OUTLINE SUMMARY: AREAS OF THE BRAIN AND NARRATIVE FUNCTIONS

Frontal Lobe

1. Maintains global coherence and tracking relationships among distant clauses within a story
2. Remembers information over relatively long periods of time, supported by the continued firing of neurons following the removal of the eliciting stimuli[14]
3. Bilateral frontal areas activated with fictional imagery[15]
4. Right side—apparent episodic buffer—integrates, manipulates, and maintains complex information from all the sensory modalities,[16] models hypothetical situations,[17] and modulates attention to achieve integration (through the selective and organized recruitment of other cortical areas)

Prefrontal Cortex*

1. Left side—associated with autobiographical memory[18]
2. Lateral area—part of a core network also extended to the medial prefrontal, the lateral part of the temporal cortex, and to areas of the occipital cortices involving autobiographical memory and theory of mind
3. Ventral areas—maintain the phonological loop and a visuospatial sketchpad[19]

---

*The prefrontal cortex exerts control over behavior by biasing the salience of memories and adjudicating among competing, context-dependent rules. According to D'Esposito and Postle, in their article published in *Psychology,* "The Cognitive Neuroscience of Working Memory," the "control of the controller" emerges from a complex interplay between the prefrontal cortex and striatal circuits and ascending dopaminergic neuromodulatory signals.

Dorsolateral Prefrontal Cortex (BA 6, 8, 9, and 46)*

1. Processes across time and across the sensory modalities, needed for understanding a story[20]

2. Linked to manipulation of information consistent with central executive function[21]

3. Area 8 only on the left side activates when stories with characters who have mental states are compared to stories without characters with mental states

Mid-dorsolateral Prefrontal Cortex (BA 9 and 46 Only)

1. Monitors and manipulates the contents of working memory (Brodmann's areas 9, 46)

2. Encodes and retrieves episodic and autobiographical memories[22]

3. Right side supports the ordering of events in time and the processing of sequential information[23]

Ventrolateral Frontal Cortex (BA 47)

1. Specifies and maintains cues for long-term memory retrieval and encoding

2. Encodes and retrieves episodic and autobiographical memories[24]

3. Part of an emotional empathy circuit that also includes the amygdalae, the insula, the superior temporal cortex, and the inferior prefrontal gyrus[25]

---

*According to findings of Martins, Simard, and Monchi, in their *Plos One* article, "Differences between Patterns of Brain Activity," young adults show increased activity in the dorsolateral prefrontal cortex, the ventrolateral prefrontal cortex, the fusiform gyrus, the ventral temporal lobe, and the caudate nucleus during semantic decisions, and in the posterior Broca's area (area 44), the temporal lobe (area 37), the temporoparietal junction (area 40), and the motor cortical regions during phonological decisions. On the other hand, older individuals show increased activity in the dorsolateral prefrontal cortex and motor cortical regions during both semantic and phonological decisions; in older individuals, the semantic and phonological routes seem to merge into a single pathway. These findings seem to represent neural reserve/compensation mechanisms, characterized by a decrease in specificity, on which the elderly rely to maintain an adequate level of performance.

Ventromedial Frontal Cortex (BA 11, 13, and 25)

1. Rejects the products of memory retrieval
2. Encodes and retrieves episodic and autobiographical memories[26]

Ventromedial Prefrontal Cortex

1. Part of the default mode network of the brain[27]
2. Mediates mentalizing or theory of mind, person perception, and representation of self-knowledge[28]

Anterior Prefrontal Cortex (BA 10)

1. Accepts the products of memory retrieval[29]
2. Encodes and retrieves episodic and autobiographical memories[30]

Medial Prefrontal Cortex*

1. Theory of mind area; involved in the attribution of mental states to characters in stories[31]
2. Encodes and retrieves episodic and autobiographical memories[32]
3. Integrates self-referencing memory into an autobiographical narrative (impaired in autism)[33]
4. Left side activates when stories about characters with motives (theory of mind) are compared to stories about physical objects (physical stories)

---

*The medial prefrontal cortex is a crucial part of a paralimbic network of self-awareness. When experiences become meaningful to the self, they are linked to synchronous activity in this network, which is largely dopaminergic. This network also includes the medial parietal cortex and the posterior cingulate cortex. Transcranial magnetic stimulation of these areas may transiently impair self-awareness. This circuit is also thought to be involved in metacognition, which is the brain's conscious monitoring of its own cognitive processes. Metacognition was improved by oral administration of 100 mg dopamine. Dopamine also improved the retrieval accuracy of memories of self-judgment (autonoetic, i.e., explicitly self-conscious metacognition). Concomitantly, magnetoencephalography (MEG) reported on by Joensson, et al., in their article in *Human Brain Mapping,* "Making Sense," showed increased amplitudes of oscillations (power) preferentially in the medial prefrontal cortex.

Posterior Cingulate Cortex and Right Inferior Parietal Lobe

1. Participate in a network with the medial temporal cortex and with medial and lateral parietal areas to:
    (a) remember
    (b) project oneself forward in time (prospection)
    (c) navigate in space
    (d) maintain a theory of mind[34]
2. Part of the default mode network of the brain circuit[35]
3. Mediates self-reflection and the regulation of emotion and arousal
4. Integrates with the anterior cingulate cortex, which integrates emotional information with cognition
5. Interacts with the posterior cingulate cortex, which discerns emotional and self-relevant information
6. Part of the circuit that operates working memory[36]

Temporo-parietal Junction*

1. Theory-of-mind area
2. With the medial temporal cortex, the precuneus, the posterior cingulate cortex, and the retrosplenial cortex, participates in processing:
    (a) memory about me (autobiographical memory)
    (b) navigation
    (c) theory of mind (cognitive theory of mind recruits the precuneus and cuneus, as well as regions in both temporal lobes)[37]
    (d) default mode (making up stories)[38]

---

*According to Xu, et al., in "Language in Context," in *NeuroImage,* the temporo-parietal conjunction and the surrounding perisylvian areas are intimately involved in language and language comprehesion, recruiting the frontal operculum and temporal pole for understanding words and sentences, when both are of higher complexity. Also in *Neuroimage,* Jouen, et al., report in "Beyond the Word and Image," that further need for processing in a narrative sense (understanding complex stories) extends this recruitment to the precuneus, the medial prefrontal cortex, and the dorsal temporo-parietal-occipital cortices. As Harel, Kravitz, and Baker point out in "Deconstructing Visual Scenes," we can imagine a similar expansion in the representation of meaning as image stimuli increase in complexity from simple objects to richer spatial scenes.

3. Activates when subjects read single words and see pictures of simple objects in semantic matching tasks, thereby integrating word and visual input, and includes in its circuit the left middle temporal cortex and the inferior frontal cortex[39]

Temporal Poles*

1. Theory-of-mind area
2. Bilateral activation occurs with a story when compared to unconnected sentences—(Brodmann's area 38) and the left superior temporal gyrus (Brodmann's areas 22 and 39)
3. Activates for the comprehension of stories that require the linking of propositions[40]

Superior Temporal Gyrus†

1. Left-sided activation occurs with a story when compared to unconnected sentences (Brodmann's areas 22 and 39)
2. Posterior area on the left activates in processing global or discourse-level understanding of a story.[41]

Medial Temporal Cortex‡

1. Participates in a network with the medial prefrontal cortex and with medial and lateral parietal areas to:

---

*The temporal poles have a role in both social and emotional processes, including face recognition and theory of mind, which goes beyond semantic memory. They bind complex, highly processed perceptual inputs to visceral emotional responses. In their article in *Brain*, "The Enigmatic Temporal Pole," Olson, Plotzker, and Ezzyat point out that perceptual inputs remain segregated into dorsal (auditory), medial (olfactory), and ventral (visual) streams, so that the integration of emotion with perception is channel specific.

† Only the left superior temporal gyrus and the putamen are critical in auditory lexical tone processing. Activation in the superior temporal cortex associated with lexical tone perception is modality-dependent, according to Kwok, et al., in "Neural Signatures of Lexical Tone Reading," *Human Brain Mapping*.

‡ Lesions of the medial temporal lobe (MTL) interfere with the recall of even well-established, remembered stories. Seven amnesic patients, five with lesions restricted to the MTL and two with lesions extending into lateral temporal cortex were asked to

(a) remember

(b) project oneself forward in time (prospection)

(c) navigate in space

(d) maintain a theory of mind[43]

2. With the precuneus, the posterior cingulate gyrus, the retrosplenial cortex, and the temporo-parietal junction, participates in processing:

(a) memory about me (autobiographical memory)

(b) navigation

(c) theory of mind

(d) default mode (making up stories)[44]

3. Participates in a network with the medial prefrontal cortex and with medial and lateral parietal areas to:

(a) remember

(b) project oneself forward in time (prospection)

(c) navigate in space

(d) maintain a theory of mind[45]

4. Part of the default mode network of the brain[46]

Anterior Cingulate Cortex

1. Associated with motivation and probably involved in paying attention to the salient details of a story[47]

(continued from page 244) recount fairy tales and Bible stories that they rated as familiar. Narratives were scored for number and type of details, number of main thematic elements, and order in which the main thematic elements were recounted. In comparison to controls, patients with MTL lesions produced fewer details, but the number and order of main thematic elements generated was intact. By contrast, when the lesions were extended into the lateral temporal cortex, patients showed a pervasive impairment, affecting not only the generation of details, but also the generation and ordering of details. These findings, reported by Verfaellie, Bousquet, and Keane, in "Medial Temporal and Neocortical Contributions to Remote Memory," in *Neuropsychologia*, challenge the notion that, once consolidated, semantic memories are no longer dependent on the hippocampus for retrieval. In the context of verbs of motion ("to come" or "to go" as opposed to "to be"), "close places" elicited more activity than "distant places" around the parahippocampal gyrus, suggesting projection of the reader's self-relevant information, or retrieval of geographical episodic memories.[42]

2. Integrates emotional information with cognition
3. Interacts with the posterior cingulate cortex, which discerns emotional and self-relevant information
4. Interacts with the medial prefrontal cortex, which allows for self-reflection and the regulation of emotion and arousal
5. Part of the circuitry that holds working memory

Posterior Cingulate Gyrus

1. Spatial tracking and visual imagery associated with listening to or reading a story
2. Bilateral activation occurs with a story when compared to unconnected sentences (Brodmann's areas 23 and 31)
3. Both sides activate when stories about characters with motives (theory of mind) are compared to stories about physical objects (physical stories)
4. Activated during any story but not for unlinked sentences
5. Thought to be associated with the incorporation of information into a burgeoning story structure[48]
6. With the medial temporal cortex, the precuneus, the retrosplenial cortex, and the temporo-parietal junction, participates in processing:
   (a) memory about me (autobiographical memory)
   (b) navigation
   (c) theory of mind
   (d) default mode (making up stories)[49]
7. Involved with episodic and autobiographical memory retrieval,[50] visuospatial mental imagery, prospection, and self-projection[51]
8. Discerns emotional and self-relevant information
9. Interacts with the anterior cingulate gyrus, which integrates emotional information with cognition
10. Interacts with the medial prefrontal cortex, which allows for self-reflection and the regulation of emotion and arousal

Orbitofrontal Cortex*

1. Anomaly detector
2. Serves to inhibit the maintenance of information irrelevant to the story being heard[52]
3. Helps to maintain attention[53]
4. Involved in effective communication of descriptions of objects, in a circuit of social coordination

Interior Parietal Cortex†

1. Right side activates when stories about characters with motives (theory of mind) are compared to stories about physical objects (physical stories)
2. Part of the default mode network of the brain[54]

Medial Parietal Areas‡

1. Participate in a network with the medial prefrontal cortex and with medial temporal cortex and lateral parietal areas to:

---

*Among people with behavioral variant frontotemporal dementia with atrophy, particularly in the medial prefrontal and orbitofrontal cortices, although patients did not have difficulty identifying the features of objects, they produced descriptions that included insufficient or inappropriate adjectives and thus struggled to communicate effectively to others. As Healey, et al. point out in "Getting on the Same Page," in *Neuropsychologia,* nonlanguage brain areas (those outside the perisylvian fissure region) are important parts of a large-scale neurocognitive network for social coordination.

†According to Healey, et al., in "Getting on the Same Page," diffusion tensor imaging has identified an indirect pathway passing through the inferior parietal cortex that is involved in semantically based language functions. The classical pathway connects Broca's region (in the inferior frontal cortex) and Wernicke's region (in the middle temporal cortex) and serves phonological language functions. This parietal area has been called Geschwind's territory in Brodmann's areas 39 and 40 and Lichtheim's concept center.

‡Medial parietal areas mediate self-awareness in a paralimbic core network that also includes the medial prefrontal cortex, the angular gyri, the insula, and subcortical regions, which may be common to all forms of self-awareness. This network has generally been termed the "default network," referring to the fact that while it is exceedingly metabolically active in idleness and tasks relevant to the self, it is often decreased in activity during goal-directed action in the outside world.

    (a) remember

    (b) project oneself forward in time (prospection)

    (c) navigate in space

    (d) maintain a theory of mind[55]

2. Part of the default mode network of the brain[56]

Lateral Parietal Cortex

1. Participates in a network with the medial prefrontal cortex and with medial temporal cortex and medial parietal areas to:

    (a) remember

    (b) project oneself forward in time (prospection)

    (c) navigate in space

    (d) maintain a theory of mind[57]

2. Part of the default mode network of the brain[58]

Posterior Lateral Parietal Cortex

1. Part of the circuitry that manages working memory[59]

Precuneus*

1. With the medial temporal cortex, the posterior cingulate cortex, the retrosplenial cortex, and the temporo-parietal junction, participates in processing:

    (a) memory about me (autobiographical memory)

    (b) navigation

    (c) theory of mind

    (d) default mode (making up stories)[60]

2. Part of the default mode network of the brain[61]

---

*Processing in a narrative sense includes the precuneus, along with the medial prefrontal cortex and the dorsal temporo-parietal-occipital circuitry, according to Jouen, et al., in "Beyond the Word and Image," *NeuroImage*.

Retrosplenial Cortex*

1. With the medial temporal cortex, the precuneus, the posterior cingulate cortex, and the temporo-parietal junction, participates in processing:

    (a) memory about me (autobiographical memory)

    (b) navigation

    (c) theory of mind

    (d) default mode (making up stories)[62]

Hippocampus[†]

1. Encodes and preserves the temporal order of experiences

2. Contributes to sequence learning[63]

3. Supports the integration of individual story elements into coherent and cohesive stories in complex verbal accounts

4. Plays a critical role in the effective communication of information to others[64]

Amygdalae[‡]

1. Part of a set of neural structures involved in processing emotion-laden stories, including the lateral prefrontal cortex, the anterior

---

*Conjunction of activity in understanding sentences and pictures reveals a common fronto-temporo-parietal network that includes the middle and inferior frontal gyri, the parahippocampal-retrosplenial complex, the anterior and middle temporal gyri, the inferior parietal lobe in particular the temporo-parietal cortex, according to Jouen, et al., in "Beyond the Word and Image."

†The mental simulation of the future and past also relies on common processes supported by the hippocampus. Patients with hippocampal lesions have striking reductions in their capacity to produce integrated (cohesive and coherent) stories about future and past events. These deficits remained when patients were asked to produce stories that came solely from pictures. According to Race, Keane, and Verfaellie, in "Losing Sight of the Future," *Hippocampus,* patients with adult-onset hippocampal damage have difficulty not only projecting back in time to mentally simulate the past (retrospection), but also projecting forward in time to mentally simulate novel and specific future scenarios (prospection).

‡Functioning is augmented by high levels of stress (opposite to hippocampal functioning), according to Elzinga and Bremner, "Are the Neural Substrates of Memory," in *Journal of Affective Disorders.*

temporal cortex, and the temporo-parietal cortex—regions associated with:

(a) story comprehension

(b) high-level semantic integration

(c) theory-of-mind processing

2. Plays an important role in stories involving intrusive, traumatic memories, in association with projections to the superior parietal areas and to the insula[65]

3. Shows elevated responsiveness in PTSD patients who are processing trauma memories in association with reduced functioning of the medial prefrontal cortex[66]

OUTLINE SUMMARY: THE TASKS INVOLVED IN STORYING AND THE BRAIN AREAS THAT ACCOMPLISH THEM

Maintaining Global Coherence and Tracking Relationships among Distant Clauses within the Story

1. Frontal lobe

Remembering Information over Relatively Long Periods of Time, Supported by Continued Firing of Neurons following Removal of Eliciting Stimuli

1. Frontal lobe[67]

Managing Fictional Imagery

1. Frontal lobe

Episodic Buffer—Integrating, Manipulating, and Maintaining Complex Information from All Sensory Modalities, Modeling Hypothetical Situations

1. Right frontal lobe[68]

Modulation of Attention to Achieve Integration through
Selective and Organized Recruitment of other
Cortical Areas
  1. Right frontal lobe

Managing Autobiographical Memory
  1. Left prefrontal cortex[69]

Managing Autobiographical Memory Involving Theory of Mind
  1. Lateral prefrontal cortex
  2. Medial prefrontal cortex
  3. Lateral part of the temporal cortex
  4. Areas of the occipital cortex

Maintaining the Phonological Loop and a Visuospatial
Sketchpad
  1. Ventral prefrontal cortex[70]

Processing across Time and Sensory Modalities
  1. Dorsolateral prefrontal cortex (Brodmann's areas 6, 8, 9, and 46)[71]

Manipulating Information Consistent with
Central Executive Function
  1. Dorsolateral prefrontal cortex (Brodmann's areas 6, 8, 9, and 46)[72]

Comparing Stories with Characters Who Have Mental States and
Motives to Stories with Characters (such as physical objects)
Lacking Mental States
  1. Left sided frontal cortex in Brodmann's area 8
  2. Left medial prefrontal cortex[73]
  3. Posterior cingulate cortex[74]
  4. Right inferior parietal lobe[75]

Monitoring, Operating, and Manipulating the Contexts of Working Memory

1. Mid-dorsolateral frontal cortex, Brodmann's areas 9 and 46
2. Medial prefrontal cortex[76]
3. Posterior lateral parietal cortex[77]

Encoding and Retrieving Episodic and Autobiographical Memories

1. Mid-dorsolateral prefrontal cortex[78]
2. Ventrolateral frontal cortex (Brodmann's area 47)[79]
3. Ventromedial frontal cortex (Brodmann's areas 11, 13, and 25)[80]
4. Anterior prefrontal cortex (Brodmann's area 10)[81]
5. Medial prefrontal cortex[82]
6. Posterior cingulate cortex[83]

Ordering Events in Time and Processing Sequential Information

1. Right mid-dorsolateral prefrontal cortex (Brodmann's Areas 9 and 46)[84]

Specifying and Maintaining Cues for Long-Term Memory Retrieval and Encoding

1. Ventrolateral frontal cortex (Brodmann's area 47)

Rejecting the Products of Memory Retrieval

1. Ventromedial frontal cortex (Brodmann's Areas 11, 13, 25)

Default Mode Network (Storytelling Brain)

1. Ventromedial prefrontal cortex[85]
2. Medial prefrontal cortex[86]
3. Medial temporal cortex[87]
4. Inferior parietal cortex[88]

5. Medial parietal cortex[89]
6. Lateral parietal cortex[90]
7. Precuneus[91]

Mediating Mentalization or Theory of Mind, Person Perception, and Representation of Self-Knowledge
1. Ventromedial prefrontal cortex[92]

Accepting the Products of Memory Retrieval
1. Anterior prefrontal cortex (Brodmann's area 10)[93]

Attributing Mental States to Characters in Stories (Theory of Mind)
1. Medial prefrontal cortex[94]
2. Temporo-parietal junction
3. Temporal poles

Remembering, Projecting Oneself Forward in Time (Prospection), Navigating in Space, and Maintaining a Theory of Mind
1. Medial prefrontal cortex[95]
2. Medial temporal cortex[96]
3. Medial parietal cortical areas[97]
4. Lateral parietal cortical areas[98]

Mediating Self-Reflection and the Regulation of Emotion and Arousal
1. Medial prefrontal cortex
2. Anterior cingulate cortex (which also integrates emotional information with cognition)
3. Posterior cingulate cortex (which also discerns emotional and self-relevant information)

*Processing Autobiographical Memory, Navigation in Space,
Theory of Mind, and Default Mode (Making Up Stories)**
1. Temporo-parietal junction
2. Medial temporal cortex
3. Precuneus
4. Posterior cingulate cortex
5. Retrosplenial cortex[99]

Recognizing a Story Over Unconnected Sentences
1. Bilateral temporal poles (Brodmann's area 38)
2. Left superior temporal gyrus (Brodmann's areas 22 and 39)
3. Bilateral posterior cingulate cortex (Brodmann's areas 23 and 31)

Comprehending Stories That Require the Linking of Propositions
1. Temporal poles[100]

Processing Global or Discourse-Level Understanding of a Story
1. Superior temporal gyrus[101]

*Associated with Motivation and Attention to the Salient
Details of a Story[102]*
1. Anterior cingulate cortex

*Integrating Emotional Information with Cognition;
Discerning Emotional and Self-Relevant Information;
Managing Self-Reflection and Regulation of Emotion and Arousal[103]*
1. Anterior cingulate cortex
2. Posterior cingulate cortex
3. Medial prefrontal cortex

---

*Schlaffke et al., in "Shared and Nonshared Neural Networks," in *Human Brain Mapping,* point out that affective theory of mind involves a neural network comprising prefrontal cortical structures, as well as smaller regions in the posterior cingulate cortex and the basal ganglia, and cognitive theory of mind recruits the precuneus, cuneus, and regions in the temporal lobes bilaterally.

Performing Spatial Tracking and Visual Imagery Associated with Hearing or Reading a Story
1. Posterior cingulate cortex

Incorporating Information into a Burgeoning Story Structure
1. Posterior cingulate cortex[104]

Prospection and Self-projection
1. Posterior cingulate cortex[105]

Detecting Anomalies
1. Orbitofrontal cortex

Inhibiting Maintenance of Information Irrelevant to the Story Being Heard
1. Orbitofrontal cortex[106]

Maintaining Attention
1. Orbitofrontal cortex[107]

Understanding Sentences and Pictures*
1. A common fronto-temporo-parietal network that includes:

---

*DTI tractography seeded from this temporo-parietal cortex hub revealed a multicomponent network reaching into the temporal pole, the ventral frontal pole, and premotor cortex. A significant correlation was found between the relative pathway density issued from the temporo-parietal cortex and the imageability of sentences for individual subjects, suggesting a potential functional link between comprehension and the temporo-parietal connectivity strength. These data help to define a "meaning" network that includes components of recently characterized systems for semantic memory, embodied simulation, and visuospatial scene representation. The network substantially overlaps with the default mode network, implicated as part of a core network of semantic representation, along with brain systems related to the formation of mental models and reasoning. These data are consistent with a model of real-world situational understanding that is highly embodied. Crucially, the neural basis of this embodied understanding is not limited to sensorimotor systems, but extends to the highest levels of cognition, including autobiographical memory, scene analysis, mental model formation, reasoning, and theory of mind.

(a) middle and inferior frontal gyri

(b) parahippocampal-retrosplenial complex

(c) anterior and middle temporal gyri, the inferior parietal lobe

(d) temporo-parietal cortex

Producing Coherent and Cohesive Integrated Narratives from Words or Pictures, Integrating Past and Future, and Effectively Communicating This Information to Others

1. Hippocampus and neighboring areas of temporal cortex[108]

Support for Recollection and Familiarity-Based Recognition

1. The medial temporal lobe and associated hippocampus and entorhinal cortex[109]

Processing Temporal Information; Temporal Order Pattern Separation and Association across Time

1. CA1 area of the hippocampus[110]

Processing Empathy

1. Anterior cingulate cortex[111]

Mentally Projecting into the Future and Past and Building Predictions and Plans for the Future Based on Prior Experience

1. Medial temporal lobe

2. Hippocampus[112]

Notes

INTRODUCTION

1. Turner, *The Literary Mind,* 5.
2. Bruner, "The Narrative Construction of Reality," 4.
3. Raichle et al., "Inaugural Article," 676–82; Raichle and Snyder, "A Default Mode of Brain Function," 1083–90.
4. Raichle, "The Brain's Dark Energy," 44–49.
5. Buckner, Andrews-Hanna, and Schacter, "The Brain's Default Network," 1–38.
6. Mehl-Madrona, *Healing the Mind,* 295.
7. Crossely, *Introducing Narrative Psychology,* 163.
8. Beckman and Frankel, "The Effect of Physician Behavior," 692–96.

CHAPTER 1.
DISCOVERING THE STORIES WE LIVE

1. Lakoff and Johnson, *Metaphors We Live By,* 3.
2. Sandelowski, "Telling Stories," 161–66.
3. Tulving, "Episodic Memory," 1–25; Wheeler, Stuss, and Tulving, "Toward a Theory of Episodic Memory," 331–54.
4. Oatley, "Why Fiction May Be Twice as True," 101–17.
5. Harris, *The Work of the Imagination,* 17.
6. Barsalou, "Perceptual Symbol Systems," 577–660; Zwaan, "The Immersed Experiencer," 35–62.
7. Zwaan, "The Immersed Experiencer," 35–62
8. Zwaan and Radvansky, "Situation Models," 162–85.

9. Vercueil and Perronne-Bertolotti, "Ictal Inner Speech Jargon," 307–9.

10. Geva et al., "The Neural Correlates of Inner Speech," 3071–82; Perronne-Bertolotti et al., "How Silent Is Silent Reading?" 17554–62.

11. Vercueil and Klinger, "Loss of Silent Reading," 705.

12. Vercueil, "Control of Inner Speech," 460–62.

13. Huang, Carr, and Cao, "Comparing Cortical Activations," 39–53; Amodio and Frith, "Meeting of Minds," 268–77.

14. Morin, "Self-Awareness Deficits," 524–29.

15. Vercueil and Perronne-Bertolotti, "Ictal Inner Speech Jargon," 307–9.

16. Morin, "Self-Awareness Deficits," 524–29.

17. Beeman, "Semantic Processing," 80–120; Beeman, "Coarse Semantic Coding, 129–41; Beeman, Bowden, and Gernsbacher, "Right and Left Hemisphere Cooperation," 310–36.

18. Oatley, "Why Fiction May Be Twice as True," 101–117; Grafman, "The Human Prefrontal Cortex," 157–74.

19. Grafman, "The Human Prefrontal Cortex," 157–74.

20. Benowitz, Moya, and Levine, "Impaired Verbal Reasoning," 231–41; Moya et al., "Covariant Defects in Visuospatial Abilities," 381–97; Wapner, Hamby, and Gardner, "The Role of the Right Hemisphere," 15–33.

21. Frisk and Milner, "The Relationship of Working Memory," 121–35; Frisk and Milner, "The Role of the Left Hippocampal Region," 349–59.

22. Tulving, "Hemispheric Encoding/Retrieval," 2016–20.

23. Larsen and Seilman, "Personal Meanings While Reading Literature," 411–29.

24. Conway et al., "Neuropsychological Correlates of Memory," 334–40.

25. Perfetti and Stafura, "Word Knowledge," 22–37.

26. Irish et al., "Right Anterior Temporal Lobe Dysfunction," 1241–53.

27. Ibid.

28. For another version of this story, see "Badger, Coyote and the Woodchucks," *Canku Ota* 117 (July 17, 2004). Available at www.turtletrack.org/Issues04/Co07172004/CO_07172004_Badger_Woodchuck.htm.

CHAPTER 2.
YOUR MIND ON STORY

1. Mar and Oatley, "The Function of Fiction," 173–92.

2. Prentice, Gerrig, and Bailis, "What Readers Bring," 416–20; Strange and

Leung, "How Anecdotal Accounts," 439–49; Wheeler, Green, and Brock, "Fictional Narratives Change Beliefs," 136–41.

3. Zunshine, *Why We Read Fiction,* 6.

4. Herman, *Basic Elements of Narrative,* 151.

5. Rolls, "The Orbitofrontal Cortex and Reward," 284–94.

6. Mar, "The Neuropsychology of Narrative," 1414–34.

7. Fuster, Bodner, and Kroger, "Cross-Modal and Cross-Temporal Association," 347–51.

8. Rolheiser, Stamatakis, and Tyler, "Dynamic Processing," 16949–57.

9. Schank and Abelson, "Knowledge and Memory," 3.

10. Bortolussi, "Minding the Text," 23–37.

11. Loftus, Miller, and Burns, "Semantic Integration," 19–31.

12. Kensinger, "Negative Emotion Enhances Memory," 213–18; LeDoux, "The Emotional Brain," 727–38.

13. Siegel, *The Developing Mind,* 350.

14. Restak, "How Our Brain Constructs," 3–11.

15. Hanson and Mendius, *Buddha's Brain,* 40.

16. Grimm, et al., "Altered Negative BOLD Responses," 932–43.

17. Beaudoin and Zimmerman, "Narrative Therapy," 1–13.

18. Ibid., 3.

19. Dantzer et al., "From Inflammation to Sickness," 46–56.

20. Larsen and Seilman, "Personal Meanings While Reading Literature," 411–29.

21. Schank, *Dynamic Memory,* 53.

22. For a similar version of this story, see "Rabbit Calls a Truce." Available at www.native-languages.org/penobscotstory.htm.

23. Hill, *Glooscap and His Magic,* 126–30.

24. Boyd, *On the Origin of Stories,* 151.

CHAPTER 3. THE COLLECTIVE SELF

1. Culler, *Structuralist Poetics,* 5–6, 130.

2. Bruner, "The Narrative Construction of Reality," 4.

3. Roberts, *Emerging Selves in Practice,* iv.

4. Ramachandran and Blakeslee, *Phantoms in the Brain,* 12, 61–62, 81.

5. Jenkins and Mitchell, "Medial Prefrontal Cortex," 211–18.

6. Raichle et al., "Inaugural Article," 676–82.

7. Broyd et al., "Default-Mode Brain Dysfunction," 279–96.

8. Barrett and Satpute, "Large-Scale Brain Networks," 361–72; Mars et al., "On the Relationship," 189; Buckner, Andrews-Hanna, and Schacter, "The Brain's Default Network," 1–38; Schilbach et al., "Minds at Rest?" 457–67; Lindquist and Barrett, "A Functional Architecture," 533–40.

9. Buckner, Andrews-Hanna, and Schacter, "The Brain's Default Network," 1–38.

10. Zhang and Li, "Functional Connectivity Mapping," 3548–62.

11. Jenkins and Mitchell, "Medial Prefrontal Cortex," 211–18; Buckner, Andrews-Hanna, and Schacter, "The Brain's Default Network," 1–38.

12. Greicius et al., "Functional Connectivity," 253–58; Raichle and Snyder, "A Default Mode of Brain Function," 1083–90.

13. Amodio and Frith, "Meeting of Minds," 268–77.

14. Spreng, Mar, and Kim, "The Common Neural Basis," 489–510.

15. Buckner, Andrews-Hanna, and Schacter, "The Brain's Default Network," 1–38.

16. Broyd et al., "Default-Mode Brain Dysfunction," 279–96.

17. Mars et al., "On the Relationship," 189; Schilbach et al., "Minds at Rest?" 457–67.

18. Mars et al., "On the Relationship," 189; Dunbar, "The Social Brain Hypothesis," 562–72.

19. Buckner, Andrews-Hanna, and Schacter, "The Brain's Default Network," 1–38.

20. Raichle and Snyder, "A Default Mode of Brain Function," 1083–90.

21. Whitfield-Gabrieli et al., "Hyperactivity and Hyperconnectivity," 1279–84; Raichle and Snyder, "A Default Mode," 1083–90.

22. Kennedy, Redcay, and Courchesne, "Failing to Deactivate," 8275–80; Whitfield-Gabrieli et al., "Hyperactivity and Hyperconnectivity," 1279–84.

23. Kolata, "Insights Give Hope."

24. Daniels et al., "Default Mode Alterations in PTSD," 56–59; Lanius et al., "Emotion Modulation in PTSD," 640–47.

25. Jang et al., "Increased Default Mode Network Connectivity," 358–62.

26. Lehrer, "Daydream Achiever."

27. Broyd et al., "Default-Mode Brain Dysfunction," 279–96.

28. Seeley et al., "Dissociable Intrinsic Connectivity Networks," 2349–56.

29. Barrett and Satpute, "Large-Scale Brain Networks," 361–72; Lindquist

and Barrett, "A Functional Architecture," 533–40; Menon and Uddin, "Saliency, Switching, Attention and Control," 655–67.

30. Seeley et al., "Dissociable Intrinsic Connectivity Networks," 2349–56.

31. Boyd, *On the Origin of Stories,* 269.

32. Ibid., 274.

33. Zunshine, *Why We Read Fiction,* 22–27.

34. Hermans, "The Dialogical Self," 243.

35. Hermans and Dimaggio, "Self, Identity and Globalization," 31–61.

36. Moghaddam, "Intersubjectivity, Interobjectivity, and the Embryonic Fallacy," 465–75.

37. Barresi, "From 'the Thought Is the Thinker,'" 237–50.

38. James, *The Principles of Psychology,* vol. 1, 291–402; James, *The Principles of Psychology,* vol. 2, 456.

39. Neisser, "The Ecological Study of Memory," 1696–1701; Gallagher, "Neurocognitive Models of Schizophrenia," 8–19.

40. Craik et al., "In Search of Self," 26–34; Kelley et al., "Finding the Self?" 785–94; Fossati et al., "In Search of the Emotional Self," 1938–45; Macrae et al., "Medial Prefrontal Activity," 647–54.

41. Mitchell, Macrae, and Banaji, "Dissociable Medial Prefrontal Contributions," 655–63.

42. Lieberman, Jarcho, and Satpute, "Evidence-Based and Intuition-Based Self-Knowledge," 421–35; Ochsner et al., "The Neural Correlates," 797–814.

43. Johnson et al., "Dissociating Medial Frontal and Posterior Cingulate Activity," 56–64.

44. Boyd, *On the Origin of Stories,* 402.

45. Hermans, "The Dialogical Self," 243–81.

46. Young and Saver, "The Neurology of Narrative," 72–84.

47. Hermans, "The Dialogical Self," 243–81.

48. Panksepp, *Affective Neuroscience,* 24–41.

49. James, *The Principles of Psychology,* vol.1, 1–11, 299–338.

50. Barrett, "Solving the Emotion Paradox," 20–46; Barrett, Wilson-Mendenhall, and Barsalou, "The Conceptual Act Theory," 83–110.

51. Tracy and Randles, "Four Models of Basic Emotions," 397–405.

52. Barrett, "Variety Is the Spice of Life," 1284–1306; Barrett, "Psychological Construction," 379–89.

53. Wilson-Mendenhall, Barrett, and Barsalou, "Neural Evidence," 947–56.

54. Lindquist et al., "The Brain Basis of Emotion," 121–202; Barrett and Satpute, "Large-Scale Brain Networks," 361–72; Mars et al., "On the Relationship" 189; Buckner, Andrews-Hanna, and Schacter, "The Brain's Default Network," 1–38; Schilbach et al., "Minds at Rest?" 457–67; Lindquist and Barrett, "A Functional Architecture," 533–40.

55. Lindquist and Barrett, "A Functional Architecture," 533–40; Bar, "The Proactive Brain," 280–89; Buckner and Carroll, "Self-Projection and the Brain," 49–57; Barrett, "Emotions Are Real," 413–29.

56. Krueger, Barbey, and Grafman, "The Medial Prefrontal Cortex," 103–9.

57. Cauda et al., "Meta-Analytic Clustering," 342–55; Craig, "How Do You Feel—Now?" 59–70; Laird et al., "Behavioral Interpretations," 4022–37; Barrett and Satpute, "Large-Scale Brain Networks," 361–72; Lindquist and Barrett, "A Functional Architecture," 533–40; Menon and Uddin, "Saliency, Switching, Attention and Control," 655–67.

58. Rosch, "On the Internal Structure," 111–44. Rosch and Mervis, "Family Resemblances," 573–605.

59. Russell and Barrett, "Core Affect, Prototypical Emotional Episodes," 805–19; Barrett and Russell, "The Structure," 10–14.

60. Wilson-Mendenhall, Barrett, and Barsalou, "Variety in Emotional Life," 4.

61. Wilson-Mendenhall, Barrett, and Barsalou, "Neural Evidence," 947–56; Wilson-Mendenhall, Barrett, and Barsalou, "Variety in Emotional Life," 62–71.

62. Wilson-Mendenhall, Barrett, and Barsalou, "Variety in Emotional Life," 62–71.

63. Barrett, "Variety Is the Spice of Life," 1284–1306.

64. Wilson-Mendenhall, Barrett, and Barsalou, "Variety in Emotional Life," 62–71; Casey, "A Reexamination of the Roles," 823–34; Larochelle and Pineau, "Determinants of Response Times," 796–823; McCloskey and Glucksberg, "Decision Processes in Verifying Category," 1–37; Russell and Fehr, "Fuzzy Concepts in a Fuzzy Hierarchy" 186–205.

65. Beck and Dozois, "Cognitive Therapy," 397–409; Masley et al., "A Systemic Review," 185–202.

CHAPTER 4. STORIES, BELIEFS, AND ANOMALIES

1. Zwaan, "The Immersed Experiencer," 35–62.
2. Pribram, Nuwer, and Baron, "The Holographic Hypothesis," 416–57.

3. Hasher, Zacks, and May, "Inhibitory Control," 653–75; Hasher and Zacks, "Working Memory, Comprehension, and Aging," 193–225.

4. Baddeley and Wilson, "Frontal Amnesia and the Dysexecutive Syndrome," 212–30; Just and Carpenter, "A Capacity Theory of Comprehension," 122–49.

5. Baddeley, "The Episodic Buffer," 417–23.

6. Baddeley and Wilson, "Prose Recall and Amnesia," 1737–43.

7. Baddeley, "The Episodic Buffer," 417–23.

8. Fuster, "Frontal Lobe and Cognitive Development," 373–85; Moscovitch and Winocur, "The Frontal Cortex," 188–209.

9. Fuster, "Frontal Lobe and Cognitive Development," 373–85.

10. Van Dijk and Kintsch, *Strategies of Discourse Comprehension,* 305; Johnson–Laird, *Human and Machine Thinking,* 14.

11. Kintsch, "The Role of Knowledge," 163; Clifton and Duffy, "Sentence and Text Comprehension," 167–96.

12. Graesser, Millis, and Zwaan, "Discourse Comprehension," 163–89.

13. Gernsbacher, "The Structure-Building Framework," 289–311. Gernsbacher, "Two Decades of Structure Building," 265–304.

14. Boyd, *On the Origin of Stories,* 45.

15. Schank and Abelson, *Scripts, Plans, Goals, and Understanding,* 36–51.

CHAPTER 5. MEETING THE STORYTELLERS

1. Mehl-Madrona, *Healing the Mind,* 65–69; Mahoney, *Constructive Psychotherapy,* 3.

2. Bernaerts, De Geest, Herman, Vervaeck, "Cognitive Narrative Studies," 1–20.

3. Ingarden, *The Literary Work of Art,* 162; 246.

4. Bernaerts, De Geest, Herman, Vervaeck, "Cognitive Narrative Studies," 1–20.

5. Spolsky, *Gaps in Nature,* 31.

6. Ibid., 52–53.

7. Iser, *The Act of Reading.*

8. Mar, "The Neuropsychology of Narrative," 1414–34.

9. Mar, "The Neuropsychology of Narrative," 1414–34; Frith and Frith, "The Biological Basis," 151–55; Frith and Frith, "Interacting Minds," 1692–95;

Frith and Frith, "Development and Neurophysiology of Mentalizing," 459–73.

10. Rolls, "The Orbitofrontal Cortex and Reward," 284–94; Rolls, "Memory Systems in the Brain," 599–630.

11. Grön et al., "Brain Activation during Human Navigation," 404–8.

12. Robin et al., "Functional Connectivity," 81–93.

13. Virtue, Parrish, and Jung-Beeman, "Inferences During Story Comprehension," 2274–84; Virtue et al., "Neural Activity," 104–14.

14. Virtue, Parrish, and Jung-Beeman, "Inferences During Story Comprehension," 2274–84; Virtue et al., "Neural Activity of Inferences," 104–14.

15. Zalla, Phipps, and Grafman, "Story Processing," 215–31.

16. Burin et al., "The Role of Ventromedial Prefrontal Cortex," 58–64.

17. Gadamer, *Truth and Method*, 308.

18. Jauss, *Literaturgeschichte als Provokation der Literaturwissenschaft*, 187.

19. Iser, "The Reading Process," 285.

20. Lewis, *Narrative Psychiatry*, 45.

21. Gladwell, *Blink*, 10–12.

22. Lahad, "Finding Coping Resources," 55–70.

23. Boyd, *On the Origin of Stories*, 381–82.

CHAPTER 6. CREATING NEW STORIES, *IMAGINING* TRANSFORMATION

1. Whitehead, "Social Mirrors," 3–36.

2. Ibid.

3. Roberts, *Emerging Selves in Practice*, 4.

4. Brafman and Brafman, *Sway*, 7.

5. Tart, *Altered States of Consciousness*, 1.

6. Leading Cloud, *Spotted Eagle and Black Crow*.

CHAPTER 7. MAGICAL POTIONS, ALCHEMICAL SOLUTIONS

1. Colloca et al., "Reevaluating the Placebo," 124–27.

2. Colloca et al., "Overt Versus Covert Treatment," 679–84; Bingel et al., "The Effect of Treatment Expectation," 1–9.

3. Koyama et al., "The Subjective Experience of Pain," 12950–55.

4. Mathers and Hodgkin, "The Gatekeeper and the Wizard," 172.

5. Dominguez et al., "A Double-Blind Placebo-Controlled Study," 84–87; Goldberg and Finnerty, "Trazadone in the Treatment of Neurotic Depression," 430–34; Kiev and Okerson, "Comparison of the Therapeutic Efficacy," 68–72; Rickels et al., "Amoxapine and Imipramine," 20–24.

6. Kirsch et al., "Initial Severity and Antidepressant Benefits," e45.

7. Mayberg et al., "The Functional Neuroanatomy of the Placebo Effect," 728–37.

8. Dominguez et al., "A Double-Blind Placebo-Controlled Study," 84–87; Goldberg and Finnerty, "Trazadone in the Treatment of Neurotic Depression," 430–34; Kiev and Okerson, "Comparison of the Therapeutic Efficacy," 68–72; Rickels et al., "Amoxapine and Imipramine," 20–24.

9. Lifson et al., "Long-Term Human Immunodeficiency Virus Infection," 959–65.

10. Quitkin, "Placebos, Drug Effects, and Study Design," 829–36.

11. Servick, "Outsmarting the Placebo Effect," 1446–47.

12. Hall et al., "Catechol-O-Methyltransferase Val158met Polymorphism," e48135.

13. Furmark et al., "Serotonin Transporter Polymorphism," 189–92.

14. Colloca et al., "Reevaluating the Placebo Effect," 124–27.

15. Beecher, "Surgery as Placebo," 1102–7.

16. Cobb et al., "Evaluation of Internal-Mammary-Artery Ligation," 1115–18; Dimond, Kittle, and Crockett, "Comparison of Internal Mammary Artery Ligation." 483–86.

17. Talbot, "The Placebo Prescription," 34.

18. Moseley et al., "Arthroscopic Treatment of Osteoarthritis of the Knee," 28–34.

19. Talbot, "The Placebo Prescription," 34.

20. Moseley et al., "Controlled Trial of Arthroscopic Surgery," 81–88.

21. Ibid., 82.

22. Olanow et al., "Double-Blind Controlled Trial of Bilateral Fetal Nigral Transplantation," 403–14.

23. Weiner, "Placebo Surgery in Trials of Therapy," 353.

24. Holmes, "Currents and Counter-Currents in Medical Science," 467.

25. Beecher, "The Powerful Placebo," 1602–6.

26. Vase, Amanzio, and Price, "Nocebo vs. Placebo," 143–50.

27. Kuten-Shorrer et al., "Placebo Effect in Burning Mouth Syndrome," 1–6.

28. Loder, Goldstein, and Biondi, "Placebo Effects in Oral Triptan Trials" 124–31.

29. Häuser et al., "Systematic Review," 1709–17.

30. Lidstone, "Great Expectations," 139–47.

31. Espay et al., "Placebo Effect of Medication Cost," 794–802.

32. Dunlop and McCormack, "Placebo Surgery," 240–47.

33. Talbot, "The Placebo Prescription," 34.

34. Kaptchuk et al., "Placebos Without Deception," doi:10.1371/journal. pone.15591.

35. Finniss et al., "Biological, Clinical, and Ethical Advances of Placebo," 686–95; Jones, Barraclough, and Dowrick, "When No Diagnostic Label Is Applied," doi: http://dx.doi.org/10.1136/bmj.c2683; Annoni, "Highlights from the 2013 Science of Placebo," 4.

36. Klosterhalfen and Enck, "Neurophysiology and Psychobiology of the Placebo," 189–95.

37. Sullivan, Rogers, and Kirsch, "Catastrophizing, Depression and Expectancies for Pain," 147–54; Branthwaite and Cooper, "Analgesic Effects of Branding in Treatment of Headaches," 1576–78; Mondloch, Cole, and Frank, "Does How You Do Depend on How You Think You'll Do?" 174–79.

38. Colloca and Grillon, "Understanding Placebo and Nocebo Responses," 419.

39. Murray and Stoessl, "Mechanisms and Therapeutic Implications of the Placebo," 306–18.

40. Bittar and Nascimento, "Placebo and Nocebo Effects in the Neurological Practice," 58–63.

41. Tippens et al., "Expectancy, Self-Efficacy, and Placebo," 181–88.

42. Ibid.

43. Kennedy, "The Nocebo Reaction," 203–5.

44. Ibid.; Enck, Benedetti, and Schedlowski, "New Insights into the Placebo and Nocebo," 195–206; Hull et al., "Patients' Attitudes about the Use of Placebo Treatments," doi: http://dx.doi.org/10.1136/bmj.f3757; Tilburt et al., "Prescribing 'Placebo Treatments'" doi: http://dx.doi.org/10.1136/bmj. a1938; Louhiala, "What Do We Really Know about the Deliberate Use

of Placebos," 403–5; Colloca and Miller, "Harnessing the Placebo Effect," 1922–30.

45. Annoni, "Highlights from the 2013 Science of Placebo Thematic Workshop."

46. Benedetti et al., "Conscious Expectation and Unconscious Conditioning," 4315–23.

47. Ploghaus et al., "Exacerbation of Pain by Anxiety Is Associated with Activity," 9896–903.

48. Annoni, "Highlights from the 2013 Science of Placebo," 1; Kaptchuk et al., "'Maybe I Made Up the Whole Thing'," 382–411; Bingel and Placebo Competence Team, "Avoiding Nocebo Effects to Optimize Treatment," 693–94.

49. Stetler, "Adherence, Expectations and the Placebo," 127–40.

50. Carlino, Frisaldi, and Benedetti, "Pain and the Context," 348–55.

51. Ibid.

52. Talbot, "The Placebo Prescription," 34–40.

53. Olesen, "Beyond the Placebo," 6–7.

54. Ibid.; Derksen, Bensing, and Lagro-Janssen, "Effectiveness of Empathy in General Practice," 76–84; Thompson, Ritenbaugh, and Nichter, "Reconsidering the Placebo Response," 112; Finniss et al., "Biological, Clinical, and Ethical Advances of Placebo," 686–95.

55. Thomas, "The Placebo in General Practice," 1066–67; Thomas, "General Practice Consultations" 1200–2.

56. Thomas, "The Placebo in General Practice," 1066–67.

57. Ibid., 1067.

58. Thomas, "General Practice Consultations," 1200–2.

59. Olesen, "Beyond the Placebo," 6–7.

60. Ibid., 6.

61. *Patch Adams,* Universal Studios, 1998.

62. Jones, Barraclough, and Dowrick, "When No Diagnostic Label Is Applied," doi: http://dx.doi.org/10.1136/bmj.c2683.

63. Thomas, "Temporarily Dependent Patient in General Practice," 625–26.

64. Derksen, Bensing, and Lagro-Janssen, "Effectiveness of Empathy in General Practice," 76–84; Thompson, Ritenbaugh, and Nichter, "Reconsidering the Placebo Response," 112–52; Finniss et al., "Biological, Clinical, and Ethical Advances of Placebo," 686–95; Jones, Barraclough, and Dowrick,

"When No Diagnostic Label Is Applied," doi: http://dx.doi.org/10.1136/bmj.c2683.

65. Olesen, "Beyond the Placebo," 6–7; Thompson, Ritenbaugh, and Nichter, "Reconsidering the Placebo Response," 112–52; Finniss et al., "Biological, Clinical, and Ethical Advances of Placebo," 686–95; Annoni, "Highlights from the 2013 Science of Placebo."

66. Annoni, "Highlights from the 2013 Science of Placebo," 1–11.

67. Oleson, "Beyond the Placebo," 6–7.

68. Stephens, Silbert, and Hasson, "Speaker–Listener Neural Coupling," 14425–30.

69. Ibid., 14427–28.

70. Van Tulder et al., "Spinal Radiographic Findings," 427–34.

71. Panksepp, *Affective Neuroscience*, 150.

72. Koyama et al., "The Subjective Experience of Pain," 12950–55.

73. Galak and Meyvis, "The Pain Was Greater if It Will Happen Again," 63–75.

74. Koyama et al., "The Subjective Experience of Pain," 12950–55.

75. Ibid.

76. Stannard, Coupe, and Pickering, *Opioids in Non-Cancer Pain*, 43-47.

77. Panksepp et al., "Endogenous Opioids and Social Behavior," 473–87; Lieberman and Eisenberger, "A Pain by Any Other Name," 167–89.

CHAPTER 8.
OUR BODIES: MAKERS OF MEANING

1. Shorter, *From Paralysis to Fatigue*, 1–20.

2. Nachmanovitch, *Free Play*, 152–98.

3. Johnson, "Developmental Transformations," 89–116.

4. Ibid., 89.

5. Ibid., 95.

6. Rotie, "Between Fabric and Flesh," 18.

7. Keri Brandt, "Intelligent Bodies," 141.

8. Ziemke and Franck, "Introduction: The Body Eclectic," 1–16.

9. Lakoff and Johnson, *Philosophy in the Flesh*, 16.

10. Wiener and Oxford, *Action Therapy with Families and Groups*, 15–17.

11. Gendlin, *Focusing*, 3.

12. Halprin, *The Expressive Body in Life, Art and Therapy*, 20.

13. Rothschild, *The Body Remembers,* 5.

14. Kirmayer, "The Cultural Diversity of Healing," 33–48.

15. Sherman, "Conversation with Mary Whitehouse," 29–32.

16. Werner and Kaplan, *Symbol Formation,* 63–200.

17. Ziemke and Franck, "Introduction: The Body Eclectic," 1–16.

18. Jones, *Drama as Therapy,* vol. 2, *Clinical Work and Research Into Practice,* 35.

19. Ibid. 35–37.

20. Ibid.

21. Zwaan and Madden, "Embodied Sentence Comprehension," 224–45.

22. Glenberg and Kaschak, "Grounding Language in Action," 558–65.

23. Grainger, "Artistic Expression and the Embodiment of Social Constructs," 139.

24. Ibid., 138.

25. Ibid., 139.

26. Mar, "The Neuropsychology of Narrative," 1414–34.

27. Grainger, "Artistic Expression and the Embodiment of Social Constructs," 139.

28. Jones, *Drama as Therapy,* vol. 1, *Theory, Practice and Research,* 312.

29. Courtney, "Aristotle's Legacy," 1–10.

30. Lakoff and Johnson, *Philosophy in the Flesh,* 9; Landy, *Persona and Performance,* 22–26.

31. Goodman, "Trance Postures," 55.

APPENDIX. AREAS OF THE BRAIN PROMINENT IN UNDERSTANDING AND PRODUCING STORY

1. Fuster, "Frontal Lobe and Cognitive Development," 373–85; Fuster, Bodner, and Kroger, "Cross-Modal and Cross-Temporal Association," 347–51.

2. Moscovitch and Winocur, "The Frontal Cortex and Working with Memory," 188–209.

3. Cabeza et al., "Task-Independent and Task-Specific Age Effects," 364–75.

4. Fuster, "Executive Frontal Functions," 66–70.

5. Sutherland et al., "Neurobiological Impact of Nicotinic Acetylcholine Receptor Agonists," http://dx.doi.org/10.1016/j.biopsych.2014.12.021.

6. Cabeza et al., "Task-Independent and Task-Specific Age Effects," 364–75.

7. Carpenter, Miyake, and Just, "Language Comprehension," 91–120.

8. Jouen et al., "Beyond the Word and Image," 72–85.

9. Cabeza et al., "Task-Independent and Task-Specific Age Effects," 364–75.

10. Schlaffke et al., "Shared and Nonshared Neural Networks," 29–39.

11. Robertson et al., "Functional Neuroanatomy of the Cognitive Process," 255–60; Crozier et al., "Distinct Prefrontal Activations in Processing," 1469–76.

12. Rubin and Greenberg, "The Role of Narrative in Recollection," 53–85.

13. Cabeza et al., "Task-Independent and Task-Specific Age Effects," 364–75.

14. Rolls, "The Functions of the Orbitofrontal Cortex," 354–75.

15. Conway et al., "Brain Imaging Autobiographical Memory," 229–64.

16. Baddeley, "The Episodic Buffer," 417–23.

17. Baddeley and Wilson, "Prose Recall and Amnesia," 1737–43.

18. Conway et al., "Brain Imaging Autobiographical Memory," 229–63.

19. D'Esposito and Postle, "The Cognitive Neuroscience of Working Memory," 115.

20. Fuster, "Frontal Lobe and Cognitive Development," 373–85.

21. D'Esposito and Postle, "The Cognitive Neuroscience of Working Memory," 115.

22. Conway et al., "Neurophysiological Correlates of Memory," 334–40.

23. Moscovitch and Winocur, "The Frontal Cortex and Working with Memory," 188–209; Fuster, "Executive Frontal Functions," 66–70.

24. Conway et al., "Brain Imaging Autobiographical Memory," 229–63; Conway et al., "Neurophysiological Correlates of Memory," 334–40.

25. Vemuri and Surampudi, "Evidence of Stimulus Correlated Empathy Modes," 32–43.

26. Conway et al., "Brain Imaging Autobiographical Memory," 229–64; Conway et al., "Neurophysiological Correlates of Memory," 334–40.

27. O'Callaghan et al., "Shaped by Our Thoughts," 1–10; Spunt, Meyer, and Lieberman, "The Default Mode of Human Brain Function," 1–9.

28. Bzdok, Groß, and Eickhoff, "The Neurobiology of Moral Cognition," 127–48; Mascaro et al., "The Neural Mediators of Kindness-Based Meditation," 109.

29. Mar, "Neuropsychology of Fiction," 1414–34.

30. Conway et al., "Brain Imaging Autobiographical Memory," 229–64; Conway et al., "Neurophysiological Correlates of Memory," 334–40.

31. Astington, "Narrative and the Child's Theory of Mind," 151–71.

32. Conway et al., "Brain Imaging Autobiographical Memory," 229–64; Conway et al., "Neurophysiological Correlates of Memory," 334–40.

33. Brezis, "Memory Integration in the Autobiographical Narratives," 76.

34. Buckner and Carroll, "Self-Projection and the Brain," 49–57.

35. Ward et al., "Relationships between Default-Mode Network Connectivity," 265–72.

36. Morrison and Chein, "Does Working Memory Training Work?" 46–60.

37. Schlaffke et al., "Shared and Nonshared Neural Networks," 29–39.

38. Mar and Oatley, "The Function of Fiction," 173–92.

39. Vandenberghe et al., "The Associative-Semantic Network," 264–72.

40. Astington, "Narrative and the Child's Theory of Mind," 151–71.

41. Ibid.

42. Buckner and Carroll, "Self-Projection and the Brain," 49–57.

43. Mar and Oatley, "The Function of Fiction," 173–92.

44. Buckner and Carroll, "Self-Projection and the Brain," 49–57.

45. Ward et al., "Relationships between Default-Mode Network Connectivity," 265–72.

46. De Vega et al., "Neurophysiological Traces of the Reader's Geographical Perspective," 108–18.

47. Fuster, "Executive Frontal Functions," 66–70; Mar, "The Neuropsychology of Narrative," 1414–34.

48. Astington, "Narrative and the Child's Theory of Mind," 151–71.

49. Mar and Oatley, "The Function of Fiction," 173–92.

50. O'Callaghan et al., "Shaped by Our Thoughts," 1–10.

51. Andrews-Hanna, Smallwood, and Spreng, "The Default Network and Self-Generated Thought," 29–52.

52. Fuster, "Frontal Lobe and Cognitive Development," 373–85.

53. Mar, "Neuropsychology of Narrative," 1414–34.

54. Wise and Braga, "Default Mode Network," 116–17.

55. Buckner and Carroll, "Self-Projection and the Brain," 49–57.

56. Raichle, "The Brain's Default Mode Network"; Lou, "Self-Awareness," 121–22.

57. Buckner and Carroll, "Self-Projection and the Brain," 49–57.

58. Raichle, "The Brain's Default Mode Network."

59. Morrison and Chein, "Does Working Memory Training Work?" 46–60.

60. Mar and Oatley, "The Function of Fiction," 173–92.

61. Raichle, "The Brain's Default Mode Network."

62. Mar and Oatley, "The Function of Fiction," 173–92.

63. Davachi and DuBrow, "How the Hippocampus Preserves Order," 92–99.

64. Race, Keane, and Verfaellie, "Sharing Mental Simulations and Stories," 271–81.

65. Peri and Gofman, "Narrative Reconstruction," 176–83.

66. Francati, Vermetten, and Bremner, "Functional Neuroimaging Studies," 202–18.

67. Rolls, "The Functions of the Orbitofrontal Cortex," 354–75.

68. Baddeley, "The Episodic Buffer," 417–23.

69. Conway et al., "Brain Imaging Autobiographical Memory," 229–64.

70. D'Esposito and Postle, "The Cognitive Neuroscience of Working Memory," 115.

71. Fuster, Bodner, and Kroger, "Cross-Modal and Cross-Temporal Association," 347–51.

72. Ibid.

73. Ziemke and Franck, "Introduction: The Body Eclectic," 1–16.

74. Ibid.

75. Ibid.

76. Morrison and Chein, "Does Working Memory Training Work?" 46–60.

77. Ibid.

78. Conway et al., "Brain Imaging Autobiographical Memory," 229–64; Conway et al., "Neurophysiological Correlates of Memory," 334–40.

79. Ibid.

80. Ibid.

81. Ibid.

82. Ibid.

83. D'Esposito and Postle, "The Cognitive Neuroscience of Working Memory," 115.

84. Fuster, "Frontal Lobe and Cognitive Development," 373–85; Moscovitch and Winocur, "The Frontal Cortex and Working with Memory," 188–209.

85. Rubin and Greenberg, "The Role of Narrative in Recollection," 53–85; Rolls, "The Functions of the Orbitofrontal Cortex," 354–75.

86. Baddeley, "The Episodic Buffer," 417–23.

87. Ibid.

88. Conway et al., "Neurophysiological Correlates of Memory," 334–40.

89. Ibid.

90. Ibid.

91. Ibid.

92. Conway et al., "Brain Imaging Autobiographical Memory," 229–64.

93. Mar, "The Neuropsychology of Narrative," 1414–34.

94. Astington, "Narrative and the Child's Theory of Mind," 151–71.

95. Buckner and Carroll, "Self-Projection and the Brain," 49–57; Buckner, Andrews-Hanna, and Schacter, "The Brain's Default Network," 1–38.

96. Ibid.

97. Ibid.

98. Ibid.

99. Spreng, Mar, and Kim, "The Common Neural Basis," 489–510.

100. Astington, "Narrative and the Child's Theory of Mind," 151–71.

101. Ibid.

102. Fuster, "Frontal Lobe and Cognitive Development," 373–85; Mar, "The Neuropsychology of Narrative," 1414–34.

103. Mar, "The Neuropsychology of Narrative," 1414–34.

104. Astington, "Narrative and the Child's Theory of Mind," 151–71.

105. Martins, Simard, and Monchi, "Differences between Patterns of Brain Activity," e99710.

106. Fuster, "Frontal Lobe and Cognitive Development," 373–85.

107. Mar, "The Neuropsychology of Narrative," 1414–34.

108. Race, Keane, and Verfaellie, "Sharing Mental Simulations and Stories," 271–81.

109. Yonelinas, Goodrich, and Borders, "Dissociating Processes Within Recognition," 83–98.

110. Kesner and Rolls, "A Computational Theory of Hippocampal Function," 92–147.

111. Poletti et al., "Catechol-O-methyltransferase (COMT) Genotype Biases," 181–86.

112. Race, Keane, and Verfaellie, "Sharing Mental Simulations and Stories," 271–81.

Bibliography

Amodio, D. M., and C. D. Frith. "Meeting of Minds: The Medial Frontal Cortex and Social Cognition." *Nature Reviews Neuroscience* 7 (2006): 268–77.

Andrews-Hanna, J. R., J. Smallwood, and R. N. Spreng. "The Default Network and Self-Generated Thought: Component Processes, Dynamic Control, and Clinical Relevance." *Annals of the New York Academy of Sciences* 1316, no. 1 (2014): 29–52.

Annoni, M. "Highlights from the 2013 Science of Placebo Thematic Workshop." Robert Wood Johnson Foundation, "Seminar Series on the Power of the Placebo," www.rwjf.org/en/grants/grantees/placebo-forum.html (accessed February 10, 2015).

Astington, J. W. "Narrative and the Child's Theory of Mind." In *Narrative Thought and Narrative Language,* edited by Bruce K. Britton and Anthony D. Pellegrini. Hillsdale, N.J.: Lawrence Erlbaum Associates, 1990.

Baddeley, A. D., and B. Wilson. "Frontal Amnesia and the Dysexecutive Syndrome." *Brain and Cognition* 7, no. 2 (1988): 212–30.

———. "Prose Recall and Amnesia: Implications for the Structure of Working Memory." *Neuropsychologia* 40, no. 10 (2002): 1737–43.

Baddeley, A. D. "The Episodic Buffer: A New Component of Working Memory?" *Trends in Cognitive Sciences* 4, no. 11 (2000): 417–23.

Bar, M. "The Proactive Brain: Using Analogies and Associations to Generate Predictions." *Trends in Cognitive Sciences* 11, no. 7 (2007): 280–89.

Barresi, J. "From 'the Thought Is the Thinker' to 'the Voice Is the Speaker': William James and the Dialogical Self." *Theory and Psychology* 12, no. 2 (2002): 237–50.

Barrett, L. F., and A. B. Satpute. "Large-Scale Brain Networks in Affective and Social Neurosceince: Towards an Integrative Functional Architecture of the Brain." *Current Opinion in Neurobiology* 23, no. 3 (2013): 361–72.

Barrett, L. F., and J. A. Russell. "The Structure of Current Affect Controversies and Emerging Consensus." *Current Directions in Psychological Science* 8, no. 1 (1999): 10–14.

Barrett, L. F., C. D. Wilson-Mendenhall, and L. Barsalou. "The Conceptual Act Theory: A Roadmap." Chap. 4 in *The Psychological Construction of Emotion,* edited by Lisa F. Barrett, James A. Russell, and Joseph E. LeDoux. New York: Guilford Press, 2014.

Barrett, L. F. "Emotions Are Real." *Emotion* 12, no. 3 (2012): 413–29.

———. "Psychological Construction: A Darwinian Approach to the Science of Emotion." *Emotion Review* 5, no. 4 (2013): 379–89.

———. "Solving the Emotion Paradox: Categorization and the Experience of Emotion." *Personality and Social Psychology Review* 10, no. 1 (2006): 20–46.

———. "Variety Is the Spice of Life: A Psychological Construction Approach to Understanding Variability in Emotion." *Cognitive Emotion* 23, no. 7 (2009): 1284–1306.

Barsalou, L. W. "Perceptual Symbol Systems." *Behavioral and Brain Sciences* 22, no. 4 (1999): 577–660.

Beaudoin, M. N., and J. Zimmerman. "Narrative Therapy and Interpersonal Neurobiology: Revisiting Classic Practices, Developing New Emphases." *Journal of Systemic Therapies* 30, no. 1 (2011): 1–13.

Beck, A. T., and D. J. Dozois. "Cognitive Therapy: Current Status and Future Directions." *Annual Review of Medicine* 62 (2011): 397–409.

Beckman, H. B., and R. M. Frankel. "The Effect of Physician Behavior on the Collection of Data." *Annals of Internal Medicine* 101, no. 5 (1984): 692–96.

Beecher, H. K. "The Powerful Placebo." *Journal of the American Medical Association* 159, no. 17 (1955): 1602–6.

———. "Surgery as Placebo: A Quantitative Study of Bias." *Journal of the American Medical Association* 176, no. 13 (1961): 1102–7.

Beeman, M. "Coarse Semantic Coding and Discourse Comprehension." Chap. 10 (129–41) in *Right Hemisphere Language Comprehension: Perspectives from Cognitive Neuroscience,* edited by Mark J. Beeman and Christine Chiarello. Mahwah, N.J.: Lawrence Erlbaum Associates, 1998.

———. "Semantic Processing in the Right Hemisphere May Contribute to

Drawing Inferences from Discourse." *Brain and Language* 44, no. 1 (1993): 80–120.

Beeman, M. J., E. M. Bowden, and M. A. Gernsbacher. "Right and Left Hemisphere Cooperation for Drawing Predictive and Coherence Inferences during Normal Story Comprehension." *Brain and Language* 71, no. 2 (2000): 310–36.

Benedetti, F., A. Pollo, L. Lopiano, M. Lanotte, S. Vighetti, and I. Raniero. "Conscious Expectation and Unconscious Conditioning in Analgesic, Motor and Hormonal Placebo/Nocebo Responses." *Journal of Neuroscience* 23, no. 10 (2003): 4315–23.

Benowitz, L. I., K. L. Moya, and D. N. Levine. "Impaired Verbal Reasoning and Constructional Apraxia in Subjects with Right Hemisphere Damage." *Neuropsychologia* 28, no. 3 (1990): 231–41.

Bernaerts, L., D. De Geest, L. Herman, B. Vervaeck. "Cognitive Narrative Studies: Themes and Variations." Introduction in *Stories and Minds: Cognitive Approaches to Literary Narratives,* edited by Lars Bernaerts, Dirk De Geest, Luc Herman, and Bart Vervaeck. Lincoln: University of Nebraska Press, 2013.

Bingel, U., and Placebo Competence Team. "Avoiding Nocebo Effects to Optimize Treatment Outcome." *Journal of the American Medical Association* 312, no. 7 (2014): 693–94.

Bingel, U., V. Wanigasekera, K. Wiech, R. Ni Mhuircheartaigh, M. C. Lee, M. Ploner, and I. Tracey. "The Effect of Treatment Expectation on Drug Efficacy: Imaging the Analgesic Benefit of the Opioid Remifentanil." *Science Translational Medicine* 3, no. 70 (2011): 70ra14.

Bittar, C., and O. J. M. Nascimento. "Placebo and Nocebo Effects in the Neurological Practice." *Arquivos de Neuro-Psiquiatria* 73, no. 1 (2015): 58–63.

Bortolussi, M., and P. Dixon. "Minding the Text: Memory for Literary Narrative." Chap. 1 in *Stories and Minds: Cognitive Approaches to Literary Narratives,* edited by Lars Bernaerts, Dirk De Geest, Luc Herman, and Bart Vervaeck. Lincoln: University of Nebraska Press, 2013.

Boyd, Brian. *On the Origin of Stories: Evolution, Cognition, and Fiction.* Cambridge, Mass.: Harvard University Press, 2009.

Brafman, Ori, and Rom Brafman. *Sway: The Irresistible Pull of Irrational Behavior.* New York: Random House, 2009.

Branthwaite, A., and P. Cooper. "Analgesic Effects of Branding in Treatment of Headaches." *British Medical Journal (Clin Res Ed)* 282, no. 6276 (1981): 1576–78.

Brezis, R. S. "Memory Integration in the Autobiographical Narratives of Individuals with Autism." *Frontiers in Human Neuroscience* 9 (2015): 76.

Broyd, S. J., C. Demanuele, S. Debener, S. K. Helps, C. J. James, and E. J. Sonuga-Barke. "Default-Mode Brain Dysfunction in Mental Disorders: A Systematic Review." *Neuroscience and Biobehavioral Reviews* 33, no. 3 (2009): 279–96.

Brandt, K. "Intelligent Bodies: Women's Embodiment and Subjectivity in the Human-Horse Communication Process." Dissertation, Boulder, University of Colorado, 2005.

Bruner, J. "The Narrative Construction of Reality." In *Advances in Consciousness Research,* edited by Michael Mateas and Phoebe Sengers. Amsterdam: John Benjamins Publishing, 2003.

———. "The Narrative Construction of Reality." *Critical Inquiry* 18, no. 1 (1991): 1–21.

Buckner, R. L., and D.C. Carroll. "Self-Projection and the Brain." *Trends in Cognitive Sciences* 11, no. 2 (2007): 49–57.

Buckner, R. L., J. R. Andrews-Hanna, and D. L. Schacter. "The Brain's Default Network: Anatomy, Function, and Relevance to Disease." *Annals of the New York Academy of Sciences* 1124, no. 1 (2008): 1–38.

Burin, D. I., L. Acion, J. Kurczek, M. C. Duff, D. Tranel, and R. E. Jorge. "The Role of Ventromedial Prefrontal Cortex in Text Comprehension Inferences: Semantic Coherence or Socio-Emotional Perspective?" *Brain and Language* 129 (2014): 58–64.

Bzdok, D., D. Groß, and S. B. Eickhoff. "The Neurobiology of Moral Cognition: Relation to Theory of Mind, Empathy, and Mind-Wandering." In *Handbook of Neuroethics,* edited by Jens Clausen and Neil Levy. New York: Springer Netherlands, 2015.

Cabeza, R., S. M. Daselaar, F. Dolcos, S. E. Prince, M. Budde, and L. Nyberg. "Task-Independent and Task-Specific Age Effects on Brain Activity during Working Memory, Visual Attention and Episodic Retrieval." *Cerebral Cortex* 14, no. 4 (2004): 364–75.

Carlino, E., E. Frisaldi, and F. Benedetti. "Pain and the Context." *Nature Reviews Rheumatology* 10 (2014): 348–55.

Carpenter, P. A., A. Miyake, and M. A. Just. "Language Comprehension: Sentence and Discourse Processing." *Annual Review of Psychology* 46 (1995): 91–120.

Casey, P. J. "A Reexamination of the Roles of Typicality and Category Dominance in Verifying Category Membership." *Journal of Experimental Psychology: Learning, Memory, and Cognition* 18, no. 4 (1992): 823–34.

Catani, M., D. K. Jones, and D. H. Ffytche. "Perisylvian Language Networks of the Human Brain." *Annals of Neurology* 57, no. 1 (2005): 8–16.

Cauda, F., T. Costa, D. M. Torta, K. Sacco, F. D'Agata, S. Duca, G. Geminiani, P. T. Fox, and A. Vercelli. "Meta-Analytic Clustering of the Insular Cortex: Characterizing the Meta-Analytic Connectivity of the Insula When Involved in Active Tasks." *NeuroImage* 62, no. 1 (2012): 343–55.

Clifton Jr, C., and S. A. Duffy. "Sentence and Text Comprehension: Roles of Linguistic Structure." *Annual Review of Psychology* 52, no. 1 (2001): 167–96.

Cobb, L. A., G. I. Thomas, D. H. Dillard, K. A. Merendino, and R. A. Bruce. "An Evaluation of Internal-Mammary-Artery Ligation by a Double-Blind Technic." *New England Journal of Medicine* 260, no. 22 (1959): 1115–18.

Colloca, L., and C. Grillon. "Understanding Placebo and Nocebo Responses for Pain Management." *Current Pain and Headache Reports* 18, no. 6 (2014): 419.

Colloca, L., W. B. Jonas, J. Killen, F. G. Miller, D. Shurtleff. "Reevaluating the Placebo Effect in Medical Practice." *Zeitschrift für Psychologie* 222, no. 3 (2014): 124–27.

Colloca, L., L. Lopiano, M. Lanotte, and F. Benedetti. "Overt Versus Covert Treatment for Pain, Anxiety, and Parkinson's Disease." *Lancet Neurology* 3, no. 11 (2004): 679–84.

Colloca, L., and F. G. Miller. "Harnessing the Placebo Effect: The Need for Translational Research." *Philosophical Transactions of the Royal Society of London, Series B* 366 (2011): 1922–30.

Conway, M. A., C. W. Pleydell-Pearce, S. E. Whitecross, and H. Sharpe. "Brain Imaging Autobiographical Memory." In *The Psychology of Learning and Motivation*, vol. 41, edited by Brian H. Ross. New York: Academic Press, 2002.

———. "Neurophysiological Correlates of Memory for Experienced and Imagined Events." *Neuropsychologia* 41, no. 3 (2003): 334–40.

Courtney, R. "Aristotle's Legacy." *Indiana Theatre Bulletin* 20, no. 3 (1981): 1–10.

Craig, A. D. "How Do You Feel—Now? The Anterior Insula and Human Awareness." *Nature Reviews Neuroscience* 10, no. 1 (2009): 59–70.

Craik, F. I. M., T. M. Moroz, M. Moscovitch, D. T. Stuss, G. Winocur, E. Tulving, and S. Kapur. "In Search of the Self: A Positron Emission Tomography Study." *Psychological Science* 10, no. 1 (1999): 26–34.

Crossely, Michele. *Introducing Narrative Psychology: Self, Trauma, and the Construction of Meaning.* Buckingham, U.K.: Open University Press, 2000.

Crozier, S., A. Siriqu, S. Lehéricy, P. F. van der Moortele, B. Pillon, J. Grafman, Y. Agid, B. Dubois, and D. LeBihan. "Distinct Prefrontal Activations in Processing Sequence at the Sentence and Script Level: An fMRI Study." *Neuropsychologia* 37, no. 13 (1999): 1469–76.

Culler, Jonathan D. *Structuralist Poetics.* London: Routledge, 1975.

Daniels, J. K., P. Frewen, M. C. McKinnon, and R. A. Lanius. "Default Mode Alterations in Posttraumatic Stress Disorder Related to Early-Life Trauma: A Developmental Perspective." *Journal of Psychiatry and Neuroscience* 36, no. 1 (2011): 56–59.

Dantzer, R., J. C. O'Connor, G. G. Freund, R. W. Johnson, and K. W. Kelley. "From Inflammation to Sickness and Depression: When the Immune System Subjugates the Brain." *Nature Reviews Neuroscience* 9, no. 1 (2008): 46–56.

Davachi, L., and S. DuBrow. "How the Hippocampus Preserves Order: The Role of Prediction and Context." *Trends in Cognitive Sciences* 19, no. 2 (2015): 92–99.

Derksen, F., J. M. Bensing, and A. Lagro-Janssen. "Effectiveness of Empathy in General Practice: A Systematic Review." *British Journal General Practice* 63 (January 2013): 76–84.

D'Esposito, M., and B. R. Postle. "The Cognitive Neuroscience of Working Memory." *Annual Review of Psychology* 66, no. 1 (2015): 115–42.

De Vega, M., D. Beltrán, E. García-Marco, and H. Marrero. "Neurophysiological Traces of the Reader's Geographical Perspective Associated with the Deictic Verbs of Motion to go and to come." *Brain Research* 1597 (February 2015): 108–18.

Dimond, E. G., C. F. Kittle, and J. E. Crockett. "Comparison of Internal Mammary Artery Ligation and Sham Operation for Angina Pectoris." *American Journal of Cardiology* 5, no. 4 (1960): 483–86.

Dominguez, R. A., B. J. Goldstein, A. F. Jacobson, and R. M. Steinbook. "A Double-Blind Placebo-Controlled Study of Fluvoxamine and Imipramine in Depression." *Journal of Clinical Psychiatry* 46, no. 3 (1985): 84–87.

Dunbar, R. I. "The Social Brain Hypothesis and Its Implications for Social Evolution." *Annals of Human Biology* 36, no. 5 (2009): 562–72.

Dunlop, Susan Rebecca, and Margaret McCormick. "Placebo Surgery in Clinical Research Trials for Parkinson Disease." *The Journal for Nurse Practitioners* 11, no. 2 (2015): 240–47.

Elzinga, B. M., and J. D. Bremner. "Are the Neural Substrates of Memory the Final Common Pathway in Posttraumatic Stress Disorder (PTSD)?" *Journal of Affective Disorders* 70, no.1 (2002): 1–17.

Enck, P., F. Benedetti, and M. Schedlowski. "New Insights into the Placebo and Nocebo Responses." *Neuron* 59, no. 2 (2008): 195–206.

Espay, Alberto J., Matthew M. Norris, James C. Eliassen, Alok Dwivedi, Matthew S. Smith, Christi Banks, Jane B. Allendorfer et al., "Placebo Effect of Medication Cost in Parkinson Disease: A Randomized Double-Blind Study." *Neurology* 84, no. 8 (2015): 794–802.

Finniss, D. G., T. J. Kaptchuk, F. Miller, and F. Benedetti. "Biological, Clinical, and Ethical Advances of Placebo Effects." *Lancet* 375, no. 9715 (2010): 686–95.

Fossati, P., S. J. Hevenor, S. J. Graham, C. Grady, M. L. Keightley, F. Craik, and H. Mayberg. "In Search of the Emotional Self: An fMRI Study Using Postive and Negative Emotional Words." *American Journal of Psychiatry* 160, no. 11 (2003): 1938–45.

Francati, V., E. Vermetten, and J. D. Bremner. "Functional Neuroimaging Studies in Posttraumatic Stress Disorder: Review of Current Methods and Findings." *Depression and Anxiety* 24, no. 3 (2007): 202–18.

Frisk, V., and B. Milner. "The Relationship of Working Memory to the Immediate Recall of Stories Following Unilateral Temporal or Frontal Lobectomy." *Neuropsychologia* 28, no.2 (1990): 121–35.

———. "The Role of the Left Hippocampal Region in the Acquisition and Retention of Story Content." *Neuropsychologia* 28, no. 4 (1990): 349–59.

Frith, C. D., and U. Frith. "Interacting Minds—A Biological Basis." *Science* 286, no. 5445 (1999): 1692–95.

Frith, U., and C. D. Frith. "The Biological Basis of Social Interaction." *Current Directions in Psychological Science* 10, no. 5 (2001): 151–55.

———. "Development and Neurophysiology of Mentalizing." *Philosophical Transactions of the Royal Society of London B, Biological Sciences* 358, no. 1431 (2003): 459–73.

Furmark, T., M. Tilfors, H. Garpenstrand, I. Marteinsdottir, B. Langström, L. Oreland, and M. Fredrikson. "Serotonin Transporter Polymorphism Related to Amygdala Excitability and Symptom Severity in Patients with Social Phobia." *Neuroscience Letters* 362, no. 3 (2004): 189–92.

Fuster, J. M. "Executive Frontal Functions." *Experimental Brain Research* 133, no. 1 (2000): 66–70.

———. "Frontal Lobe and Cognitive Development." *Journal of Neurocytology* 31, nos. 3–5 (2002): 373–85.

Fuster, J. M., M. Bodner, and J. K. Kroger. "Cross-Modal and Cross-Temporal Association in Neurons of Frontal Cortex." *Nature* 405, no. 6784 (2000): 347–51.

Gadamer, Hans-Georg. *Truth and Method*. London: Sheed and Ward, 1979.

Galak, J., and T. Meyvis. "The Pain Was Greater if It Will Happen Again: The Effect of Continuation on Retrospective Discomfort." *Journal of Experimental Psychology* 140, no.1 (2011): 63–75.

Gallagher, S. "Neurocognitive Models of Schizophrenia: A Neurophenomenological Critique." *Psychopathology* 37, no. 1 (2004): 8–19.

Gendlin, Eugene. *Focusing*. New York: Bantam Books, 1982.

Gernsbacher, M. A. "The Structure-Building Framework: What It Is, What It Might Also Be, and Why." Chap. 11 in *Models of Understanding Text*, edited by Bruce K. Britton and Arthur C. Graesser. Hillsdale, N.J.: Lawrence Erlbaum Associates, 1995.

———. "Two Decades of Structure Building." *Discourse Processes* 23, no. 3 (1997): 265–304.

Geva, S., P. S. Jones, J. T. Crinion, C. J. Price, J. C. Baron, and E. A. Warburton. "The Neural Correlates of Inner Speech Defined by Voxel-Based Lesion-Symptom Mapping." *Brain* 134 (2011): 3071–82.

Gladwell, Malcolm. *Blink: The Power of Thinking without Thinking*. New York: Little, Brown and Company, 2005.

Glenberg, A. M., and M. P. Kaschak. "Grounding Language in Action." *Psychonomic Bulletin and Review* 9, no. 3 (2002): 558–65.

Goldberg, H. L., and R. J. Finnerty. "Trazadone in the Treatment of Neurotic Depression." *Journal of Clinical Psychiatry* 41, no. 12 (1980): 430–34.

Goodman, F. "Ritual Body Postures, Channeling and the Ecstatic Body Trance," *Anthropology of Consciousness* 10, no. 1 (1999): 54–59.

Graesser, A. C., K. K. Millis, and R. A. Zwaan. "Discourse Comprehension." *Annual Review of Psychology* 48 (1997): 163–89.

Grafman, J. "The Human Prefrontal Cortex Has Evolved to Represent Components of Structured Event Complexes." In *Handbook of Neuropsychology* 7, edited by Jordan Grafman. Amsterdam: Elsevier, 2002: 157–74.

Grainger, R. "Artistic Expression and the Embodiment of Social Constructs." *The Arts in Psychotherapy* 23, no. 2 (1996): 137–40.

Greicius, M. D., B. Krasnow, A. L. Reiss, and V. Menon. "Functional Connectivity in the Resting Brain: A Network Analysis of the Default Mode Hypothesis." *Proceedings of the National Academy of Sciences* U.S.A. 100, no. 1 (2003): 253–58.

Grimm, S., P. Boesiger, J. Beck, D. Schuepbach, F. Bermpohl, M. Walter, J. Ernst, D. Hell, H. Boeker, and G. Northoff. "Altered Negative BOLD Responses in the Default-Mode Network During Emotion Processing in Depressed Subjects." *Neuropsychopharmacology* 34, no. 4 (2009): 932–43.

Grön, G., A. P. Wunderlich, M. Spitzer, R. Tomczak, and M. W. Riepe. "Brain Activation during Human Navigation: Gender-Different Neural Networks as Substrate of Performance." *Nature Neuroscience* 3, no. 4 (2000): 404–8.

Hall, K. T., A. J. Lembo, I. Kirsch, D. C. Ziogas, J. Douaiher, K. B. Jensen, L. A. Conboy, J. M. Kelley, E. Kokkotou, and T. J. Kaptchuk. "Catechol-O-Methyltransferase Val158met Polymorphism Predicts Placebo Effect in Irritable Bowel Syndrome." *PLoS One* 7, no. 10 (2012): e48135.

Halprin, Daria. *The Expressive Body in Life, Art and Therapy: Working with Movement, Metaphor and Meaning.* London: Jessica Kingsley, 2003.

Hanson, Rick, and Richard Mendius. *Buddha's Brain: The Practical Neuroscience of Happiness, Love and Wisdom.* Oakland, Calif.: New Harbinger Publications, 2009.

Harel, A., D. J. Kravitz, and C. I. Baker. "Deconstructing Visual Scenes in Cortex Gradients of Object and Spatial Layout Information." *Cerebral Cortex* 23, no. 4 (2013): 947–57.

Harris, Paul L. *The Work of the Imagination.* Oxford: Wiley-Blackwell, 2000.

Hasher, L., and R. T. Zacks. "Working Memory, Comprehension, and Aging: A Review and a New View." In *The Psychology of Learning and Motivation*, vol. 22 *Advances in Research and Theory*, edited by Gordon H. Bower, 193–225. New York: Academic Press, 1988.

Hasher, L., R. T. Zacks, and C. P. May. "Inhibitory Control, Circadian Arousal, and Age." In *Attention and Performance 17: Cognitive Regulation of Performance; Interaction of Theory an Application,* edited by Daniel Gopher and Asher Koriat, 653–75. Cambridge, Mass.: MIT Press, 1999.

Häuser, W., E. Bartram-Wunn, C. Bartram, H. Reinecke, and T. Tölle. "Systematic Review: Placebo Response in Drug Trials of Fibromyalgia Syndrome and Painful Peripheral Diabetic Neuropathy-Magnitude and Patient-Related Predictors." *Pain* 152, no. 8 (2011): 1709–17.

Healey, M. L., C. T. McMillan, S. Golob, N. Spotorno, K. Rascovsky, D. J. Irwin, R. Clark, and M. Grossman. "Getting on the Same Page: The Neural Basis for Social Coordination Deficits in Behavioral Variant Frontotemporal Degeneration." *Neuropsychologia* 69C (January 2015): 56–66.

Herman, David. *Basic Elements of Narrative.* Malden, Mass.: Wiley-Blackwell, 2009.

Hermans, H. J. M. "The Dialogical Self: Toward a Theory of Personal and Cultural Positioning." *Culture Psychology* 7, no. 3 (2001): 243–81.

Hermans, H. J. M., and G. Dimaggio. "Self, Identity and Globalization in Times of Uncertainty: A Dialogical Analysis." *Review of General Psychology* 11, no. 1 (2007): 31–61.

Heyes, C. "Four Routes of Cognitive Evolution." *Psychological Review* 110, no. 4 (2003): 713–27.

Hill, Kay. *Glooscap and His Magic: Legends of the Wabanaki Indians.* Toronto: McClelland and Stewart, 1970.

Holmes, O. W. "Currents and Counter-Currents in Medical Science." *American Journal of the Medical Sciences* 40 (1860): 462–74.

Hsu, C. T., A. M. Jacobs, and M. Conrad. "Can Harry Potter Still Put a Spell on Us in a Second Language? An fMRI Study on Reading Emotion-Laden Literature in Late Bilinguals." *Cortex* 63 (2015): 282–95.

Huang, J., T. H. Carr, and Y. Cao. "Comparing Cortical Activations for Silent and Overt Speech Using Event-Related fMRI." *Human Brain Mapping* 15, no.1 (2002): 39–53.

Hull, S. C., L. Colloca, A. Avins, N. P. Gordon, C. P. Somkin, T. J. Kaptchuk, and F. G. Miller. "Patients' Attitudes about the Use of Placebo Treatments: Telephone Survey." *BMJ* 347 (July 2013): doi: http://dx.doi.org/10.1136/bmj.f3757.

Ingarden, Roman. *The Literary Work of Art: An Investigation of the Borderlines of Ontology, Logic, and Theory of Language*. Evanston, Ill.: Northwestern University Press, 1973.

Irish, M., J. R. Hodges, and O. Piquet. "Right Anterior Temporal Lobe Dysfunction Underlies Theory of Mind Impairments in Semantic Dementia." *Brain* 137 (April 2014): 1241–53.

Iser, Wolfgang. *The Act of Reading: A Theory of Aesthetic Response*. Baltimore: Johns Hopkins University Press, 1978.

———. "The Reading Process: A Phenomenological Approach." *New Literary History* 3, no. 2 (1972): 279–99.

James, William. *The Principles of Psychology*, vol. 1. New York: Henry Holt, 1890.

———. *The Principles of Psychology*, vol. 2. New York: Henry Holt, 1892.

Jang, J. H., W. H. Jung, D. H. Kang, M. S. Byun, S. J. Kwon, C. H. Choi, and J. S. Kwon. "Increased Default Mode Network Connectivity Associated with Meditation." *Neuroscience Letters* 487, no. 3 (2011): 358–62.

Jauss, Hans R. *Literaturgeschichte als Provokation der Literaturwissenschaft*. Frankfort am Main, Deutschland: Suhrkamp Verlag, 1970.

Jenkins, A. C., and J. P. Mitchell. "Medial Prefrontal Cortex Subserves Diverse Forms of Self-Reflection." *Social Neuroscience* 6, no. 3 (2011): 211–18.

Joensson, M., K. R. Thomsen, L. M. Andersen, J. Gross, K. Mouridsen, K. Sandberg, L. Østergaard, and H. C. Lou. "Making Sense: Dopamine Activates Conscious Self-Monitoring through Medial Prefrontal Cortex." *Human Brain Mapping* (2015): doi: 10.1002/hbm.22742.

Johnson, D. R. "Developmental Transformations: Towards the Body as Presence." Chap. 6 (89–116) in *Current Approaches in Drama Therapy*, edited by David R. Johnson and Penny Lewis. Springfield, Ill.: Charles C. Thomas, 2000.

Johnson, M. K., C. L. Raye, K. J. Mitchell, S. R. Touryan, E. J. Greene, and S. Nolen-Hoeksema. "Dissociating Medial Frontal and Posterior Cingulate Activity During Self-Reflection." *Social Cognitive and Affective Neuroscience* 1, no. 1 (2006): 56–64.

Johnson-Laird, P. N. *Human and Machine Thinking*. Hillsdale, N.J.: Lawrence Erlbaum Associates, 1993.

Jones, Phil. *Drama as Therapy. Vol. 1, Theory, Practice and Research*. New York: Routledge, 2007.

———. *Drama as Therapy. Vol. 2. Clinical Work and Research Into Practice*. New York: Routledge, 2010.

Jones, R. M., K. Barraclough, and C. Dowrick. "When No Diagnostic Label Is Applied." *BMJ 340* (May 2010): doi: http://dx.doi.org/10.1136/bmj.c2683.

Jouen, A. L., T. M. Elmore, C. J. Madden, C. Pallier, P. F. Dominey , and J. Ventre-Dominey. "Beyond the Word and Image: Characteristics of a Common Meaning System for Language and Vision Revealed by Functional and Structural Imaging." *NeuroImage* 106 (2015): 72-85.

Just, M. A., and P. A. Carpenter. "A Capacity Theory of Comprehension: Individual Differences in Working Memory." *Psychological Review* 99, no. 1 (1992): 122–49.

Kaptchuk, T. J., E. Friedlander, J. M. Kelley, M. N. Sanchez, E. Kokkotou, J. P. Singer, M. Kowalczykowski, F. G. Miller, I. Kirsch, and A. J. Lembo. "Placebos Without Deception: A Randomized Controlled Trial for Irritable Bowel Syndrome." *PloS ONE* 5, no. 12 (December 2010): doi:10.1371/journal.pone.15591.

Kaptchuk, T. J., J. Shaw, C. E. Kerr, L. A. Conboy, J. M. Kelley, T. J. Csordas, A. J. Lembo, and E. E. Jacobson. "'Maybe I Made Up the Whole Thing': Placebos and Patients' Experiences in a Randomized Controlled Trial." *Culture, Medicine and Psychiatry* 33 (2009): 382–411.

Kelley, W. M., C. N. McRae, C. L. Wyland, S. Caglar, S. Inati, and T. F. Heatherton. "Finding the Self? An Event-Related fMRI Study." *Journal of Cognitive Neuroscience* 14, no. 5 (2002): 785–94.

Kennedy, D. P., E. Redcay, and E. Courchesne. "Failing to Deactivate: Resting Functional Abnormalities in Autism." *Proceedings of the National Academy of Sciences* 103, no. 21 (2006): 8275–80.

Kennedy, W. P. "The Nocebo Reaction." *Medical World* 95 (September 1961): 203–5.

Kensinger, E. A. "Negative Emotion Enhances Memory Accuracy: Behavioral and Neuroimaging Evidence." *Current Directions in Psychological Science* 16, no. 4 (2007): 213–18.

Kesner, R. P., and E. T. Rolls. "A Computational Theory of Hippocampal Function, and Tests of the Theory: New Developments." *Neuroscience and Biobehavioral Reviews* 48 (2015): 92–147.

Kiev, A., and L. Okerson. "Comparison of the Therapeutic Efficacy of Amoxapine with That of Imipramine." *Clinical Trials Journal* 16, no. 3 (1979): 68–72.

Kintsch, W. "The Role of Knowledge in Discourse Comprehension: A

Construction-Integration Model." *Psychological Review* 95, no. 2 (1988): 163–82.

Kirsch, I., B. J. Deacon, T. B. Huedo-Medina, A. Scoboria, T. J. Moore, and B. T. Johnson. "Initial Severity and Antidepressant Benefits: A Meta-Analysis of Data Submitted to the Food and Drug Administration." *PLoS Medicine* 5, no. 2 (2008): e45.

Kirmayer, L. "The Cultural Diversity of Healing: Meaning, Metaphor and Mechanism." *British Medical Bulletin* 69, no. 1 (2004), 33–48.

Klosterhalfen, S., and P. Enck. "Neurophysiology and Psychobiology of the Placebo Response." *Current Opinion in Psychiatry* 21, no. 2 (2008): 189–95.

Kolata, G. "Insights Give Hope for New Attack on Alzheimer's." *New York Times,* December 14, 2010. http://www.nytimes.com/2010/12/14/health/14alzheimers.html (accessed February 11, 2015).

Koyama, T., J. G. McHaffie, P. J. Laurienti, R. C. Coqhill. "The Subjective Experience of Pain: Where Expectations Become Reality." *Proceedings of the National Academy of Sciences* 102, no. 36 (2005): 12950–55.

Krueger, F., A. K. Barbey, and J. Grafman. "The Medial Prefrontal Cortex Mediates Social Event Knowledge." *Trends in Cognitive Sciences* 13, no. 3 (2009): 103–9.

Kuten-Shorrer, M., J. M. Kelley, S. T. Sonis, N. S. Treister. "Placebo Effect in Burning Mouth Syndrome: A Systematic Review." *Oral Diseases* 20, no. 3 (2014): 1–6.

Kwok, V. P., T. Wang, S. Chen, K. Yakpo, L. Zhu, P. T. Fox, and L. H. Tan. "Neural Signatures of Lexical Tone Reading." *Human Brain Mapping* 36, no. 1 (2015): 304–12.

Lahad, M. "Finding Coping Resources by Means of Six-Part Storymaking, the BASIC Ph Model." In *Psychology in the School and the Community: Models of Intervention during Times of Calm and Emergency,* edited by S. Levinson, 55–70. Tel Aviv: Hadar, 1993.

Laird, A. R., P. M. Fox, S. B. Eickhoff, J. A. Turner, K. L. Ray, D. R. McKay, D. C. Glahn, C. F. Beckmann, S. M. Smith, and P. T. Fox. "Behavioral Interpretations of Intrinsic Connectivity Networks." *Journal of Cognitive Neuroscience* 23, no. 12 (2011): 4022–37.

Lakoff, George, and Mark Johnson. *Metaphors We Live By.* Chicago: University of Chicago Press, 1980.

————. *Philosophy in the Flesh: The Embodied Mind and Its Challenge to Western Thought.* New York: Basic Books, 1999.

Landy, Robert J. *Persona and Performance: The Meaning of Role in Drama, Therapy and Everyday Life.* London: Guilford Press, 1996.

Lanius, R. A., E. Vermetten, R. J. Loewenstein, B. Brand, C. Schmahl, J. D. Bremner, D. Spiegel. "Emotion Modulation in PTSD: Clinical and Neurobiological Evidence for a Dissociative Subtype." *American Journal of Psychiatry* 167, no. 6 (2010): 640–47.

Larochelle, S., and H. Pineau. "Determinants of Response Times in the Semantic Verification Task." *Journal of Memory and Language* 33, no. 6 (1994): 796–823.

Larsen, S. F., and U. Seilman. "Personal Meanings While Reading Literature." *Text & Talk* 8, no. 4 (1988): 411–29.

Leading Cloud, J. *Spotted Eagle and Black Crow.* As told by Jenny Leading Cloud in White River, Rosebud Indian Reservation, South Dakota, 1967. Recorded by Richard Erdoes. www.angelfire.com/ca/Indian/SpottedEagle .html (accessed February 14, 2015).

LeDoux, J. "The Emotional Brain, Fear, and the Amygdala." *Cellular and Molecular Neurobiology* 23, nos. 4–5 (2003): 727–38.

————. *The Emotional Brain: The Mysterious Underpinnings of Emotional Life.* New York: Simon & Schuster, 1996.

Lehrer, J. "Daydream Achiever." *Boston Globe,* August 31, 2008. http://www .boston.com/bostonglobe/ideas/articles/2008/08/31/daydream_achiever. (accessed February 14, 2015).

Lewis, Bradley. *Narrative Psychiatry: How Stories Shape Clinical Practice.* Baltimore: Johns Hopkins University Press, 2011.

Lidstone, S. C. "Great Expectations: The Placebo Effect in Parkinson's Disease." *Handbook of Experimental Pharmacology* 225 (2014): 139–47.

Lieberman, M. D., and N. I. Eisenberger. "A Pain by Any Other Name (Rejection, Exclusion, Ostracism) Still Hurts the Same: The Role of Dorsal Anterior Cingulate Cortex in Social and Physical Pain." In *Social Neuroscience: People Thinking about Thinking People,* edited by John T. Cacioppo, Penny S. Visser, and Cynthia L. Pickett, 167–89. Cambridge, Mass.: MIT Press, 2006.

Lieberman, M. D., J. M. Jarcho, and A. B. Satpute. "Evidence-Based and Intuition-Based Self-Knowledge: An fMRI study." *Journal of Personality and Social Psychology* 87 (2004): 421–35.

Lifson, A. R., S. P. Buchbinder, H. W. Sheppard, A. C. Mawle, J. C. Wilbur, M. Stanley, C. E. Hart, N. A. Hessol, and S. D. Holmberg. "Long-Term Human Immunodeficiency Virus Infection in Asymptomatic Homosexual and Bisexual Men with Normal CD4+ Lymphocyte Counts: Immunologic and Virologic Characteristics." *Journal of Infectious Diseases* 163, no. 5 (1991): 959–65.

Lindquist, K. A., and L. F. Barrett. "A Functional Architecture of the Human Brain: Emerging Insights from the Science of Emotion." *Trends in Cognitive Sciences* 16, no. 11 (2012): 533–40.

Lindquist, K. A., T. D. Wager, H. Kober, E. Bliss-Moreau, and L. F. Barrett. "The Brain Basis of Emotion: A Meta-Analytic Review." *Behavioral and Brain Sciences* 35, no. 3 (2012): 121–202.

Loder, E., R. Goldstein, and D. Biondi. "Placebo Effects in Oral Triptan Trials: The Scientific and Ethical Rationale for Continued Use of Placebo Controls." *Cephalalgia* 25, no. 2 (2005): 124–31.

Loftus, E. F., D. G. Miller, and H. J. Burns. "Semantic Integration of Verbal Information into a Visual Memory." *Journal of Experimental Psychology. Human Learning and Memory* 4 no. 1 (1978): 19–31.

Lou, H. C. "Self-Awareness: An Emerging Field in Neurobiology." *Acta Paediatrica* 104, no. 2 (2015): 121–22.

Louhiala, P. "What Do We Really Know about the Deliberate Use of Placebos in Clinical Practice." *Journal of Medical Ethics* 38 (2012): 403–5.

Macrae, C. N., J. M. Moran, T. F. Heatherton, J. F. Banfield, and W. M. Kelley. "Medial Prefrontal Activity Predicts Memory for Self." *Cerebral Cortex* 14, no. 6 (2004): 647–54.

Mahoney, Michael. *Constructive Psychotherapy: A Practical Guide.* New York: The Guilford Press, 2003.

Mar, R. A. "The Neuropsychology of Narrative: Story Comprehension, Story Production and Their Interrelation." *Neuropsychologia* 42, no. 10 (2004): 1414–34.

Mar, R. A., and K. Oatley. "The Function of Fiction Is the Abstraction and Simulation of Social Experience." *Perspectives on Psychological Science* 3, no. 3 (2008): 173–92.

Mars, R. B., F. X. Neubert, M. P. Noonan, J. Sallet, I. Toni, and M. F. S. Rusworth. "On the Relationship between the 'Default Mode Network' and the 'Social Brain.'" *Frontiers in Human Neuroscience* 6 (2012): 189.

Martins, R., F. Simard, and O. Monchi. "Differences between Patterns of Brain Activity Associated with Semantics and Those Linked with Phonological Processing Diminish with Age." *PloS ONE* 9, no. 6 (2014): doi: 10.1371/journal.pone.0099710.

Mascaro, J. S., A. Darcher, L. T. Negi, and C. L. Raison. "The Neural Mediators of Kindness-Based Meditation: A Theoretical Model." *Frontiers in Psychology* 6 (2015): 109.

Masley, S. A., D. T. Gillanders, S. G. Simpson, and M. A. Taylor. "A Systemic Review of the Evidence Base for Schema Therapy." *Cognitive Behavioral Therapy* 41, no. 3 (2012): 185–202.

Mathers, N., and P. Hodgkin. "The Gatekeeper and the Wizard: A Fairy Tale." *British Medical Journal* 298, no. 6667 (1989): 172–74.

Mayberg, H. S., J. A. Silva, S. K. Brannan, J. L. Tekell, R. K. Mahurin, S. McGinnis, and P. A. Jerabek. "The Functional Neuroanatomy of the Placebo Effect." *American Journal of Psychiatry* 158, no. 5 (2002): 728–37.

McCloskey, M., and S. Glucksberg. "Decision Processes in Verifying Category Membership Statements: Implications for Models of Semantic Memory." *Cognitive Psychology* 11, no. 1 (1979): 1–37.

Mehl-Madrona, Lewis. *Coyote Healing: Miracles from Native America*. Rochester, Vt.: Bear & Company, 2004.

———. *Healing the Mind through the Power of Story: The Promise of Narrative Psychiatry*. Rochester, Vt.: Bear & Company, 2010.

Menon, V., and L. Q. Uddin. "Saliency, Switching, Attention and Control: A Network Model of Insula Function." *Brain Structure and Function* 214, nos. 5–6 (2010): 655–67.

Mitchell, J. P., C. N. Macrae, and M. R. Banaji. "Dissociable Medial Prefrontal Contributions to Judgments of Similar and Dissimilar Others." *Neuron* 50, no. 4 (2006): 655–63.

Moghaddam, F. M. "Intersubjectivity, Interobjectivity, and the Embryonic Fallacy in Developmental Science." *Culture & Psychology* 16, no. 4 (2010): 465–75.

Mondloch, M. V., D. C. Cole, and J. W. Frank. "Does How You Do Depend on How You Think You'll Do? A Systematic Review of the Evidence for a Relationship between Patients' Recovery Expectations and Health Outcomes." *Canadian Medical Association Journal* 165, no. 2 (2001): 174–79.

Morin, A. "Self-Awareness Deficits Following Loss of Inner Speech: Dr. Jill Bolte Taylor's Case Study." *Consciousness and Cognition* 18, no. 2 (2009): 524–29.

Morrison, A. B., and J. M. Chein. "Does Working Memory Training Work? The Promise and Challenges of Enhancing Cognition by Training Working Memory." *Psychonomic Bulletin and Review* 18, no. 1 (2011): 46–60.

Moscovitch, M., and G. Winocur. "The Frontal Cortex and Working with Memory." In *Principles of Frontal Lobe Function,* edited by Donald T. Stuss and Robert K. Knight, 188–209. New York: Oxford University Press, 2002.

Moseley, J. B., K. O'Malley, N. J. Petersen, T. J. Menke, B. A. Brody, D. H. Kuykendall, J. C. Hollingsworth, C. M. Ashton, and N. P. Wray. "A Controlled Trial of Arthroscopic Surgery for Osteoarthritis of the Knee." *New England Journal of Medicine* 347, no. 2 (2002): 81–88.

Moseley, J. B., N. P. Wray, D. Kuykendall, K. Willis, and G. Landon. "Arthroscopic Treatment of Osteoarthritis of the Knee: A Prospective, Randomized, Placebo-Controlled Trial; Results of a Pilot Study." *American Journal of Sports Medicine.* 24, no. 1 (1996): 28–34.

Moya, K. L., L. I. Benowitz, D. N. Levine, and S. Finklestein. "Covariant Defects in Visuospatial Abilities and Recall of Verbal Narrative after Right Hemisphere Stroke." *Cortex* 22, no. 3 (1986): 381–97.

Murray, D., and A. J. Stoessl. "Mechanisms and Therapeutic Implications of the Placebo Effect in Neurological and Psychiatric Conditions." *Pharmacology and Therapeutics* 140, no. 3 (2013): 306–18.

Nachmanovitch, Stephen. *Free Play: Improvisation in Life and Art.* New York: Putnam, 1990.

Neisser, U. "The Ecological Study of Memory." *Philosophical Transactions of the Royal Society of London B: Biological Sciences* 352, no. 1362 (1997): 1696–1701.

Oatley, K. "Why Fiction May Be Twice as True as Fact: Fiction as Cognitive and Emotional Stimulation." *Review of General Psychology* 3, no. 2 (1999): 101–17.

O'Callaghan, C., J. M. Shine, S. J. Lewis, J. R. Andrews-Hanna, and M. Irish. "Shaped by Our Thoughts: A New Task to Assess Spontaneous Cognition and Its Associated Neural Correlates in the Default Network." *Brain and Cognition* 93 (February 2015): 1–10.

Ochsner, K. N., J. S. Beer, E. R. Robertson, J. C. Cooper, J. D. E. Gabrieli,

J. F. Kihsltrom, and M. D. Esposito. "The Neural Correlates of Direct and Reflected Self-Knowledge." *NeuroImage* 28 (2005): 797–814.

Olanow, C. W. et al. "A Double-Blind Controlled Trial of Bilateral Fetal Nigral Transplantation in Parkinson's Disease." *Annals of Neurology* 54, no. 3 (2003): 403–14.

Olesen, F. "Beyond the Placebo: Understanding the Therapeutic Context." *British Journal of General Practice* 65, no. 630 (2015): 6–7.

Olson, I. R., A. Plotzker, and Y. Ezzyat. "The Enigmatic Temporal Pole: A Review of Findings on Social and Emotional Processing." *Brain* 130, no. 7 (2007): 1718–31.

Panksepp, Jaak. *Affective Neuroscience: The Foundations of Human and Animal Emotions.* New York: Oxford University Press, 1998.

Panksepp, J., B. H. Herman, T. Vilberg, P. Bishop, and F. G. DeEskinazi. "Endogenous Opioids and Social Behavior." *Neuroscience and Behavioral Reviews* 4, no. 4 (1980): 473–87.

Perfetti, C., and J. Stafura. "Word Knowledge in a Theory of Reading Comprehension." *Scientific Studies of Reading* 18, no. 1 (2013): 22–37.

Peri, T., and M. Gofman. "Narrative Reconstruction: An Integrative Intervention Module for Intrusive Symptoms in PTSD Patients." *Psychological Trauma: Theory, Research, Practice, and Policy* 6, no.2 (2014): 176–83.

Perronne-Bertolotti, M. et al. "How Silent Is Silent Reading? Intracerebral Evidence for Top-Down Activation of Temporal Voice Areas During Reading." *Journal of Neuroscience* 32, no. 49 (2012): 17554–62.

Ploghaus, A., C. Narain, C. F. Beckmann, S. Clare, S. Bantick, R. Wise, P. M. Matthews, J. N. Rawlins, and I. Tracey. "Exacerbation of Pain by Anxiety Is Associated with Activity in a Hippocampal Network." *Journal of Neuroscience* 21, no. 24 (2001): 9896–903.

Poletti, S., D. Radaelli, R. Cavallaro, M. Bosia, C. Lorenzi, A. Pirovano, E. Smeraldi, and F. Benedetti. "Catechol-O-methyltransferase (COMT) Genotype Biases Neural Correlates of Empathy and Perceived Personal Distress in Schizophrenia." *Comprehensive Psychiatry* 54, no. 2 (2013): 181–86.

Prentice, D. A., R. J. Gerrig, and D. S. Bailis. "What Readers Bring to the Processing of Fictional Texts." *Psychonomic Bulletin and Review* 4, no. 3 (1997): 416–20.

Pribram, K., M. Nuwer, and R. Baron. "The Holographic Hypothesis of

Memory Structure in Brain Function and Perception." In *Contemporary Developments in Mathematical Psychology,* vol. 2, edited by David H. Krantz, 416–57. New York: W. H. Freeman, 1974.

Quitkin, F. M. "Placebos, Drug Effects, and Study Design: A Clinician's Guide." *American Journal of Psychiatry* 156, no. 6 (1999): 829–36.

Race, E., M. M. Keane, and M. Verfaellie. "Losing Sight of the Future: Impaired Semantic Prospection Following Medial Temporal Lobe Lesions." *Hippocampus* 23, no. 4 (2013): 268–77.

———. "Sharing Mental Simulations and Stories: Hippocampal Contributions to Discourse Integration." *Cortex* 63 (2015): 271–81.

Raichle, M. E. "The Brain's Dark Energy." *Scientific American* 302 (March 2010): 44–49.

———. "The Brain's Default Mode Network." *Annual Review of Neuroscience* 38 (forthcoming, August 2015).

Raichle, M. E., A. M. MacLeod, A. Z. Snyder, W. J. Powers, D. A. Gusnard, and G. L. Shulman. "Inaugural Article: A Default Mode of Brain Function." *Proceedings of the National Academy of Sciences* 98, no. 2 (2001): 676–82.

Raichle, M. E., and A. Z. Snyder. "A Default Mode of Brain Function: A Brief History of an Evolving Idea." *NeuroImage* 37, no. 4 (2007): 1083–90.

Ramachandran, V. S., and Sandra Blakeslee. *Phantoms in the Brain: Probing the Mysteries of the Human Mind*. New York: William Morrow, 1998.

Restak, R. "How Our Brain Constructs Our Mental World." Chap. 1 in *The Jossey-Bass Reader on the Brain and Learning,* edited by J. B. Publishers, 3–11. San Francisco: John Wiley, 2007.

Rickels, K., W. G. Case, J. Werblowsky, I. Csanalosi, A. Schless, and C. C. Weiise. "Amoxapine and Imipramine in the Treatment of Depressed Outpatients: A Controlled Study." *American Journal of Psychiatry* 138, no. 1 (1981): 20–24.

Roberts, P. *Emerging Selves in Practice: How Do I and Others Create My Practice and How Does My Practice Shape Me and Influence Others?* Bath, U.K.: University of Bath, 2003.

Robertson, D. A., M. A. Gernsbacher, S. J. Guidotti, R. R. Robertson, W. Irwin, B. J. Mock, and M. E. Campana. "Functional Neuroanatomy of the Cognitive Process of Mapping during Discourse Comprehension." *Psychological Science* 11, no. 3 (2000): 255–60.

Robin, J., M. Hirshhorn, R. S. Rosenbaum, G. Winocur, M. Moscovitch, and

C. L. Grady. "Functional Connectivity of Hippocampal and Prefrontal Networks During Episodic and Spatial Memory Based on Real-World Environments." *Hippocampus* 25, no. 1 (2015): 81–93.

Rolheiser, T., E. A. Stamatakis, and L. K. Tyler. "Dynamic Processing in the Human Language System: Synergy between the Arcuate Fascicle and Extreme Capsule." *The Journal of Neuroscience* 31, no. 47 (2011): 16949–57.

Rolls, E. T. "Memory Systems in the Brain." *Annual Review of Psychology* 51 (2000): 599–630.

———. "The Functions of the Orbitofrontal Cortex." In *Principles of Frontal Lobe Function,* edited by Donald T. Stuss and Robert K. Knight. New York: Oxford University Press, 2002.

———. "The Orbitofrontal Cortex and Reward." *Cerebral Cortex* 10, no. 3 (2000): 284–94.

Rosch, E. "On the Internal Structure of Perceptual and Semantic Categories." In *Cognitive Development and the Acquisition of Language,* edited by Timothy E. Moore, 111–44. New York: Academic Press, 1973.

Rosch, E., and C. B. Mervis. "Family Resemblances: Studies in the Internal Structure of Categories." *Cognitive Psychology* 7, no. 4 (1975): 573–605.

Rothschild, Babette. *The Body Remembers: The Psychophysiology of Trauma and Trauma Treatment.* New York: Norton, 2000.

Rotie, M. "Between Fabric and Flesh." *Blue Pages Newsletter of the Society of British Theatre Designers* 3 (2009): 18.

Rubin, D. C., and D. L. Greenberg. "The Role of Narrative in Recollection: A View from Cognitive and Neuropsychology." In *Narrative and Consciousness: Literature, Psychology, and the Brain,* edited by Gary Fireman, Ted E. McVay Jr, and Owen J. Flanagan. New York: Oxford University Press, 2003.

Russell, J. A., and L. F. Barrett. "Core Affect, Prototypical Emotional Episodes, and Other Things Called Emotion: Dissecting the Elephant." *Journal of Personality and Social Psychology* 76, no. 5 (1999): 805–19.

Russell, J. A., and B. Fehr. "Fuzzy Concepts in a Fuzzy Hierarchy: Varieties of Anger." *Journal of Personality and Social Psychology* 67 (1994): 186–205.

Sandelowski, M. "Telling Stories: Narrative Approaches in Qualitative Research." *Image: The Journal of Nursing Scholarship* 23, no. 3 (1991): 161–66.

Schank, Roger C. *Dynamic Memory: A Theory of Reminding and Learning in Computers and People.* New York: Cambridge University Press, 1983.

Schank, Roger C., and Robert P. Abelson. "Knowledge and Memory: The

Real Story." Chap. 1 in *Knowledge and Memory: The Real Story; Advances in Social Cognition,* edited by Robert S. Wyer Jr., 1–85. Hillsdale, N.J.: Lawrence Erlbaum Associates, 1995.

———. *Scripts, Plans, Goals, and Understanding: An Inquiry into Human Knowledge Structures.* Hillsdale, N.J.: Lawrence Erlbaum Associates, 1977.

Schilbach, L., S. B. Eickhoff, A. Rotarska-Jaqiela, G. R. Fink, and K. Vogeley. "Minds at Rest? Social Cognition as the Default Mode of Cognizing and Its Putative Relationship to the 'Default System' of the Brain." *Consciousness and Cognition* 17, no. 2 (2008): 457–67.

Schlaffke, L., S. Lissek, M. Lenz, G. Juckel, T. Schultz, M. Tegenthoff, T. Schmidt-Wilcke, and M. Brüne. "Shared and Nonshared Neural Networks of Cognitive and Affective Theory-of-Mind: A Neuroimaging Study Using Cartoon Picture Stories." *Human Brain Mapping* 36, no. 1 (2015): 29–39.

Seeley, W. W., V. Menon, A. F. Schatzberg, J. Keller, G. H. Glover, H. Kenna, A. L. Reiss, and M. D. Greicius. "Dissociable Intrinsic Connectivity Networks for Salience Processing and Executive Control." *Journal of Neuroscience* 27, no. 9 (2007): 2349–56.

Servick, K. "Outsmarting the Placebo Effect." *Science* 345, no. 6203 (2014): 1446–47.

Sherman, F. "Conversation with Mary Whitehouse." In *Authentic Movement: Essays by Mary Starks Whitehouse, Janet Adler and Joan Chodorow,* edited by Patrizia Pallaro, 29–32. London: Jessica Kingsley Publishers, 1999.

Shorter, Edward. *From Paralysis to Fatigue: A History of Psychosomatic Illness in the Modern Era.* New York: The Free Press, 1992.

Siegel, Daniel J. *The Developing Mind: Toward a Neurobiology of Interpersonal Experience.* New York: Guilford Press, 1999.

Spivey, M. J., M. J. Tyler, D. C. Richardson, and E. E. Young. "Eye Movements During Comprehension of Spoken Scene Descriptions." In *Proceedings of the Twenty-Second Annual Meeting of the Cognitive Science Society,* 487–92. Mahwah, N.J.: Lawrence Erlbaum Associates, 2000.

Spolsky, Ellen. *Gaps in Nature: Literary Interpretation and the Modular Mind.* Albany: State University of New York Press, 1993.

Spreng, R. N., R. A. Mar, and A. S. Kim. "The Common Neural Basis of Autobiographical Memory, Prospection, Navigation, Theory of Mind, and the Default Mode: A Quantitative Meta-Analysis." *Journal of Cognitive Neuroscience* 21, no. 3 (2009): 489–510.

Spunt, R. P., M. L. Meyer, and M. D. Lieberman. "The Default Mode of Human Brain Function Primes the Intentional Stance." *Journal of Cognitive Neuroscience* (January 2015): doi:10.1162/jocn_a_00785.

Stannard, Cathy, Michael Coupe, and Tony Pickering, eds. *Opioids in Non-Cancer Pain.* Oxford: Oxford University Press, 2013.

Stephens, G. J., L. J. Silbert, and U. Hasson. "Speaker–Listener Neural Coupling Underlies Successful Communication." *Proceedings of the National Academy of Sciences* 107, no. 32 (2010): 14425–30.

Stetler, C. "Adherence, Expectations and the Placebo Response: Why Is Good Adherence to an Inert Treatment Beneficial?" *Psychology & Health* 29, no. 2 (2013): 127–40.

Strange, J. J., and C. C. Leung. "How Anecdotal Accounts in News and in Fiction Can Influence Judgments of a Social Problem's Urgency, Causes, and Cures." *Personality and Social Psychology Bulletin* 25, no. 4 (1999): 439–49.

Sullivan, M., W. Rogers, and I. Kirsch. "Catastrophizing, Depression and Expectancies for Pain and Emotional Distress." *Pain* 91 (2001): 147–54.

Sutherland, M. T., K. L. Ray, M. C. Reidel, J. A. Yanes, E. A. Stein, and A. L. Laird. "Neurobiological Impact of Nicotinic Acetylcholine Receptor Agonists: An ALE Meta-Analysis of Pharmacological Neuroimaging Studies." *Biological Psychiatry* (January 2015): doi: http://dx.doi.org/10.1016/j.biopsych.2014.12.021 (accessed February 12, 2015).

Talbot, M. "The Placebo Prescription." *New York Times Magazine,* January 9, 2000. www.nytimes.com/2000/01/09/magazine/the-placebo-prescription.html (accessed February 10, 2015).

Tart, Charles C. *Altered States of Consciousness.* New York: John Wiley, 1969.

Thomas, K. B. "General Practice Consultations: Is There Any Point in Being Positive?" *British Medical Journal* (Clin Res Ed) 294, no. 6581 (1987): 1200–2.

———. "The Placebo in General Practice." *Lancet* 334, no. 8929 (1994): 1066–67.

———. "Temporarily Dependent Patient in General Practice." *British Medical Journal* 1, no. 5908(1974): 625–26.

Thompson, J. J., C. Ritenbaugh, and M. Nichter. "Reconsidering the Placebo Response from a Broad Anthropological Perspective." *Culture, Medicine and Psychiatry* 33, no. 1 (March 2009): 112–52.

Tilburt, J. C., E. J. Emanuel, T. J. Kaptchuk, F. A. Curlin, and F. G. Miller. "Prescribing 'Placebo Treatments': Results of a National Survey of US Internists and Rheumatologists." *BMJ* 337 (October 2008): doi: http://dx.doi.org/10.1136/bmj.a1938.

Tippens, K. M., J. Q. Purnell, W. L. Gregory, E. Connelly, D. Hanes, B. Oken, and C. Calabrese. "Expectancy, Self-Efficacy, and Placebo Effect of a Sham Supplement for Weight Loss in Obese Adults." *Journal of Evidence-Based Complementary & Alternative Medicine* 19, no. 3 (2014): 181–88.

Tracy, J. L., and D. Randles. "Four Models of Basic Emotions: A Review of Ekman and Cordaro, Izard, Levenson, and Panksepp and Watt." *Emotion Review* 3, no. 4 (2011): 397–405.

Tulving, E. "Episodic Memory: From Mind to Brain." *Annual Review of Psychology* 53, no. 2 (2002): 1–25.

Tulving, E., S. Kapur, F. I. Craik, M. Moscovitch, and S. Houle. "Hemispheric Encoding/Retrieval Asymmetry in Episodic Memory: Positron Emission Tomography Findings." *Proceedings of the National Academy of Sciences* 91, no. 6 (1994): 2016–20.

Turner, Mark. *The Literary Mind: The Origins of Thought and Language.* New York: Oxford University Press, 1996.

Van Dijk, Teun A., and Walter Kintsch. *Strategies of Discourse Comprehension.* New York: Academic Press, 1983.

Vandenberghe, R., Y. Wang, N. Nelissen, M. Vandenbulcke, T. Dhollander, S. Sunaert, and P. Dupont. "The Associative-Semantic Network for Words and Pictures: Effective Connectivity and Graph Analysis." *Brain and Language* 127, no. 2 (2013): 264–72.

Van Tulder, M., W. J. Assendelft, B. W. Koes, and L. M. Bouter. "Spinal Radiographic Findings and Non-Specific Low Back Pain: A Systematic Review of Observational Studies." *Spine* 22, no. 4 (1999): 427–34.

Vase, L., M. Amanzio, and D. Price. "Nocebo vs. Placebo: The Challenges of Trial Design in Analgesia Research." *Clinical Pharmacology & Therapeutics* (2015): 143–50.

Vemuri, K., and B. R. Surampudi. "Evidence of Stimulus Correlated Empathy Modes: Group ICA of fMRI Data." *Brain and Cognition* 94C (January 2015): 32–43.

Vercueil, L. "Control of Inner Speech and Gilles de la Tourette's Syndrome." *Encéphale* 29, no. 5 (2003): 460–62 (in French).

Vercueil, L., and H. Klinger. "Loss of Silent Reading in Frontotemporal Dementia: Unmasking the Inner Speech." *Journal of Neurology, Neurosurgery and Psychiatry* 70, no. 5 (2001): 705–6.

Vercueil, L., and M. Perronne-Bertolotti. "Ictal Inner Speech Jargon." *Epilepsy & Behavior* 27, no. 2 (2013): 307–9.

Verfaellie, M., K. Bousquet, and M. M. Keane. "Medial Temporal and Neocortical Contributions to Remote Memory for Semantic Narratives: Evidence from Amnesia." *Neuropsychologia* 61 (2014): 105–12.

Virtue, S., J. Haberman, Z. Clancy, T. Parrish, and M. Jung Beeman. "Neural Activity of Inferences During Story Comprehension." *Brain Research* 1084, no. 1 (2006): 104–14.

Virtue, S., T. Parrish, and M. Jung-Beeman. "Inferences During Story Comprehension: Cortical Recruitment Affected by Predictability of Events and Working Memory Capacity." *Journal of Cognitive Neuroscience* 20, no. 12 (2008): 2274–84

Wapner, W., S. Hamby, and H. Gardner. The Role of the Right Hemisphere in the Apprehension of Complex Linguistic Materials." *Brain and Language* 14, no. 1 (1981): 15–33.

Ward, A. M., E. C. Mormino, W. Huijbers, A. P. Schultz, T. Hedden, and R. A. Sperling. "Relationships between Default-Mode Network Connectivity, Medial Temporal Lobe Structure, and Age-Related Memory Deficits." *Neurobiology of Aging* 36, no.1 (2015): 265–72.

Weiner, W. J. "Placebo Surgery in Trials of Therapy for Parkinson's Disease." *New England Journal of Medicine* 342, no. 5 (2000): 353.

Werner, Heinz, and Bernard Kaplan. *Symbol Formation: An Organismic-Developmental Approach to Language and the Expression of Thought.* London: John Wiley, 1964.

Wheeler, M., D. Stuss, and E. Tulving. "Toward a Theory of Episodic Memory: The Frontal Lobes and Autonoetic Consciousness." *Psychological Bulletin* 121, no. 3 (1997): 331–54.

Wheeler, S. C., M. C. Green, and T. C. Brock. "Fictional Narratives Change Beliefs: Replications of Prentice, Gerrig and Bailis (1997) with Mixed Corroration." *Psychonomic Bulletin and Review* 6, no. 1 (1999): 136–41.

Whitehead, C. "Social Mirrors and Shared Experiential Worlds." *Journal of Consciousness Studies* 8, no. 4 (2001): 3–36.

Whitfield-Gabrieli, S. et al. "Hyperactivity and Hyperconnectivity of the

Default Network in Schizophrenia and in First-Degree Relatives of Persons with Schizophrenia." *Proceedings of the National Academy of Sciences* 106, no. 4 (2009): 1279–84.

Wiener, Daniel J., and Linda K. Oxford. *Action Therapy with Families and Groups: Using Creative Arts Improvisation in Clinical Practice.* Washington, D.C.: American Psychological Association, 2003.

Wilson-Mendenhall, C. D., L. F. Barrett, and L. W. Barsalou. "Neural Evidence That Human Emotions Share Core Affective Properties." *Psychological Science* 24, no. 6 (2013): 947–56.

———. "Variety in Emotional Life: Within-Category Typicality of Emotional Experiences Is Associated with Neural Activity in Large-Scale Brain Networks." *Social Cognitive and Affective Neuroscience* 10, no. 1 (2015): 62–71.

Winkelman, Michael. *Shamanism: The Neural Ecology of Consciousness and Healing.* Westport, Conn.: Bergin & Garvey, 2000.

Wise, R. J., and R. M. Braga. "Default Mode Network: The Seat of Literary Creativity?" *Trends in Cognitive Sciences* 18, no.3 (2014): 116–17.

Xu, J., S. Kemeny, G. Park, C. Frattali, and A. Braun. "Language in Context: Emergent Features of Word, Sentence, and Narrative Comprehension." *NeuroImage* 25, no. 3 (2005): 1002–15.

Yonelinas, A. P., R. I. Goodrich, and A. A. Borders. "Dissociating Processes Within Recognition, Perception, and Working Memory." Chap. 6 in *Remembering: Attributions, Processes, and Control in Human Memory,* edited by D. Stephen Lindsay, Colleen M. Kelley, Andrew P. Yonelinas, and Henry L. Roediger III. Washington, D.C.: Psychology Press, 2014.

Young, K., and J. L. Saver. "The Neurology of Narrative." *SubStance* 30, nos. 1–2 (2001): 72–84.

Zalla, T., M. Phipps, and J. Grafman. "Story Processing in Patients with Damage to the Prefrontal Cortex." *Cortex* 38, no. 2 (2002): 215–31.

Zhang, S., and C. S. Li. "Functional Connectivity Mapping of the Human Precuneus by Resting State fMRI," *NeuroImage* 59, no. 4 (2012): 3548–62.

Ziemke, T., and R. M. Franck. "Introduction: The Body Eclectic." In *Cognitive Linguistics Research: Body, Language and Mind.* Vol. 1, Embodiment, edited by Tom Ziemke, Jordan Slatev, and Roslyn M. Franck, 1–16. New York: Mouton de Gruyter, 2007.

Zunshine, Lisa. *Why We Read Fiction: Theory of Mind and the Novel.* Columbus: The Ohio State University Press, 2006.

Zwaan, R. A. "The Immersed Experiencer: Toward an Embodied Theory of Language Comprehension." In *The Psychology of Learning and Motivation,* vol. 44 edited by Brian H. Ross, 35–62. New York: Academic Press, 2003.

Zwaan, R. A. and C. J. Madden. "Embodied Sentence Comprehension." In *Grounding Cognition: The Role of Perception and Action in Memory, Language, and Thinking,* edited by Diane Pecher and Rolf A. Zwaan, 224–45. Cambridge: Cambridge University Press, 2005.

Zwaan, R.A., and G. A. Radvansky. "Situation Models in Language Comprehension and Memory." *Psychological Bulletin* 123, no. 2 (1998): 162–85.

Index

BOOKS OF RELATED INTEREST

Coyote Healing
Miracles in Native Medicine
by Lewis Mehl-Madrona, M.D., Ph.D.
Foreword by Larry Dossey, M.D.

Coyote Wisdom
The Power of Story in Healing
by Lewis Mehl-Madrona, M.D., Ph.D.

Healing the Mind through the Power of Story
The Promise of Narrative Psychiatry
by Lewis Mehl-Madrona, M.D., Ph.D.

Narrative Medicine
The Use of History and Story in the Healing Process
by Lewis Mehl-Madrona, M.D., Ph.D.

Meditations with the Cherokee
Prayers, Songs, and Stories of Healing and Harmony
by J. T. Garrett

The Cherokee Herbal
Native Plant Medicine from the Four Directions
by J. T. Garrett

Medicine of the Cherokee
The Way of Right Relationship
by J. T. Garrett and Michael Tlanusta Garrett

Walking on the Wind
Cherokee Teachings for Harmony and Balance
by Michael Tlanusta Garrett

INNER TRADITIONS • BEAR & COMPANY
P.O. Box 388
Rochester, VT 05767
1-800-246-8648
www.InnerTraditions.com

Or contact your local bookseller